Super-Flexibility for Knowledge Enterprises

Second edition

Super-Flexibility for Knowledge Enterprises

A Toolkit for Dynamic Adaptation

Second edition

 Springer

Professor Homa Bahrami
Haas School of Business
University of California
Berkeley
CA 94720-1900
USA
bahrami@haas.berkeley.edu
homa@pdgy.com

Professor Stuart Evans
Carnegie Mellon University
Silicon Valley
NASA Ames Research Park
Moffet Field
CA 94035-1000
USA
Stuart.evans@sv.cmu.edu
stuart@pdgy.com

ISBN 978-3-642-43154-8   ISBN 978-3-642-02447-4 (eBook)
DOI 10.1007/978-3-642-02447-4
Springer Heidelberg Dordrecht London New York

© Springer-Verlag Berlin Heidelberg 2005, 2010
Softcover re-print of the Hardcover 2nd edition 2010
This work is subject to copyright. All rights are reserved, whether the whole or part of the material is concerned, specifically the rights of translation, reprinting, reuse of illustrations, recitation, broadcasting, reproduction on microfilm or in any other way, and storage in data banks. Duplication of this publication or parts thereof is permitted only under the provisions of the German Copyright Law of September 9, 1965, in its current version, and permission for use must always be obtained from Springer. Violations are liable to prosecution under the German Copyright Law.
The use of general descriptive names, registered names, trademarks, etc. in this publication does not imply, even in the absence of a specific statement, that such names are exempt from the relevant protective laws and regulations and therefore free for general use.

Cover design: WMXDesign GmbH, Heidelberg

Cover page layout: Rys Art & Design

Printed on acid-free paper

Springer is part of Springer Science+Business Media (www.springer.com)

Preface 2nd Edition

Since the first edition of the book was published five years ago, the world has gone through a metamorphic transformation. The global financial crisis has led to a fundamental re-assessment of conventional business practices. Emerging economies have taken center-stage. The pace of technological innovation continues unabated. The "Millennial" generation has come of age and is entering the workforce. Collectively, these forces have propelled us towards a new, dynamic era. The only certainty today is that the future will be different from the past.

We believe this transformation is not just a cyclical phenomenon, but rather a fundamental sea change. We live in an inter-dependent world where revision-triggers come fast and furious, from many different, often unexpected, sources. The capacity to dynamically adapt to new realities is a critical success factor and a major source of competitive advantage. How do we dynamically adapt when we don't have the luxury of time and resources to predict and plan?

This situation presents a dilemma; although the game is changing, from predictable stability to dynamic fluidity, we continue to rely on the old rules to play this new game. We suggest that today knowledge workers need a different toolkit to harness uncertainty and to thrive on dynamic adaptation. It is imperative to use diagnostic frameworks to help us assess situations on the fly and devise appropriate solutions "*in situ*".

This second edition is, in essence, a distillation and synthesis of diagnostic frameworks and core principles that can help knowledge workers interpret unfolding situations, create shared reality and develop a common vocabulary among diverse stakeholders. Instead of relying on complex approaches and outside experts, analogous to performing "open-heart surgery", we hope to equip a new generation of "enterprise cardiologists", knowledge workers who can make just-in-time interventions and devise practical solutions on the fly. They are close to action and in the best position to figure out what makes sense. What they need are shared diagnostic tools that can help them think through, categorize and interpret dynamic realities in a complex world.

Since the book was first published, we have had the opportunity to teach these frameworks at business seminars to a cross-section of knowledge workers in different parts of the world. The goal of many of these forums has been to bring together leaders from different functions so they can cross-pollinate and develop a sense of shared reality. Yet, despite all the talk about cross-functional teamwork, we are struck by how rigid our silos are and how firmly our views are anchored in our core disciplines. We talk about the importance of cross-silo teamwork, but we rarely walk the talk. Therefore a second key driver for this new edition is to present a 'general management", cross-disciplinary approach to enterprise adaptation. We discuss strategy, but we also focus on execution. We talk about organizational design, and also reflect on leadership practices. Our assumption is that in a dynamic world, leaders at all levels, have to constantly switch gears, wear different hats, and navigate at different altitudes. They have to think about the "total" enterprise, not in terms of compartmentalized silos or fields of functional expertise. Much like a general contractor, they have to draw on specialized expertise, as and when needed, yet keep the big picture in mind. Our hope is that our diagnostic tools can help teams develop a shared frame of reference and generate cross-functional dialogue.

The third driving force behind this second edition is the gradual convergence between the worlds of entrepreneurial start-ups and challenges facing established corporations. Innovation, agility, and initiative are no longer the exclusive preserve of start-ups. Established companies are looking for ways to re-invent themselves, to innovate, to think creatively, and to make their enterprises more flexible, agile and entrepreneurial. We have had the good fortune to sit at the intersection of these two worlds. We hope our ideas can benefit both groups. We set out to provide a "buffet table", a menu of options that can be helpful for the two ends of the spectrum.

Finally, we try to bridge the gap between the worlds of academic, research-based scholarship, and its practical application. Many knowledge workers we come across are interested in the theoretical foundations of practical ideas. In this revised edition, we set out to pull together seminal contributions from different scholars across a wide range of disciplines, as can be seen from the extended conceptual analysis in chapter 2.

We have been fortunate to test-drive the ideas with our graduate students at Homa's "Global Organizational Innovation" class at Berkeley and at Stuart's "Innovation & Entrepreneurship" class at Carnegie Mellon's Silicon Valley campus. In addition, we have discussed the ideas in many executive seminars and in-company programs. Our students and executive audiences have challenged our views, questioned our assumptions, improved our ideas, and shown us how to apply the frameworks to diagnose real-time challenges. We have learned a great deal in the process, and are grateful for their input, contributions, and refinements.

In revising the book, we are indebted to many business leaders and technology entrepreneurs who have shared their experiences and perspectives and in the process refined our ideas. Special thanks to Larry Boucher, Raphael Bracho, Tom Campbell, Bill Davidow, Carl Everett, Ken Coleman, Eric Dunn, Mark Emkjer, Sheridan Foster, Christian Frei, Tim Haley, Greg Heibel, Nigel Keen, Igor Khandros, Hap Klopp, Dave Lacey, Rita Lane, Lothar Maier, Giacomo Marini, Tom Mitchell, Helga Nes, Jon Peters, Jim Prestridge, Peter Rip, Patricia Roller, Mario Ruscev, Carol Sands, Radhika Shah, Christophe Soutter, Robin Vasan, and Harvey Wagner for sharing their front line observations, experiences and insights only possible by those close to action.

Our colleagues at Berkeley, Cambridge, CMU and other universities have been a source of inspiration and encouragement over the years. We are grateful to Ulrike Baumöl, Jenny Chatman, John Child, Keith Cotterill, Whitney Hischier, Drew Isaacs, Ralph Keeney, Reinhard Jung, Gladys Mercier and Terry Pearce.

We'd like to express our special thanks to Juliette Rys for her creative artwork, and for her diligence and dedication in producing the manuscript, and to Dr. Werner Müller and Ruth Milewski at Springer, who have been patient and supportive throughout the publication process. Finally, we owe a special thanks to our families and friends for their encouragement, and to James, who is a constant source of inspiration.

Menlo Park, California	Homa Bahrami
January 2010	Stuart Evans

Preface 1st Edition

The origin of the ideas presented in this book can be traced back to 1982 when we first came to Silicon Valley. After studying several European multinationals as part of our doctoral field research, the contrast with Silicon Valley was somewhat startling. At the time, the Valley was going through its formative years. The first IBM PC and the Apple Macintosh had yet to be introduced. Many of today's technology giants were fledgling start-ups; some, like Cisco, had yet to be founded. We were fortunate to have "ringside" seats, the opportunity to witness the meteoric rise and growth of entrepreneurial companies and emerging industries.

During the first few years, our research interests, while complementary, were pursued along separate tracks. Homa's focus was on organizational design: how entrepreneurial companies were architected to address the combined challenges of innovation, speed, and growth in turbulent domains. Stuart's focus was on flexibility, especially as it related to developing product and business strategies. These parallel tracks gradually converged as we realized the close inter-linkages between the two fields, especially in practice.

For the past twenty years, we have observed Silicon Valley during several evolutionary phases. Our path has taken us to many technology companies during various stages of growth, ranging from emerging start-ups, to mid-sized adolescents, and global giants. Our journey has taken us to different technology domains, including semiconductors (packaging, equipment, processors and devices), e-business and enterprise software (databases, helpdesk, multimedia, financial industry specialists), disk drives, controllers and peripherals manufacturers, networking and storage archiving products, telecommunications equipment, and life sciences. We have talked to hundreds of entrepreneurs, executives, and knowledge workers, and served on several advisory boards over the years, giving us "unfiltered", first-hand perspectives on critical realities and business challenges. We have immersed ourselves in the phenomenon by conducting field research, observing events close up, participating in various projects, and interacting with venture capitalists, lawyers, accountants and other professionals associated with technology ventures and corporations.

Collectively our observations and experiences lead us to conclude that Silicon Valley and its technology enterprises have experimented with novel approaches to "management", "organization" and "strategy". These experiments cannot be solely attributed to a "quirky Californian mentality", or the need to be just different and unique, although these factors have been clearly influential. We suggest that pioneering entrepreneurs and executive teams of the new generation companies are continually developing novel recipes because they face unique and unprecedented challenges.

This book is a synthesis of our collective learnings and field observations in Silicon Valley. We have set out to distill the most salient themes that have practical implications, and that would be of interest to entrepreneurs, executives, and investors. Our approach is unconventional in several ways. We do not confine ourselves to traditional disciplinary boundaries in that we propose frameworks for developing strategy as well as organizational design and leadership practices. We examine the dynamics of the broad ecosystem as well as the recipes used by individual firms. Our approach is partly descriptive, partly interpretive, and partly prescriptive, drawing on detailed case studies, cross-sectional field research, and action-based reflections. We draw as much on pathological cases of failure as well as the experiences of successful entities.

Our overarching goal is to synthesize our combined research, teaching, and practical experiences of Silicon Valley and its enterprises, as they relate to the challenge of super-flexibility, and to propose conceptual frameworks that underpin pragmatic action steps. We do not pretend to have all the answers to these complex questions. Rather, our hope is that the proposed action principles provide conceptual "coat hangers", helping executives and entrepreneurs examine their current assumptions, reflect on their unique challenges, and devise their own action recipes, using our frameworks as "food for thought". We think the time is ripe for reflection and introspection, as our business entities are clearly experiencing novel and unprecedented challenges worldwide.

Our learning journey would not have been possible without the critical insights and thoughtful contributions of many entrepreneurs, executives, and knowledge workers who have shared their experiences with us during the past twenty years. We have also had the opportunity to discuss many of the frameworks presented in this book with our MBA students at Berkeley and Cambridge, with multi-cultural knowledge workers in executive programs and business seminars around the world, and with business and government leaders visiting Silicon Valley during the past ten years. Their critical insights and constructive feedback have influenced our thinking, helped us refine the ideas, and prompted us to relate them to the practical challenges facing front-line executives. We are truly grateful for all their insights and contributions. Naturally, we are solely responsible for any errors or misinterpretations.

While there are too many people to thank individually, we are especially indebted to several entrepreneurs, investors, and executives who have been willing to share their experiences over time and to provide us with candid, longitudinal perspectives. Among entrepreneurial founders and venture capitalists, we are particularly grateful to Larry Boucher, Ken Coleman, Eric Dunn, Larry Garlick, John Glynn, Till Guldimann, Jim Guzy, Tim Hayley, Trip Hawkins, John Hendrickson, Mark Hoffman, Nigel Keen, Igor Khandros, Roger Lang, Giacomo Marini, Bob Maxfield, Doug Merritt, Bob Metcalfe, Tom Mitchell, Ken Oshman, Will Pape, Jim Patterson, Jon Peters, Carol Sands and George Sollman. A number of senior executives and board members have been generous in sharing their perspectives and experiences. They include Faruq Ahmad, Mark Allen, Deborah Barber, Bob Baxter, Janet Beach, Chris Carlton, Caretha Coleman, Keith Cotterill, Debra Engel,

Steve Engle, Mats Engstrand, David Foster, Charlotte Gubler, Jim Illich, Barry Karlin, Barbara Kerr, Tracy Koon, Meghan Leader, Dennis Paboojian, Lynn Phillips, Pete Peterson, Dennis Rohan, Rosemary Remacle, Clent Richardson, Kevin Sullivan and Phil Wilson.

In addition, several academic colleagues have influenced our thinking, and given us critical feedback over the years. We owe special thanks to John Child, Hal Leavitt, Robert Burgelman, Glenn Carroll, Sandra Dawson, John Freeman, Stig Hagstrom, Ralph Keeney, Martin Kenney, Gianni Lorenzoni, Barry Staw, and the late Gunnar Hedlund. We'd also like to express our warm gratitude and sincere thanks to Ulrike Baumoel for her expert advice and professional guidance.

Special thanks are due to our international associates who have encouraged us to relate the experiences of Silicon Valley to broader challenges facing global companies in different industries. They include Tony Andersson, Jacinta Calverley, Ake Ekblad, Hamish Fordwood, Christian Jenny, Reinhard Jung, Guiliana Lavendel, Nils Mehr, Ken Miki, Christophe Soutter, Markus Stricker, Beat Umbricht, and Hubert Weber. We would also like to extend our sincere thanks to Dr. Werner Mueller and the team at Springer-Verlag, who have been patiently supportive throughout the publication process, and to Claire Dolan for her creative artwork. Last but not least, we truly appreciate the inspiration, support and encouragement of our parents, families and friends.

Menlo Park, California
June 2004

Homa Bahrami
Stuart Evans

Contents

1 Super-Flexibility: A Toolkit for Dynamic Adaptation 1
   1.1 Revision-Triggers and Super-Flexibility 4
   1.2 Silicon Valley and Dynamic Adaptation 5
   1.3 The Concept of Super-Flexibility 7
   1.4 The Organization of the Book 9

2 Conceptual Foundations of Super-Flexibility 15
   2.1 Flexibility: Multi-Disciplinary Contributions 16
   2.2 Flexibility: Related Concepts 20
      2.2.1   Adaptability 22
      2.2.2   Agility 23
      2.2.3   Ambidexterity 24
      2.2.4   Hedging 25
      2.2.5   Liquidity 26
      2.2.6   Malleability 27
      2.2.7   Mobility 28
      2.2.8   Modularity 28
      2.2.9   Plasticity 30
      2.2.10 Resilience 32
      2.2.11 Robustness 34
      2.2.12 Versatility 36
   2.3 Integrating Different Senses of Flexibility 36
   2.4 Conclusion 40

3 The Research Laboratory: Silicon Valley's Knowledge Ecosystem 43
   3.1 Conceptual Underpinnings 44
   3.2 The Evolution of Silicon Valley 45
   3.3 The Building Blocks 47
      3.3.1 The Knowledge Originators 48
      3.3.2 The Knowledge Hatcheries 50
      3.3.3 The Knowledge Generators 51
      3.3.4 The Knowledge Lubricants 53
   3.4 The Ecosystem's "Climate" 54
      3.4.1 Goal-Driven Work Ethic and Eternal Optimism 55
      3.4.2 Limited "Safety Net" and Minimal "Life Support System" ... 56
      3.4.3 Collaborative Partnerships and Recombinant Innovations 58
   3.5 Super-Flexibility and the Ecosystem 59

4 Super-Flexible Ecosystems: Innovating by Recycling 61
4.1 Recycling Catalysts 62
4.1.1 Recycling by Re-Creating: High Birth Rates for New Ventures 63
4.1.2 Recycling by Cross-Pollinating: Talent Re-Deployment and Information Diffusion 66
4.1.3 Recycling by Recursive Learning: Exploring, Prototyping and Failing 68
4.1.4 Recycling by Re-Inventing: Re-Financing, Re-Packaging and Re-Purposing 69
4.2 Case History 71
4.3 Recycling and Super-Flexibility 75

5 Super-Flexible Strategies: Shifting Gears and Maneuvering Swift Turns 77
5.1 Conceptual Underpinnings 77
5.2 Revision-Triggers 79
5.3 Maneuvering: The "Time" Dimension 81
5.4 Maneuvering: The "Intent" Dimension 82
5.5 Maneuvering to Achieve Super-Flexibility: A Conceptual Framework 84
5.5.1 Pre-emptive Maneuvers 85
5.5.2 Protective Maneuvers 89
5.5.3 Corrective Maneuvers 91
5.5.4 Exploitive Maneuvers 93
5.6 Maneuvering and Super-Flexibility 95

6 Super-Flexible Execution: Experimenting, Iterating and Recalibrating 99
6.1 Conceptual Underpinnings 99
6.2 The Framework: Recalibration 103
6.3 Case History: ROLM Corporation 106
6.3.1 Phase 1: Experimentation 108
6.3.2 Phase 2: Escalation 110
6.3.3 Phase 3: Integration 112
6.4 Recalibration in Action 114
6.5 Guidelines for Implementation 116
6.6 Recalibration and Super-Flexibility 119

7 Super-Flexible Organizations:
Orgitechting Geo-Distributed Federations 123
- 7.1 Conceptual Underpinnings 123
- 7.2 Organizational Challenges of Knowledge Enterprises 125
- 7.3 Contrasting Static and Dynamic Architectures 126
- 7.4 Diagnostic Framework:
  Building Blocks of Dynamic Organizations 128
- 7.5 Organizational "Anatomy" 129
- 7.6 Organizational "Circulation" 134
- 7.7 Organizational "Personality" 141
- 7.8 Illustrative Case Study 144
- 7.9 Implementation Guidelines 146
- 7.10 Geo-Distributed Organizations and Super-Flexibility 150

8 Super-Flexible Leadership:
Aligning Knowledge Workers Through Peer-Peer Practices 153
- 8.1 Who Are Knowledge Workers? 153
- 8.2 What Makes Knowledge Workers Tick? 154
- 8.3 Peer-Peer Leadership 156
- 8.4 Front-Line Practices 158
  - 8.4.1 Ensuring Knowledge Worker Fit 160
  - 8.4.2 Providing Structured Freedom 161
  - 8.4.3 Creating Shared Reality 162
  - 8.4.4 Orchestrating Distributed Teamwork 164
- 8.5 Aligning and Super-Flexibility 166

9 Becoming Super-Flexible: The Enterprise in Motion 169
- 9.1 New Game/ Old Rules 169
- 9.2 Concluding Thoughts 173

10 References and Additional Readings 177

11 Index 205

12 Biographies 209

Figures

Figure 1	Alternative methods for dealing with uncertainty	2
Figure 2	Categories of revision-triggers	4
Figure 3	Defining super-flexibility: Critical attributes	8
Figure 4	Overview of the book	10
Figure 5	The "polymorphous" nature of flexibility	37
Figure 6	The arc of super-flexibility	38
Figure 7	Silicon Valley's knowledge originators	48
Figure 8	Recycling mechanisms	62
Figure 9	Categories of personal and professional networks	67
Figure 10	Spinoffs from Shugart in the disk drive industry	73
Figure 11	Super-flexible strategies: The maneuvering framework	85
Figure 12	The deliberate model	100
Figure 13	The emergent model	101
Figure 14	The recalibration model	104
Figure 15	The three phases of the recalibration process	105
Figure 16	The experimentation phase	109
Figure 17	The escalation phase	111
Figure 18	The integration phase	113
Figure 19	Contrasting organizational models	127
Figure 20	The nodal architecture: A diagnostic framework	128
Figure 21	Evolution of the "anatomy" or "base" structure in high tech companies	132
Figure 22	The circulation: Different types of connective tools	135
Figure 23	Connecting silos: Horizontal 'circulation'	138
Figure 24	Cross-pollinators and hubs	140
Figure 25	Differentiated task portfolio for corporate/ HQ functions	148
Figure 26	Categories of knowledge workers	154
Figure 27	Comparing "parent-child" and peer-peer" leadership practices	157
Figure 28	Super-Flexibility in action: A toolkit for dynamic adaptation	175

Tables

Table 1	Multi-disciplinary contributions to understanding flexibility	18
Table 2	Concepts resembling flexibility	21
Table 3	Super-Flexibility and its different nuances	40
Table 4	Silicon Valley's major areas of economic activity 2007	47
Table 5	Top twenty firms in Silicon Valley, 1982 and 2002	58
Table 6	Annual number of venture-funded start-ups	64
Table 7	Spin-offs from leading firms in Silicon Valley and the Boston area	66
Table 8	Different attributes of super-flexibility and their impact	174

1 Super-Flexibility: A Toolkit for Dynamic Adaptation

These are challenging times for business entities. We face the restructuring of the global financial system, complex geopolitical challenges, environmental concerns, generational differences, social tensions, ethical dilemmas, widespread diffusion of technology and legislative demands for compliance and transparency. Knowledge workers struggle to create balanced life styles, to prioritize in the face of overwhelming demands, and to juggle the combined pressures of collaborative teamwork and personal impact. The world of business is ready for innovation and creative thinking. We are truly at a critical inflection point, prompting us to think out of the box, and to pioneer new approaches and novel practices.

The collective impacts of these game-changing developments have eroded the core assumptions of stability and predictability and point to a very different future. The key to success, we argue, is to harness and thrive on uncertainty. We need flexible business strategies, dynamic leadership capabilities, and fluid organizational architectures, actionable tools and practical frameworks that can help business leaders diagnose situations on the fly, and develop innovative solutions for solving complex and novel challenges.

Thriving on uncertainty is easier said than done. We are creatures of habit and do not change unless we have to. The same can be said of business entities. Although it is common sense to suggest that leadership teams should look ahead, anticipate, and take proactive steps, this seldom happens. As we have seen with the financial crisis of 08-09, many leaders act after the fact, when the crisis has already unfolded. Weak signals of impending change are usually ignored or rationalized away (Roberto, Bohmer & Edmondson 2006). Examples of proactive adaptation are hard to come by. As research indicates, established entities have a difficult time "innovating" (Christensen 1997). Disruptive technologies and pioneering products are typically introduced by nimble start-ups, not by resource-rich incumbents. Active inertia takes over and "sudden left turns" are hard to make.

Despite the prevalence of active inertia, the dark clouds of the recent global crisis may have a silver lining; business leaders and knowledge workers are searching for novel recipes to reinvent themselves for the new world. This task presents a major challenge because the kernels of our leadership tools and conceptual frameworks were forged in a different era, when the business scene was relatively stable and predictable. Major breakthroughs took time to unfold and could be anticipated, and planned for, in advance. In fact, the assumption of stability and predictability has been the cornerstone of our strategic, organizational and managerial thought and practice during the last few decades. Now this has all changed, possibly forever.

Even before the onset of the global financial crisis, business ecosystems had become more interdependent and turbulent. As a result, front-line business practices have evolved during the past decade to make companies more flexible and adaptive. Examples of gradual adaptation include reliance on partnering and outsourcing, variable use of contractors and contingent workers, deployment of cross-functional teams and geo-distributed virtual groups, dissemination of knowledge management systems and e-business tools, and the re-engineering of core business processes.

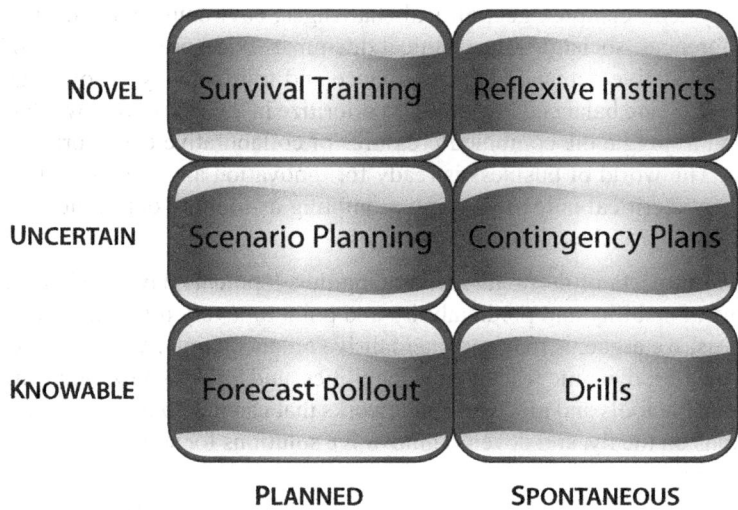

Figure 1. Alternative methods for dealing with uncertainty

Conventional wisdom, as indicated in Figure 1, suggests that the optimal way to prepare for the future is to plan ahead, forecast different scenarios, and develop contingency plans. This approach makes sense when we face "knowable" contexts. The problem is that planning is not enough when we face novel situations. Although it may be costly to wait until the disaster hits, as was the case with Hurricane Katrina and the global financial crisis, the "real" impact of a crisis is only "revealed" when it actually unfolds. Knowledge workers need conceptual tools that can help them diagnose situations on the fly and to develop realistic solutions spontaneously and almost instinctively.

Navigating dynamic reality is challenging enough even when we know what to expect. It becomes especially perplexing when we get into new domains and uncharted territories. Analogous to driving through foggy conditions or sand storms, this is a time when business leaders must rely on their collective instincts and act quickly and often intuitively, under immense pressure. How can we sharpen our instincts? How can we navigate in novel situations? Where can we learn how to harness novelty and extreme forms of uncertainty?

Although many established companies have deployed flexible business practices in recent years, these have been superimposed on their old foundations, In order to understand recipes for dynamic adaptation, we need to look beyond established firms trying to remodel themselves. It is important to observe and gain insights from a new generation at work; business entities that thrive on novelty, but that in addition, are not constrained by tradition, history, and active inertia. They can think creatively without having their hands tied behind their backs.

Silicon Valley is an ideal research laboratory for studying dynamic adaptation. In this setting, rapid adaptation is a "must-have" capability, not just a "nice-to-have" benefit. The pace of change is frenzied and intense. Products, markets, distribution channels and competitive boundaries are in a state of continuous flux. The environment has a high propensity for "kaleidoscopic" change. A firm can be seriously impaired by the departure of a key executive, the unexpected loss of a critical account, personality clashes, in addition to challenges related to product performance and market traction in pioneering domains. Indeed, the nature of change in this arena can be best defined as a "Kuhnian inversion"; long periods of frenzied change, punctuated briefly by stable interludes.[1] *Based on the experience of knowledge enterprises in Silicon Valley's Darwinian ecosystem, this book presents diagnostic frameworks and business practices that can facilitate the process of dynamic adaptation.*

Our central thesis is that:
- In today's turbulent and interconnected world, a multitude of "revision-triggers" bombard firms and force them to deviate from planned courses of action. Revision-triggers operate at different altitudes. Some operate at the super-macro or at the 50,000 feet altitude and redefine the broader context within which businesses operate; examples include the end of the "Cold War", the tragedy of September 11, the revolutionary impact of the Internet, the rise of emerging economies, and the global financial crisis. Others operate on the ground or at zero altitude; the sudden departure of a key team member, the unexpected loss of a critical account, clashes among the core leadership team, or surprising competitive moves, are examples of "micro" revision-triggers.
- The challenge, as illustrated in Figure 1, is not only to predict, but more importantly, to be prepared for rapid adaptation. It is impossible to anticipate and plan ahead for every possible eventuality. We need the capability to draw on our "reflexive instincts", to act "in situ", to improvise quickly and spontaneously, as new triggers unfold. Our leadership "toolkit" should enable us to diagnose on the fly, and to take rapid action as new realities unfold. We need to continuously adapt and to re-adapt to novel situations.
- The key to dynamic adaptation, we argue, is to become super-flexible. Super-flexibility is a complex construct that does not fit our traditional "either/or" perspectives. On the one hand, it refers to the capacity to change course, to transform, to evolve, and to reinvent; just like a chameleon changing its color, a snake shedding its skin, or a tadpole evolving into a frog. On the

---

[1] In his seminal work, Kuhn (1962) emphasized that scientific revolutions follow a similar pattern; long periods of relative stability are periodically ruptured by a major discontinuity. Our view is that today the business environment can be best depicted in terms of a "Kuhnian inversion", long periods of frenzied change, followed by brief, stable interludes.change, followed by brief, stable interludes.

other hand, it is about the capacity to withstand turbulence, to bounce back, to weather stormy conditions, and to stay the course, like a starfish re-growing its arm, or a camel surviving in desert conditions.

1.1 Revision-Triggers and Super-Flexibility

What causes entrepreneurs, business leaders, and knowledge workers to make "sudden left turns" and to veer away from planned courses of action? Why are the themes of adaptability, flexibility, and dynamic recipes critical success factors in today's turbulent world? What are the underlying forces that may prompt us to embark on dynamic adaptation?

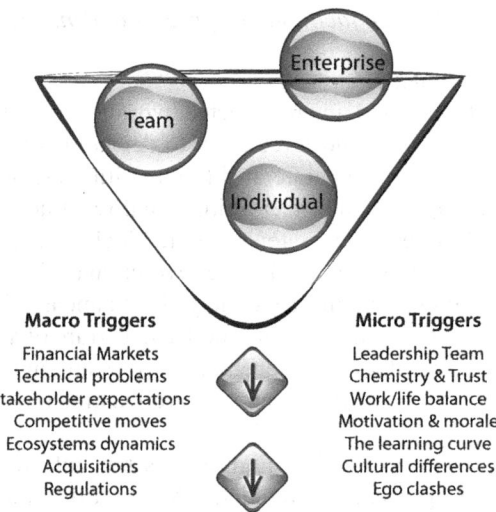

Figure 2. Categories of revision-triggers

As depicted in Figure 2, a myriad of "revision-triggers" can come into play. They include personality clashes between the key players; surprising moves by competitors, invention of new technologies and products, and shifting market conditions and consumer confidence; In the grander scheme of things, geopolitical, regulatory, environmental, technological, cultural, and economic forces can drive adaptation. When the price of oil dropped from $140 a barrel to less than $40, energy companies had to reexamine their portfolios and reprioritize their programs.

Consider a few examples of revision-triggers at work:
- A biotech company derives most of its profits from a single "block-buster" product. The product gets FDA approval and sales soar. Some time later, clinical trials, conducted in other geographies, begin to show signs of undesir-

able side effects. Although, with hindsight, the weak signals may have been visible, it took some time to respond to the crisis and restructure the business.
- The co-founder of a software start-up, funded by a leading venture firm, falls out with a key investor when they argue over the appointment of a seasoned CEO. The prototype is well received by the pundits; several venture firms are eager to fund the next round. However, personality clashes on the board fester and attention shifts to internal power dynamics. The feud leads to the parting of the ways. The founders have to look for alternative sources of funding. The action delays work on product development; the team loses momentum and misses the market window for an exit strategy.
- A start-up launches its website and gets several hundred thousand hits. The company looks set to succeed. Within a month of launch, the initial surge subsides and it is clear that the company needs a new trajectory. The CEO convenes an emergency off-site; a junior engineer comes up with a new idea for redeploying its core technology. This results in a highly successful product launch. The company secures its series "B" funding with a high valuation.

As we can see from these examples, revision-triggers have differential impact on businesses. Although weak signals are clearly visible with hindsight, they are initially ignored or go unnoticed. Many leaders are slow to respond; some rationalize the situation, others have selective hearing. The point to note is that in today's interconnected world, revision-triggers come in different shapes and sizes. As is the case with monitoring blood sugar or cholesterol levels, critical business triggers should be identified, categorized and monitored as a prelude to dynamic adaptation.

1.2 Silicon Valley and Dynamic Adaptation

Silicon Valley is an ideal research laboratory for studying the process of dynamic adaptation. This knowledge ecosystem is intensely competitive, continuously innovative, and lives with uncertainties about which there can be limited prior knowledge. Firms are inundated with a myriad of revision-triggers. Typically, there is little lead-time to anticipate and develop contingency plans ahead of time. In order to succeed, technology firms need to continually evolve their trajectories real-time, and to refocus resources on successive targets, often with different rules of engagement.

The need for dynamic adaptation is highlighted when we consider the complex set of challenges facing technology companies during different stages of growth:
- Raising successive rounds of funding to ramp-up and scale a new venture.
- Competing with, yet cooperating selectively, with competitors.
- Migrating the business trajectory from end-of-life products and services to innovative solutions and emerging market segments.
- Remaining disciplined, focused, and frugal, while innovating, experimenting and learning.

- Getting input and buy-in from experts and opinionated knowledge workers, yet ensuring fast and timely decisions.
- Connecting a globally-distributed organization through the hard wire of IT while ensuring the development of a community-based culture that nurtures emotional connectivity.
- Developing simple and standard templates, metrics, and formats for systematic knowledge sharing, whilst ensuring the capability for customized approaches that cater for unique, one-off, situations.
- Balancing the need for local accountability and responsiveness, in the context of a well-coordinated global approach.
- Reorganizing to address emerging realities, in the context of a few stable anchors that don't change as frequently.

The challenge is aptly captured in the following comment:

"High technology obeys the iron law of revolution, ...the more you change, the more you have to change..., you have to be willing to accept the fact that in this game the rules keep changing."[2]

Many firms create, or quickly enter, pioneering markets with innovative products without the benefit of role models and blueprints for success. They are founded by entrepreneurial teams, populated by cosmopolitan "knowledge workers" with a multitude of career options and complex expectations of self-actualization. In this Darwinian ecosystem, the challenge is to grasp fleeting opportunities, innovate continuously, and compete globally from the outset. As such, Silicon Valley and its innovative, entrepreneurial firms have provided a fertile research laboratory for understanding the core principles and practices of dynamic adaptation.

Swift action, mobility, and ephemeral enterprises are the critical features of Silicon Valley. Organizational structures are fluid; they undergo frequent adjustments and constant realignments. Today's successful business models only endure for a short time. Incumbent firms must find new business propositions and reinvent themselves, before they become obsolete. Pioneering products quickly become commodities, and today's premium pricing strategy, with high gross margins, hits the bottom of the "waterfall" abruptly. Successful start-ups can unexpectedly turn into black holes. In such a turbulent setting, dynamic adaptation is highly prized.

Our point of view is that Silicon Valley and its entrepreneurial companies can help us learn about the process of dynamic adaptation. Their business strategies and organizational structures typically deal with fleeting opportunities and novel tasks. Even long-standing Valley companies strive to be "forever adolescent". They constantly reinvent themselves by re-assessing market opportunities, killing old products, and introducing new products in rapid succession. Apple has transformed itself from a personal computer company, to a consumer electronics and mobile comput-

---

[2] Bill Joy (co-founder of Sun Microsystems) in a speech at the Churchill Club, Palo Alto, California, 1990.

ing pioneer. Hewlett Packard has evolved from a product-based company to a services and solutions entity. Intel reinvented itself as a processor company and exited the memory business. Google has leveraged its blockbuster search engine to diversify into a whole host of web-based solutions. Adobe has evolved from a printing and document company to web-based authoring across all media types. Most of a high tech firm's revenues derive from products and services that are typically less than 18 months old. The key imperative is to continuously innovate, to adapt, and to reinvent.

The challenge is to organize, strategize and manage for the moment, and keep options open for the long haul. There is no "buffering", no slack, no cushion, to shield enterprises and entrepreneurs from market realities. What counts is *de facto* market acceptance, rather than *de jure* norms imposed by committees. Does my product have major benefits valued by a target group of potential customers, or is it just a cool technology? Is someone willing to pay for this benefit? Can I continue to deliver value or is this just a quick one-off? Is this a "must-have" or a "nice-to-have"? No amount of spin, inspirational story, good press, prestigious venture funding, or a distinguished board is likely to sustain the firm in the long run. It may sustain it as a "living dead", supported by an artificial life support system. Given the constant turbulence, Silicon Valley is an ideal research laboratory to understand the game of dynamic adaptation and the rules by which it is played.

1.3 The Concept of Super-Flexibility

Flexibility sounds simple but it is a complex construct. As we will later discuss in chapter 2, it has been the subject of interest in many disciplines. It means being "agile", able to move rapidly, change course to take advantage of an opportunity or to sidestep a threat. It is also about being versatile; the ability to do different things and to deploy various capabilities depending on the needs of a particular situation. The concept can also mean being robust, able to absorb shocks and to withstand adversity; and about being resilient, able to recover and to spring back from the brink of disaster.

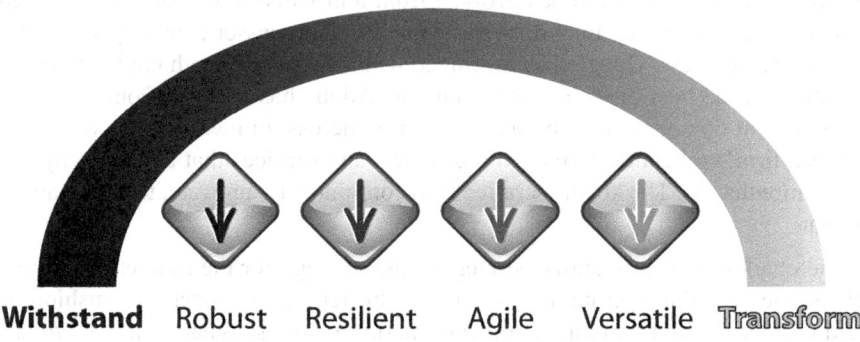

Figure 3. Defining super-flexibility: Critical attributes

These different senses point to a "polymorphous" concept. That is why we aggregate these diverse attributes under the conceptual rubric of "super-flexibility". Its practical deployment, we argue, requires a broad array of principles, capabilities, and attributes. For example, having the liquidity to exploit an unexpected opportunity is qualitatively different from possessing a resilient disposition to deal with the negative impact of an accident, or a mistake. Similarly, reliance on "redundant" mechanisms, such as insurance, buffers or slack, to protect against potentially damaging situations, is different from the dexterity needed in being agile or versatile when entering new markets. Yet clearly, these notions are in some way related. When we refer broadly to "super-flexibility", it denotes these different senses.

The term "super-flexibility", as depicted in Figure 3, is used in this book to describe an enterprise's ability to address the entire spectrum; the capability to reinvent and transform, by being agile and versatile, much like an entrepreneurial company, combined with the capacity to withstand turbulence, by remaining robust and resilient, attributes historically associated with established corporations. The challenge is to harness novelty, move swiftly, and manage for the moment, while simultaneously withstanding turbulence and providing anchors of stability. Although this dialectical goal may be unattainable in its purest form, knowledge workers have to surf successive waves of market turbulence and technological innovation, without losing a sense of cohesion, identity and stability.

Super-flexibility refers to the dialectical capacity of *withstanding while transforming*. A truly super-flexible entity should move quickly and adopt a variable posture, with the built-in capacity to withstand turbulence. It must deploy the most appropriate capability, depending on the context and the revision-triggers. In an evolutionary context, we argue that it needs a diverse "gene pool", capable of exhibiting what biologists term "phenotype plasticity".

1.4 The Organization of the Book

What are the underlying principles that can help explain how super-flexibility can be implemented in dynamic settings? How do the innovative firms of Silicon Valley evolve their strategic trajectories when they can only predict a few weeks ahead? How do they organize for rapid growth on the one hand, and sudden downturns on the other? How do they give their knowledge workers anchors of stability and yet retain the flexibility to switch "on and off" at short notice? How do they embark on, and commit to, major initiatives when they have imperfect information and limited resources?

This book is about the strategic, the organizational and the leadership principles that have shaped Silicon Valley as the innovation engine of the digital age. The game is partly about dynamic adaptation, thriving on perpetual novelty; the rules of the game are about creating and surfing successive waves of innovation. Our over arching objective in this book is to translate the core principles of dynamic adaptation into conceptual frameworks and practical tools that can help knowledge workers diagnose situations on the fly and to develop customized solutions. Our focus is on business practices that can proactively harness, not just retroactively respond to, novelty and uncertainty.

Our findings are the result of 25 years of exposure to the phenomena, including field research, advisory work, and professional experience in Silicon Valley. We have studied and worked with many technology companies during various stages of growth, ranging from emerging start-ups, to mid-sized adolescents, and global giants. Our learning journey has taken us to different technology domains, including semiconductors, enterprise software, hardware, storage systems, peripherals, telecommunications equipment, Internet portals, search companies, biotech and life science firms. In addition, we have served on several public, private, and advisory boards, giving us "unfiltered", first-hand perspectives on critical realities and business challenges.

The core principles of super-flexibility are described in the following eight chapters. Chapter 2 focuses on the concept of flexibility, its historical antecedents, and its treatment in various disciplines. We explore the various senses of flexibility; from agility, liquidity, and versatility, to robustness and resilience. A super-flexible entity, we suggest, is agile and versatile, and robust and resilient. It is capable of balancing both: withstanding turbulence and evolving as new realities unfold. This chapter may be of special interest to research students and academic scholars interested in the foundational building blocks of flexibility and its treatment in different disciplines.

10   Super-Flexibility: A Toolkit for Dynamic Adaptation

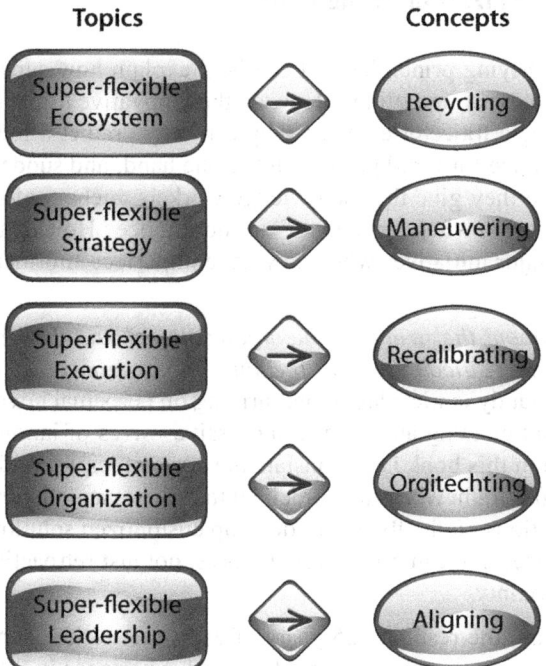

Figure 4. Overview of the book

Chapter 3 focuses on our research laboratory, the knowledge ecosystem of Silicon Valley. We describe the core building blocks of the Silicon Valley ecosystem; from originators and hatcheries, to catalysts and generators. In this Darwinian setting, the name of the game is harnessing kaleidoscopic change, focusing on innovation, changing the rules, and reinventing the future, while pruning excess to survive downturns and to withstand difficult market conditions. Entities in Silicon Valley also have to guide and motivate multi-cultural knowledge workers, whose preferences and core skills continuously evolve.

Chapters 4 through 8 are about the action principles of super-flexibility: how this capability is put into practice; how it influences strategy, structure, and leadership practices for guiding and engaging knowledge workers. As depicted in Figure 4 five interlocking principles are the foundational building blocks of super-flexibility: These are:

1. Innovating by *recycling* know-how, talent, and assets in a multi-polar ecosystem.
2. Strategizing by developing a variable portfolio of initiatives, changing gears between offensive and defensive moves, and dynamically *maneuvering* the business trajectory real-time.
3. Executing by *recalibrating* assumptions, initiatives and actions as new realities unfold, and by rapid prototyping and targeted *experimentation*.

4. Organizing by *orgitechting* a multi-polar, *geo-distributed federation*, and by clarifying *"federal/state"* rules of engagement.
5. Leading by *aligning and re-aligning* multi-cultural knowledge workers around dynamic realities and by *deploying peer-peer practices*.

Chapter 4, on "recycling", is about how the Silicon Valley ecosystem turns setbacks into opportunities. It is about learning from failure and putting that learning to effective use. Recycling is one approach for harnessing "failures". The process nurtures innovation, fosters entrepreneurship, and cross-pollinates know-how. It gives birth to new firms, blends in "failed" initiatives, and combines elements of old and new. In essence, recycling encourages life after death; the people, the know-how, and the capabilities of failed ventures and discontinued initiatives are recycled in the broader ecosystem, giving rise to new enterprises, new innovations, and new teams. Failure is viewed as a temporary "setback", to learn from, not to be punished for. It provides the foundation for future innovations.

The concept of "maneuvering" is discussed in chapter 5. Maneuvering is about how technology companies navigate their dynamic business trajectories by not putting "all eggs in one basket". It describes the process of strategizing by continually changing gears and refocusing a firm's know-how on shifting centers of gravity. The maneuvering framework proposes parallel deployment of offensive and defensive moves before, or after, revision-triggers. It focuses on a continuous search for new opportunities, and constant correction of mistakes. The goal of this chapter is to develop a conceptual framework around which intentions, capabilities, and resources can be configured to focus on successive opportunities. Four types of maneuver, pre-emtive, protective, opportunistic, and corrective, are proposed as a diagnostic framework and as an intervention tool.

Chapter 6 presents the principle of recalibrating. Recalibration is about dynamic execution. The term refers to real-time adjustments that have to be made as circumstances unfold. It describes a process of learning by probing, experimenting, prototyping, failing, succeeding, and trying again. Analogous to the scientific model of discovery, it describes the interlinked stages of experimentation, escalation, and integration. Effective recalibration is about the ability to change gears by leveraging fact-based feedback. The process is about rapid prototyping and targeted testing in uncharted fields.

In the recalibration framework, the processes of strategy formation and execution are linked together in an iterative process. In pioneering settings, it is difficult to iron out all the uncertainties and "de-risk" strategies through detailed planning and elaborate analyses, before execution. Relevant information is hard to come by; the underlying assumptions morph and evolve. It may be difficult to establish the technical feasibility of a new technology, or the market viability of a pioneering product, through "theoretical" planning. By engaging in action, new information can be brought to light, and unforeseen limitations, and new possibilities, identified.

The organizational configuration of dynamic enterprises is described in chapter 7. In contrast to the "unipolar" hierarchies of the industrial age, super-flexible entities have a multi-polar, geo-distributed, architecture. They resemble "federal" systems, have distributed "brains", and are organized around several centers of competence. The challenge is to conceptualize the organization as a living organism, not as a mechanical machine; this means that business leaders have to diagnose and fine-tune the organizational architecture on a regular basis. The goal is to orgitecht super-flexible organizations that are capable of withstanding turbulence, yet adapting, as and when needed, to harness new opportunities.

The 'multi-polar" architecture consists of 3 building blocks; the "anatomy" or the clustering dimension; the "circulation" or the connective dimension; the "personality" or the cohesive dimension. The anatomy consists of geo-distributed, cross-functional, teams with complex interdependencies. The "circulation" is about different types of interactions, enabled through core processes, virtual interactions and personal networks. The personality is about an entity's "core DNA", its non-negotiable values, leadership principles, and behavioral norms. The three building blocks are blended together to create organizational architectures that can be stable yet dynamic, uniform yet differentiated.

The critical challenge is to balance what may appear to be mutually exclusive tensions and to think in terms of trade-offs and "shades of grey". On the one hand, the organization needs to be disciplined, lean, and focused, with minimal duplication of effort, stringent accountability, and guided direction. On the other hand, it is important to minimize complex coordination, provide room for self-management, and develop the capability for rapid response to front-line realities. Innovation and speed have to be balanced with focus and control. The imperative is to strike a dynamic balance between these apparent opposites and to consider the critical "trade-offs". The key enabler is to clarify and communicate non-negotiable "federal" mandates, so that front-line "states" can exercise discretion and address dynamic realities real-time.

Chapter 8, on the principle of "aligning" refers to leadership practices that can motivate, engage, and enable knowledge workers to pool together their collective talents in realizing common goals. Creating shared reality and getting everyone on the same page is easier said than done. Leaders have to think about the "softer" themes of emotional engagement, and the "harder" elements of project management in cross-functional, geo-distributed, multi-cultural contexts. Effective leaders provide guided direction and recognize the need for personal initiative. They understand the significance of financial rewards, and the critical value of intellectual and emotional motivators.

In the spirit of peer-peer, rather than the traditional parent-child leadership, the aligning framework revolves around four sets of practices: Interactive communication of "context"; ensuring person-values "fit"; collaborating in cross-functional, geo-distributed teams, and creating defined boundaries by setting clear expectations and clarifying "non-negotiable" golden rules.

We propose these five action principles as the operational means of becoming super-flexible: being resilient and robust yet agile and versatile; managing for the moment, while keeping the long-term destination in mind; continuously reinventing, in the context fundamental core beliefs and value propositions. A super-flexible entity can shift its priorities and trajectory. It can change gears and maneuver realtime. It recalibrates its approach when faced with new realities. It recycles people, assets and technologies; and it re-align its knowledge workers as it morphs and evolves. The generals are aligned with the troops, picking up signals from the frontliners. In short, a super-flexible entity is dynamic and mobile, designed to enact change, not just react to change.

Just as scientists learn from controlled experiments in a laboratory, established firms can benefit from the experience of Silicon Valley and its high tech entities. In chapter 9, we reflect on a few lessons that traditional enterprises can take away from this entrepreneurial ecosystem. This chapter summarizes our key findings and puts forward a few practical suggestions. The focus is on how established companies can be reinvented, in order to become super-flexible.

Our target audience include entrepreneurs, business leaders, and knowledge workers whose enterprises are experiencing schizophrenia. They have one foot entrenched in the old camp of tradition, inertia, and recipes born of historic success during the industrial age. They have another foot firmly placed in the emerging world of technology, globalization and knowledge-based economies. Our goal is to help our readers learn about dynamic adaptation so they can harness new opportunities emerging in today's dynamic age. As Tom Watson, IBM's leader, observed long ago:

"Technological change demands an even greater measure of adaptability and versatility on the part of the management of a large organization. Unless management remains alert, it can be stricken with complacency, one of the most insidious dangers we face in business. In most cases it's hard to tell that you have caught the disease until its almost too late. It is frequently most infectious among companies that have already reached the top. They get to believing in the infallibility of their own judgment." (Watson 1963: 63)

2 Conceptual Foundations of Super-Flexibility: A Multi-Disciplinary Synthesis

Flexibility is often invoked as a panacea for operating in dynamic contexts. We define it as the "propensity to adapt, at times spontaneously, to fluid conditions". In practice, it is a means of enacting swift changes and making sudden turns in order to harness new opportunities and address challenging situations. Examples include rapid acceleration (such as in entering new markets, deploying new technologies, and making acquisitions), immediate disengagement (from an unattractive market), applying brakes in an emergency (such as in a financial crisis), and deploying shock absorbers (for example in dealing with hostile takeovers).

In view of its universal intuitive appeal, flexibility has been a topic of research in several disciplines. These include economics, evolutionary biology, decision analysis and game theory, information systems, manufacturing systems, strategic management, organizational design, child development and, at its most acute form, military strategy. Several terms have been used to convey the idea, including strategic flexibility, operational flexibility, internal and external flexibility, financial flexibility, agile information systems, flexible work arrangements, flexible manufacturing systems, strategic agility, and strategic resilience. Although the terminology may be different, they all refer to the capacity to make swift adjustments in order to adapt to novel situations. This chapter examines previous research on the topic through the lenses of both, a microscope and a telescope.

As is the case in the natural world, a multitude of triggers may prompt an entity to adapt. They range from mega-events to the unique conjunction of mundane coincidences. Moreover, surprises, serendipity, luck, mistakes and accidents, both good and bad, trigger the need to adapt. Often the unique conjunction of "hard factors", (such as market expansion, supply chain pipelines, IT, manufacturing and distribution systems), and "soft" factors (such as the chemistry among the top team and their ability to function in different cultural settings) coalesce to produce metamorphic moments.

These episodes can seldom be predicted or reproduced under similar conditions. Factors such as stakeholder perceptions, interactions among geo-distributed teams, relationships with key customers or government officials can unhinge or energize an entity. These forces coalesce to create novel "revision-triggers".[1] Historically, in the old world, these events occurred periodically; changes could be predicted and contingency plans put in place. Today metamorphic events occur unexpectedly, rapidly and frequently. This makes it difficult to predict or to allow time to develop an appropriate response. Leadership teams try to evade danger or seize the moment by turning swiftly, reversing, accelerating, braking hard, intensifying, disengaging, and in general, deviating from an existing trajectory

---

[1] As stated by Brock and Carpenter 2009, p.45 "Flickering may trigger regime shifts" echoing the idea that the seeds of the change-inducing episode are difficult to discern ahead of time and may be weak.

To become viable, high tech ventures often "pivot"[2] through "knot-holes" or brief periods of intense "kaleidoscopic" transformation. The ensuing metamorphosis or reinvention, if successful, can unravel a varied array of adaptive niches, and expand the range of ecosystems in which it can thrive. There are, however, serious practical considerations when a firm pivots through a "knot-hole". The "adaptive DNA" of a company is typically forged during these formative episodes. This condition is reinforced by research studies in the field of neuroscience where, *"synaptic plasticity can be modulated, sometimes dramatically, by prior synaptic activity"* because *"prior synaptic activation can leave an enduring trace that affects the subsequent induction of synaptic plasticity"*.[3]

Knowledge enterprises, from start-up ventures to global corporations, frequently need to do things differently. The frequency of unexpected or spontaneous "revision-triggers" has always been prevalent in high tech ventures. Large corporations have historically found it difficult to adapt unless they experience potentially catastrophic situations. Today, even established global corporations are trying to adapt and to reinvent themselves for a dynamic world.

2.1   Flexibility: Multi-Disciplinary Contributions

A substantial body of research on the notion of flexibility can be found across a wide range of disciplines. The earliest contributions are in the field of military strategy. Two famous French Generals, Bourcet (1888) and Guibert, pioneered the use of the "divisional structure" and faster marching speeds to improve maneuverability in battle. Decades later, Clausewitz, the grandfather of modern strategy, emphasized flexibility in three over arching areas: the significance of the moral factors, the ability to concentrate forces at a decisive point, and the value of a standing reserve (von Guyczy et al. 2003, Hahlway 1966).

Flexibility was an implicit part of General Sherman's (1860) strategy during the American Civil War. During his Atlanta campaign, he dispensed with supplies to lighten the load, enabling rapid movement. To achieve this, he deployed his scouts in an ambidextrous role, not only to forage for food, but also to provide an early warning system. His railway engineers rapidly repaired tracks and bridges to enable his forces to move quickly. Decades later, the British military historian, Liddell-Hart (1929, 1954) proposed an "indirect approach" to strategy that was "adaptable to circumstances" as the cornerstone of flexibility. Other military strategists consider flexibility as an essential principle of warfare (Eccles 1959, Taylor 1959). Recently, the topic has taken on a broader significance because of technological sophistication and logistical complexity of contemporary warfare.

---

[2] Rip, 2006.

[3] Abraham, 1996, p. 126 & p. 129; see also de Visser, 2003, who explores the role of robustness in responding to epistatic effects in genetic adaptation.

Economists focused on flexibility during and after the Great Depression by examining the impact of oscillations in the business cycle on a firm's adaptive capability.[4] Arrow describes it as *"a known though not thoroughly explored concept that seems to have been introduced by Hart"*.[5] Hart focused on how business entities adapt to uncertainty in the aftermath of the Great Depression and on the creation of new entrepreneurial firms: *"The entrepreneur's fundamental means of meeting uncertainty is the postponement of decisions till more information comes in—that is to say the preservation of flexibility in his business plan."*[6] Significantly, he proposes flexibility as a fundamental management principle for dealing with uncertainty: *"Flexibility helps an individual or a firm preserve freedom to change plans without undue sacrifice if anticipations are revised."*[7] Shackle's notion of unexpected events (Shackle 1953), resulting in kaleidoscopic change, is echoed in Schumpeter's notion of "creative destruction" (1926, 1934) brought about by technological innovations (Hammond 2007). Economists have also examined flexibility with regard to changing tastes and preferences (Koopmans 1953). Koopmans argued the need for flexibility is driven as much by evolving tastes as by physical options, currently available, or projected to be, sometime in the future.

Agricultural economists also viewed flexibility as a potential response by farmers in dealing with agricultural price fluctuations.[8] Several studies have examined how farmers can respond flexibly by considering crop selection and rotation, or by switching between products, such as milk and cheese production. This agricultural focus was further extended by later research on the subject.[9]

---

[4] Hart 1937a,b, Kindleberger 1937; Knight 1921; Lange 1944, Stigler 1939, Tinbergen 1932, McKinsey 1932.

[5] Arrow 1995, p. 9.

[6] Hart 1937a, p. 286.

[7] Hart 1940, p 49.

[8] Backman 1940 a & b, 1948, Mason 1938, Nicholls 1940, Timoshenko 1930, French et al. 1956, Kerchner 1966.

[9] Carley & Cryer 1964, Collins 1956, Cowden & Trelogan 1948, French et al. 1956, Kerchner 1966.

DISCIPLINE	AREA OF FOCUS
Military strategy	Adapting operations in the "fog" of battle; Graduated response
Economics	New firm creation
Agriculture	Price fluctuations, crop rotation, technological capabilities
Manufacturing systems	Ordering of activities, sequencing of job shops, range and volume of product Modular manufacturing, product mix
Operations management	Supply chain agility, E-business
Strategic management	Meta-flexibility; managing the "unforeseen"
Decision theory	Future options, expected value of information, viable across a range of scenarios
Child psychology	Children and teenagers rebounding from adverse experiences
Information systems	Agile IT infrastructure
Organizational design	Structural flexibility
Financial engineering	Liquidity, hedging, real options, derivative & Swaps pricing
Systems analysis & environmental research	Repairing damaged ecosystems

Table 1. Multi-disciplinary contributions to understanding flexibility

Interest in the topic was rekindled after the 1973 Oil Crisis, particularly with regard to corporate strategy.[10] Strategic flexibility was viewed as a generic response to the "unforeseen". A flexible firm was considered to have *"the ability to change itself in such a way that it remains viable"*.[11] Other researchers viewed flexibility as a means of disengaging from an arena by removing obstacles and penalties (Harrigan 1980, 1985). Several scholars have discussed the importance of organizational flexibility in rapidly changing environments.[12] The term "strategic resilience" (Hamel & Valicangas 2003) was later coined as a critical capability in addressing turbulent business conditions. Recently, strategic agility has been proposed as a critical capability for developing a "fast strategy" (Doz 2008). In aggregate, as we discuss in Chapter 5, these capabilities collectively refer to a company's ability to rapidly "maneuver".

---

[10] Ansoff 1975, Eppink 1978a, 1978b, Krijnen 1979.

[11] Krijnen 1979, p. 64.

[12] Ackoff 1977, Perrow 1970, Thompson 1967, Tomlinson 1976.

Tactical and operational challenges have also led to the development of methods for evaluating flexibility in energy generation and distribution. These studies have focused, among other things, on the ability to switch inputs as prices change and/or supplies fluctuate.[13] Later, studies on flexible manufacturing systems focused on the variability of product mix and output volume.[14] Following the deployment of flexible manufacturing systems, a substantial body of literature has also emerged on supply chain agility in high technology industries. Attention was initially focused on calculating the value of flexibility (Kulatilaka 1988). Later research set out to integrate the various senses of flexibility. The notion of "flexagility" was proposed in operations management (Wadhwa & Rao 2003a & b).

Flexibility has also been examined in the field of engineering. The concept has been used in the design of complex systems, such as energy production, aerospace and IT.[15] Recently, Saleh defined flexibility as *"the property of a system that allows it to respond to changes in its initial objectives and requirements- both in terms of capabilities and attributes- occurring after the system has been fielded."*[16] The design, development, and deployment of this capability, as these scholars have pointed out, is infinitely more complex than installing something extra at the margin to address incremental oscillations.

Formal representational progress has also been made in using flexibility as a criterion for making optimal decisions. Decision theorists have formalized the impact of evolving preferences on multi-period choices,[17] have developed probabilistic measures of flexibility[18] and have examined the "robustness" of decisions to withstand future changes.[19] This stream of research has been extended to encompass "real-options" theory.[20] Research in finance has focused on the relationship between flexibility and liquidity as related to options and portfolio theory.[21]

---

[13] Draaisma & Mol 1977, Friedman & Reklaitis 1975, Fuss 1977, Guerico 1981, Schroeder et al. 1981, Van der Vet 1977.

[14] Adler 1988, Buzacott 1982, De Meyer et al. 1989, Gerwin 1982, Hutchinson 1973, Ira-vani et al. 2003, Mandelbaum & Brill 1989, Spur et al. 1976, Tilak 1978.

[15] Fuss 1997, Chen & Lewis 1999, Hamblin 2002, Saleh et al. 2001.

[16] Saleh 2008, p. 10.

[17] Day 1969, Koopmans 1964, Kreps 1979.

[18] Heimann & Lusk 1976, Klein & Meckling 1958, Mandelbaum 1978, 1989, Marschak & Nelson 1962, Merkhofer 1975.

[19] Pye 1978, Rosenhead 1972, 1980, Rosenhead et al. 1986.

[20] Triantis & Hodder 1990, Trigeorgis 1996, Raynor 2001, Trigeorgis & Schwartz 2001, Ekstrom & Bjornsson 2003, Gamba & Fusari 2009.

[21] Frazer 1985, Goldman 1978, Jones & Ostroy 1976, 1984, Mason, 1986.

In recent years, agility has been put forward as an effective methodology for software development.[22] With the advent of "autonomic" or self-adaptive computing, this stream of research will become more significant, especially in view of its impact on the evolution of e-business (Shi & Daniels 2003). Researchers have also examined the need for different types of user and IT system flexibility (Gebaur 2007) and its broader impact on strategy and organization (Weill 2003). How to achieve adaptive IT systems is a perennial challenge. As technology continues to evolve, research on this topic will gain additional momentum.

As described in this section, there has been an extensive body of multi-disciplinary research on the subject of flexibility. Yet research contributions have been somewhat fragmented, reflecting different priorities and situational contexts. Moreover, scholars have addressed the topic at different altitudes, and use various terms to describe the notion. These include "operational flexibility", "strategic flexibility", "internal flexibility", "external flexibility", "strategic resilience", and "strategic agility". The crux of the problem is that the value of flexibility is seldom precise yet rarely in doubt. The critical challenge is how to source and deploy it. In the following section, we set out to synthesize these contributions and to examine various terms that are related to flexibility.

2.2 Flexibility: Related Concepts

As we examine these contributions in some depth, we can distinguish between two discernable approaches. The first involves the study of flexibility in specific situations, typically within a disciplinary silo. The second approach is a multi-disciplinary review of the literature in order to develop a comprehensive definition, or a mathematical formulation, of flexibility. As pointed out in one such review, there are "*50 definitions of different types of flexibility in a manufacturing context*".[23] A management scholar prefaces his contribution by suggesting flexibility is often "*used as a magic word.*"[24]

Why does this recurrent definitional problem exist when the concept is so intuitively valued? It has been 70 years since Hart's seminal work and the problem still exists in spite of many efforts to put forward a precise definition. In almost every substantive contribution to the field, we find a common starting point, namely to clarify the ill-defined nature of the concept. We suggest the source of this conundrum is the "polymorphous" nature of flexibility, as evidenced by the interchangeable use of several related terms (Evans 1982a). Related terms include, agil-

---

[22] Cockburn 2001, Del Prete et al. 2003.
[23] Saleh et.al. 2008, p. 1.
[24] Volberda, 1998, p.2; see also Kickert 1985.

ity, adaptability, versatility, resilience, and robustness. Other concepts, such as dexterity, elasticity, liquidity, malleability, modularity, mobility, and plasticity are also at times substituted for flexibility. Table 2 defines these related concepts.

CONCEPTS	DEFINITIONS
Agility	Moving nimbly into and out of areas of interest
Elasticity	Stretching & shrinking with different pressures
(Ambi)dexterity	Developing bifunctional capability, i.e. using both hands adroitly, explore and exploit simultaneously
Hedging	Mitigating against the losses associated with "downside" potential at a cost
Liquidity	Transforming assets without switching costs
Malleability	Able to be bent, molded or manipulated to meet unusual conditions or unorthodox circumstances
Mobility	Re-deployable assets and capabilities
Modularity	Self-contained re-configurable building blocks
Plasticity	Molding to unique shapes
Resilience	Recoiling or bouncing back from the brink after sustaining damage, or degrading gracefully before termination
Robustness	Taking hits with minimal damage to functional capability
Versatility	Able to wear many hats or deploy various skills to function with dexterity in different settings

Table 2. Concepts resembling flexibility

The differences between these concepts are sometimes evident, at other times unclear. For example, having the liquidity to exploit an unexpected opportunity is qualitatively different from resiliently recovering from an accident or a trauma. Similarly, buying insurance, options, buffers or slack, to protect or insulate against potentially damaging situations, is different from the agility or the dexterity needed to enter a new arena or to side-step an impending threat.

There are also important nuances embedded within these terms. For example, agility can mean being able to "dodge and weave" around competitors, or it may refer to the ability to rapidly switch direction or to accelerate into an emerging field of opportunity. Even in a defensive sense, agility is needed to avoid an approaching disaster. Similarly, resilience has several meanings. It refers to the ability to rebound from setbacks, or the ability to regenerate or to restore damaged parts; it can also mean being able to revive a system so it continues to function although it might be slowly degrading. Robustness refers to the ability to deflect threats in hostile terrains by wearing bullet proof vests, or by being "Teflon coated", or like shock absorbers, being capable of "riding over the bumps" or "traversing the treacherous rapids in a fast moving river".[25]

In evolutionary biology, resilience is defined as the time required for a system to return to equilibrium, following a disturbance, or the amount of disturbance that a system can absorb before switching to another stable regime (Brand & Jax 2007). By way of distinction, being versatile may involve multi-tasking, or like a triathlete, being competent in several different areas, reflected in the old adage of wearing many hats. These terms are clearly in some way related and have been used by scholars to give granularity to the notion of flexibility. These related concepts will be examined in the following section.

2.2.1 Adaptability

The term "adaptability" is defined as "adjusting to changing conditions". Although it is used interchangeably with flexibility, it is qualitatively different from other related terms in that successful adaptation is the goal of being flexible. Stigler (1939) made the distinction between the two terms. He suggests that adaptability implies a singular and optimal adjustment to a transformed environment, whereas flexibility enables successive, but temporary, approximations to the optimal adaptive state. The term has been used in the field of strategic management to describe an enterprise's ability to respond to foreseen changes; for example, when a projected scenario, such as deregulation of a major industry, becomes reality. Flexibility, on the other hand, refers to the ability to respond to the unanticipated.

Ansoff focused on flexibility as a means of coping with extreme turbulence (Ansoff 1975). His doctoral student, Eppink (1978a), studied adaptive responses of several firms to the first Oil Crisis of 1973. Later, building on Ansoff's insights, Volberda (1996, 1997, 1998), extended the study into how firms cope with "hyper-competitive" environments. He studied how the "repertoire" of management capabilities, augmented by a firm's organizational structure, might impact its ability to become strategically flexible. Recognizing the need for flexibility, Harrigan, (1980, 1985) examined the ability of firms to disengage from unattractive businesses. This theme was extended by Katsushiko & Hitt (2004); Hitt had previously

---

[25] Olsson et al. 2006. See also Kinzig, et al. 2006.

examined how flexibility can improve enterprise adaptation to novel conditions (Hitt et al.1998). A recent contribution is the work of Teece (2009) who has proposed the notion of "dynamic capabilities" as a means of adapting to changing conditions.

Recently, a number of researchers have explored the notion of ecosystem resilience as a means of adapting to climate change (Chapin et al. 2006). We will return to this recurring ecological theme whereby the cross-utilization of several concepts is used to pinpoint the meaning of flexibility.

2.2.2 Agility

The term "agility" describes the extent to which an individual, a team or a firm, can move nimbly with dexterity. In nature, we often think of gazelles or cheetahs as being agile. In business settings, it refers to moving out of the way of an impending disaster, for example by rapidly adopting "poison pill" measures to thwart an acquisition, or entering a new market by buying a company before others. The term has been used in the literature to characterize a firm's adaptive strategy (Doz 2008), organizational structure, supply chain, and IT infrastructure.

The concept has also transformed the software development process. With the advent of the "Agile Manifesto" software engineers have embraced the methodology with gusto (Cockburn 2002). The term has been applied broadly to information systems planning (Weill et al. 2002, 2006). Today, software engineers welcome changing requirements (Patten et al. 2005) and software releases are becoming monthly occurrences instead of biannual rollouts. However, several organizational problems have emerged with the wholesale adoption of this approach.[26] A number of researchers point to the need for ambidextrous coping strategies in implementing distributed software development projects (Lee et al. 2006). As aptly concluded *"Organizational forms and cultures conducive to innovation may embrace agile methods more easily than those built around bureaucracy and formalization"*. [27] (Nerur 2005)

Improving an enterprise's agility with IT is a recurring theme.[28] The concept of a "scrum" has recently augmented agile methods for real-time software development. The term "robustness" is also used to denote flexibility in IT development projects.[29] A critical question, highlighted by a number of studies, is how much is worth paying for IT flexibility.[30] This continues to be a difficult question to address (Copeland & Keenan 1988).

---

[26] Turk et. al 2002, Lycett et al. 2003.

[27] Nerur, 2005, p. 78.

[28] Overby, 2006; Tallon, 2007.

[29] Patten 2005 & Patten et al. 2006.

[30] Gebauer (2006 & 2007) conducted research on IT spending decisions and the deployment of mobile technologies in terms of the ability to change the use of a system (also see Schober and Gebauer, 2008).

In addition, there is a substantial body of research on supply chain agility.[31] Flexibility is addressed in terms of the variety of products produced, the volume and the logistics of shipping goods and the variability of sourcing components. Agility is perceived as either a combination of speed and flexibility, or as an extension of flexibility. As discussed earlier, the hybrid term "flexagility" was proposed to capture the overlapping meaning of the two concepts. In the turbulent environment following the 2008 financial crisis, this capability is critical for many companies, yet fraught with danger from what is termed the "bull-whip" effect.[32]

Strategic agility (Doz 2008) has also been addressed in studying innovative corporate strategies, defined as "*not just the ability to be quick, but also to take strategic turns in a timely fashion, strategic re-direction/reinvention at high speed*".[33] Another study defined marketplace agility as the "*ability to generate a steady stream of both large and small innovations in products, services, solutions, business models, and even internal processes that enable them to leapfrog and outmaneuver current and would be competitors and thus eke out a series of temporary competitive advantages that might, with luck, add up to sustained success over time.*".[34] They propose the notion of workforce scalability as the mechanism that provides "alignment and fluidity" necessary to become an agile organization.[35]

2.2.3 Ambidexterity

This term is commonly used to denote a person's ability to write with, or use, both hands with equal proficiency. It has been applied to bifunctional activities in organizational contexts (Duncan 1976), to denote the coexistence of dual structures, such as R&D to enable new product introductions, and quality control to ensure product consistency and supply chain alignment. The idea has also been incorporated in studies of teams developing complex software projects (Lee 2006). Switching between different modes of development is a desired capability; for example, when a "quick and dirty" response is needed, compared to a mission-critical project that needs extensive documentation and testing before being rolled out.

---

[31] Buzacott 1982, 2008, Spür 1976, Slack 1987, De Groote 1994, Suarez 1996, Shewchuk 1998.

[32] Lee et al. 1997, Glatzel et al. 2009.

[33] Presentation given by Doz & Kosonen on "Fostering Strategic Agility", INSEAD, 2006, P. 1.

[34] Dyer & Ericksen 2006, p.3.

[35] In a later work, the researchers propose: "a complexity-based agile enterprise configuration to enable a firm to operate on the edge of chaos to form and reform, strategize and re-strategize on the fly." (Dyer & Ericksen, 2008, p.3).

In general, the concept refers to the ability to engage in apparently contradictory activities for example, by pursuing revolutionary and evolutionary change (Tushman & O'Reilly 1996). It is proposed as a means of deploying dynamic capabilities and reconfigurable assets, and adopting an organizational architecture that promotes exploitation and exploration (Birkinshaw 2004). Several studies have also used the concept to examine strategic alliances and the performance of small-to-medium sized firms (Lin 2007).[36]

The question we must ask is how is this related to flexibility. Using both hands is an interesting metaphor to signify the accommodation of contradictory hypotheses. In this sense, we can also extend the term to denote switching between activities, using two distinctive capabilities. In defense of ambidexterity, it is often the case that contradictory factors must be accommodated in organizing a flexible enterprise (Bahrami 1992). *"ambidextrous organizations mobilize, coordinate, and integrate dispersed contradictory efforts, and allocate, reallocate, combine and recombine resources and assets across differentiated exploratory and exploitive units"*.[37]

Research has found a strong correlation between decision-making authority and a manager's ambidexterity (Mom 2009). For example, an informal top management team, interacting with formal organization integration can produce ambidexterity (Jansen, 2009). Dealing with unexpected occurrences in a timely fashion requires several capabilities, all focused on what military strategists term the shifting center of gravity. It is precisely in such circumstances that flexibility is at a premium. Whether an ambidextrous organization is more capable of managing turbulence in dynamic settings remains an open question (Raisch et al. 2009).

2.2.4 Hedging

"Hedging" is a concept evoked by the idiom of "not putting all eggs in one basket" (Ansoff 1965). It plays an important role in financial engineering, particularly in derivatives trading (Ding et al. 2007). Hedging tools can buy insurance and are shown to be effective during "normal" market conditions. Propelled to notoriety by their role in precipitating the financial collapse of 2008, the instruments of derivative hedging or swaps trading rely on complex mathematical models to price options (Lutgens 2006). It was argued that *"almost any arbitrary pay-off function can be hedged with a piecewise linear approximation using a tailored portfolio of options"*.[38] However, as exemplified by the market corrections of 2008, these linear approximations function poorly when things change kaleidoscopically. A

---

[36] See also Pauwels 2005 for a view of strategic flexibility in export markets.
[37] Jansen et al. 2009, p.797.
[38] Bartram 2008, p.10.

number of researchers have attempted to address this by modeling in "jump diffusion" phenomenon when a stock price or an asset suddenly spikes or implodes (Kennedy et al. 2009).

It has been argued that we need to distinguish between "tractable" information used as a basis for options that can be acquired, and "intractable" information (surprises for example) that can not.[39] Over the years there has been a meteoric rise of financial engineering, based on what an eminent scholar termed "econophysics" (Shubik 2007). A clear example of the relationship between flexibility and hedging is reflected in a recent theoretical work that promotes flexible contracts with hedging to be an option for dynamic portfolio management (Caldenty et al. 2008). It should be noted, however, that "hedging" only mitigates the losses associated with the downside potential, at the expense of foregoing the full benefits of any upside potential (Merkhofer & Saade 1978). In view of the losses inflicted by pursuing these strategies, the value of hedging in providing flexibility is not always demonstrable, although this may be an over-reaction to recent events.

2.2.5 Liquidity

Economists use the concept of liquidity as a means of producing financial flexibility.[40] An asset is liquid if it can be easily converted into some alternative form of wealth with little or no conversion costs or associated penalties. Hart defines liquidity as *"the maintenance of a cash balance...in excess of turnover requirements"*.[41] Liquidity considerations are an integral part of financial portfolio planning (Hong & Rady 2002) and an essential ingredient of securities design (Blais & Mariotti 2005). It has profound implications for capital generation, and can influence the configuration and deployment of securities, bonds and other financial instruments. The concept is also becoming increasingly important in the design and use of IT systems for financial trading (Mendelson & Tunca 2004).

"Slack" is an analogous concept in that it refers to unused assets and resources that can be easily converted or readily deployed. Cyert and March (1963) refer to "organizational slack" as a buffer between an organization and external discontinuities. In the context of providing a buffer, slack is another means of achieving flexibility (Bourgeois 1981).

---

[39] Mendelson & Tunca 2005.
[40] Frazer 1985, Goldman 1974, 1978, Jones & Ostroy 1976, 1984.
[41] Hart 1937a, p. 290.

2.2.6 Malleability

In the same way that snakes coil around trees, "malleability" refers to the ability to bend or be easily molded. Sometimes this is irreversible and the shape solidifies, rather like putty or clay that hardens once in place. In other cases, like a gel-pack, it may be re-molded when necessary. As a concept related to flexibility, it has received the least attention. However, economists have explored the "putty-clay" hypothesis, clarifying the differences between "*ex ante*" ability to be molded, and "*ex post*" hardening that occurs once deployed.[42] This distinction helped fuel the debate framed by Henry (1974) around the "Irreversibility Effect" and taken up later by Bernanke (1983).

In a business context, malleability allows an entity to spontaneously stretch organizational boundaries to accommodate new circumstances, for example in seeking partnerships or in forging collaborative relationships. Although the term has not been extensively used in the literature, it resembles flexibility, especially as it relates to organizational structure: "*…organization structure may be less malleable than Chandler (the famous business historian) assumed. In fact, structure can play a critical role in influencing corporate strategy*".[43] The term has also been deployed in an organizational context "*where their members are malleable beings whose sense of self is influenced by their organization's evolving social identity*".[44]

It is in this sense of a person's ability to perform unconventional tasks that other studies have contributed to our understanding (Gist & Mitchel 1992). In the field of consumer psychology, for example, researchers have examined the notion with respect to justifying extraordinary spending decisions (Cheema & Soman 1996). Indeed, to illustrate the interchangeable nature of the terms, a relevant article is sub-titled "A Flexible Model for a Malleable Concept" (DeSteno & Salovey 1997). Malleability has also been explored in the context of decision-making uncertainty (Fong & McCabe 1999) and conflict resolution (Druckman 1993).

These contributions echo the seminal work of Koopmans (1966). He discusses the problem of selecting a meal from a menu several days in advance, when preferences are not fully known. However, progress in this area remains theoretical, except in high performance computing where: "*Malleability is the ability to dynamically change the data size and number of computational entities in an application. Malleability can be used by middleware to autonomously reconfigure an application in response to dynamic changes in resource availability in an architecture-aware manner, allowing applications to optimize the use of multiple processors and diverse memory hierarchies in heterogeneous environments*".[45] It will be interesting to see

---

[42] Fuss 1977, Albrecht & Hart 1983.

[43] Greiner 1973, p. 399.

[44] Spender 1996, p. 53.

[45] Desell et al. 2007 p 323.

how this plays out when IT no longer needs a "physical" presence.

2.2.7 Mobility

Historically, mobility has been viewed as a fundamental principle of military strategy.[46] Its impact is clearly exemplified in General Sherman's Atlanta campaign and the subsequent march to the sea during the American Civil War. As he observed, *"The Atlanta campaign would simply have been impossible without the use of the railroads."*[47] Sherman went on to praise the ingenuity of his engineers in keeping the trains running, allowing him to surprise the Confederate Army by his speed of movement.[48]

The concept of mobility has also been applied in strategic management.[49] For example, inter-firm mobility of researchers and scientists has been found to lead to higher levels of innovation (as measured by patent output) due to the "cross-pollination" effect.[50] In an earlier paper, we viewed talent mobility as a critical success factor in the Silicon Valley ecosystem.[51] A study of Italian pharmaceutical inventors found that there is a *"positive association between productivity and mobility"*. [52]

Mobility that provides flexibility in this sense is different to the kind induced by the emerging explosion of mobile computing. Stimulated by the bifurcation of IT into the "cloud" and "end-points", it will lead to a transformational change in the way organizations operate.[53] The collective impact of mobile computing, collaborative software, and advances in computer and communications hardware are profound. It is time to consider how to create "mobile enterprises".

2.2.8 Modularity

Modularity is a pragmatic way of achieving flexibility in nature, as exemplified by colonial invertebrates such as barnacles, mussels and whelks (Hughes 2005).

---

[46] Liddel-Hart 1954, Fuller 1946, Shank et al. 1991.

[47] Sherman 1875 p. 399.

[48] Liddell-Hart 1929.

[49] Mascarenhas 1989.

[50] Breschi & Lissoni 2006.

[51] Bahrami & Evans 1995.

[52] Lenzi 2006, p. 30.

[53] Developing mobile systems for diverse uses and field conditions presents a special range of design and testing considerations (Oulasvirta & Nyyssönen, 2009). Mobility continues to be a critical challenge,; this was highlighted by a study that indicated the problem with existing systems is that "they all work in one direction only and do not sufficiently recognize uncertainty" Shank et al. 1991, p. vi.

Just like cells in a beehive, modularity has been proposed as a means of achieving flexibility especially in product design and organizational "scaling" (Clark 1997, Sanchez 1997). Researchers argue that by *"splitting options and decentralizing decisions, control is fragmented, (thereby enhancing) evolution"*.[54] The concept has been applied to manufacturing operations (Baldwin & Clark 1997) and has become a mantra in product design (Baldwin et al. 2000). The pioneering work of Baldwin has been extended to software (Rusnak et al. 2007), and to the evolution of regional clusters (Baldwin & Woodward 2007). Recently, the notion of modularity has been applied to capital budgeting decisions (Gamba & Fusari 2009).

Sanchez (1997, 1999) developed a prescriptive approach to modular product design that was later applied to marketing and organization design. This work was further extended to test how modular architectures impact innovation and/or imitation (Galunic & Eisenhardt 2001). Another group of researchers found that modular organizational designs facilitated innovation, whereas non-modular structures provided a stronger imitation deterrent (Ethiraj et al. 2008). The interesting question posed by this stream of research is the impact of product modularity on organizational design. An empirical study concluded that while " *modular products lead to more reconfigurable organizations ... product modularity contributes less or not at all to another part of organizational modularity, firms shifting activity out of hierarchy"*.[55]

Modularity is defined as a means of *"encapsulating interdependencies within decomposable self-contained units, called modules, and minimizing reciprocal interdependencies between modules"*.[56] In some senses it is viewed as a decomposition design heuristic to enable upscaling and downscaling of capacity with minimum interconnection penalties. Recent studies have examined the impact of modularity on product and organizational design with mixed conclusions. In essence, while it is easier to scale up and down, modularity may not enhance the ability to shift gears and make sudden turns.

The viability of this approach, when facing stochastic events, has recently been questioned: *"In highly volatile environments, modular search strategies are shown to have a high probability of becoming trapped into low fitness zones of the landscape, since they only change locally, they take too long to get out. Integral search strategies, on the contrary, perform search on a broader spectrum and can therefore jump out of low fitness zones of the landscape in which, sooner or later, everybody will fall in a highly volatile environment."*[57] Looking at the topic from a different vantage point, another study found "modular organizations do not necessarily

---

[54] Baldwin 2001, slide # 10.
[55] Hoetke 2006, p. 513.
[56] Ethiraj et al. 2008, p. 939.
[57] Brusconi, et.al. 2007 p. 130.

encourage the construction of managers' mental models with a capability to generate more strategic options and, thus, do not increase strategic flexibility."[58] In conclusion, although it is clear that modularity does enhance flexibility, its effectiveness clearly depends on the situational context.

2.2.9 Plasticity

The notion of plasticity has been proposed as an adaptive mechanism in evolutionary biology, in computational optimization, and in strategic management.[59] In evolutionary biology, the notion of "organic evolution" was introduced in the nineteenth century (Baldwin 1896). The basic idea is that ecosystems are inherently dynamic and *"no single phenotype is consistently optimal. Natural selection, therefore, will favor organisms that are capable of altering their development to track environmental changes"*.[60]

The notion of "phenotype plasticity" denotes an organism's real-time adaptation to environmental disturbances (Ancel & Fontana 2000). In evolutionary biology, it is viewed as a means of facilitating spontaneous, context-specific, adaptive adjustments. These may be either defensive in nature (Agrawal & Fishbein 2008) or they may enhance predatory activity (Hill et al. 2003) Mechanisms that facilitate organic adjustments are often hidden until brought into play (Wycliffe & Bear 1996). This is a crucial point to note. As mentioned earlier, when entrepreneurial firms pivot towards a new direction, they often go through "knot-holes", using "hidden" talents. Novelty, by definition, can not be foreseen, although prior adaptive activity can put in place mechanisms that may be tuned to the new situation (Mockett & Hulme 2008). This prior activity is referred to as "meta-plasticity" and conceptually parallels strategic flexibility (Evans 1982; De Leeuw & Volberda 1996), meta-flexibility (Epplink 1978) and "größer flexibilität" (Meffert 1986).

In a seminal work, it was concluded; *"The more variation in a plastic repertoire, the less time a sequence (of RNA) spends in its best structure. In this way plasticity is costly and, is ultimately reduced by natural selection in constant environments"*.[61] This view echoes Stigler's insight that a flexible response is, in essence, a successive approximation to the "optimal" adaptive action (Stigler 1939). In business this could imply that in a disturbed equilibrium, plasticity is a mechanism that enables firms to make adjustments to adapt to ephemeral environmental changes.

---

[58] Adamides et al. 2007, p. 10.

[59] Dewitt 1998, 2004, Paenke et al. 2007, Ancel 2000, Jedlika 2002, Daoudal 2003, Bayne 2004, Piersma 2003, Langerhans 2002, Heckhausen 2001, Wickliffe 1996, Giovanni & Rivkin 2007.

[60] DeWitt 1998, p. 466, see also Daoudal & Debanne 2003.

[61] Ancel & Fontana 2000. p. 278.

Mechanisms by which organisms create "phenotype" plasticity parallel, in some degree, research undertaken in evolutionary computation. Costs of phenotype plasticity are only warranted if the environment transforms in ways that bring embedded plasticity into play. If the environment shifts into a benign state, or a novel state, then there are limits to inherent plasticity (DeWitt 2003). In this regard, it has been shown in artificial evolutionary systems (Paenke 2007) that phenotype plasticity with non-inheritable adaptive capabilities (Baldwinian inheritance) tend to perform better in changing environments, compared to those that have them passed on from prior generations (Lamarkian inheritance, Piersma & Drent 2003).

Agrawal (2001) itemized adaptive responses by organisms in situations where there are species interactions. He distinguished between responses to competition, mutualism, predation risk, parasitism and food quality.[62] Responses varied from strategies such as defensive structures in aquatic invertebrates, to hiding, reduced feeding activity, transformation into a parasite of the predator, habitat induced camouflage,[63] increased immune functions and several more.[64] The point here is that in the natural world there are response repertoires to variations in the ecosystem. It is difficult to generalize because responses are unique to specific situations and contexts.

There are clear parallels to enterprises facing turbulent environments. Rumelt introduced the concept of organizational plasticity in exploring business strategy.[65] *"There are a number of erroneous assumptions that most economically-oriented strategy researchers continue to borrow from economics. At this moment those that are clearest are plasticity, rationality of collective action, and homogeneity of beliefs. I believe that the most important of these is plasticity—the assumption that firms readily respond to exogenous shocks and changes in competitive conditions. The centerpiece of microeconomics is the deduction of autonomous responsiveness (mediated by self-interest) to changes in prices, technology, taxes, etc. Yet the truth is that firms change only with difficulty. Changing strategy and the structural forms and administrative procedures that undergird strategy is difficult, costly, risky, and time consuming. I shall call this lack of plasticity inertia."* This term "plasticity inertia" points to the friction and the resistance an enterprise encounters when trying to deviate from its trajectory, in what strategy scholars have recently termed "stylized deviations".[66]

Smead & Zollman (2009) explore the process of adaptation by plasticity by using evolutionary game theory. Their conclusion makes an important distinction

---

[62] Bayne 2004, Roll & Shibata 1991, Unger et al. 2006.

[63] Montgomerie et al 2001.

[64] ibid.

[65] Rumelt 1995a, p. 102, see also Rumelt 1995b.

[66] Gavetti & Rivkin 2007.

between *developmental* plasticity and *behavioral* plasticity. Developmental plasticity is a function of contextual and experiential adaptive behavior as an entity matures. Behavioral plasticity focuses on the competitive and other interactive forms of adaptation. This distinction may explain why startup firms exhibit adaptive potential as they grow and develop, compared to large, established enterprises whose adaptive behavior is typically predicated on some form of crisis. It also mirrors the conclusion of neuroscientists in exploring the impact of contextual and experiential influences on plasticity. They distinguish between associative memory plasticity and the functional organization of cortical processes (Li et al. 2006).

The notion of plasticity is rich, yet its relationship to flexibility has not been explored extensively. In studying flexibility in business, researchers have concentrated on the "genotype", instead of realizing that it is at the "phenotype", or at the level of the enterprise, that flexibility has tangible value. This may help explain why generic measures or approaches to flexibility may be of limited value.

2.2.10 Resilience

Just like a starfish that can regenerate a lost limb, the term "resilience" refers to the capacity to withstand or bounce back from shocks without permanent damage or rupture, and the tendency to rebound or recoil, showing buoyancy or recuperative power. In a nuanced sense, the term also refers to a system's ability to degrade gracefully, providing minimal functionality long enough for the task at hand to be completed. The notion is extensively discussed in ecosystem management, child psychology and strategic management. Entrepreneurs exhibit this trait, frequently bouncing back from the setbacks inherent in creating a business.

Systems analysts have used the term to denote a natural ecosystem's ability to restore itself after a catastrophic event, such as a hurricane, or a radical change.[67] For example, the construction of a hydroelectric dam changes the surrounding habitat by diverting the flow of water. Resilience in this setting refers to the ability of the natural species living in the habitat to recover to their former population levels. As succinctly put, resilience in complex systems is characterized by abrupt transitions between alternative persistent states (Chisholm 2007, 2009).

As a response to environmental degradation and the threat of "global warming", resilience has become a mantra. It is proposed as a measure of an ecosystem's ability to regenerate itself [68] and to recover from a traumatic shock, such as a dam rupturing or the unintended consequences of disposing hazardous wastes.[69] This stream

---

[67] Holling 1973, Fiering 1982, Grümm & Breitenecker 1981, Hashimoto et al. 1982.

[68] Holling 1973. Grüüm 1976.

[69] Collingridge 1983, Fiering 1982, Hashimoto et al. 1982a, 1982b, Keeney 1983.

of work has been extended to consider the sustainability of natural ecosystems, such as Florida's Everglades (Carpenter & Walker 2001) and socio-technical ecosystems (Gunderson 1999).

The concept of resilience has received significant attention at the Beijer Institute for Ecological Economics[70] and the Santa Fe Institute (Jen 2004). Mäler encapsulated the rationale when he argued *"the probability for the system to flip from the currently preferred state to an alternative one- an undesirable state- would be smaller (ceteris paribus) for a higher resilient system"*.[71] This work has been extended by economists studying resilience as a form of insurance[72] and to crisis management in public sector organizations. They focus on responses to earthquakes and other natural disasters, when operating in a state of "permanent whitewater" while "shooting the rapids" (Olsson et al. 2006).

Educational psychologists use the term resilience to refer to individuals who become stronger as a result of overcoming major problems in their lives.[73] Developmental psychologists have studied how children recover from trauma during childhood and adolescence.[74] Other studies have examined how the children of parents with alcohol or drug problems rebound from dysfunctional home lives (Werner 1986).

Although the concept has many interpretations (Olsson et al. 2003) the need to put it into practice is evident (Luthar et al. 2000). While it has been viewed as an important element in recovery from childhood trauma, it needs to be analyzed at a higher level of specificity in terms of single life events versus cumulative risk (Vanderbilt-Adriance 2008).

In a business context, the term "strategic resilience" has been used to describe a firm's ability to withstand or to bounce back from a damaged state and to recover from shocks and setbacks.[75] Knowledge enterprises inevitably experience setbacks and have to deal with the challenge of recovery. Some setbacks result in damage. Whatever the cause of the damage, an enterprise must bounce back by rapidly regenerating itself. Clearly, many entities place a premium on resilience after the financial crisis of 2008.

There are clear parallels with start-ups in Silicon Valley, where entrepreneurs often become successful only after they overcome major obstacles (Bahrami & Evans 1995). These setbacks often induce transitional or metamorphic episodes, referred to as "knot-holes". Knot-holes may be precipitated by the rapid demise of a

---

[70] Mäler, 2007, 2009; Carpenter et al. 2009.

[71] Mäler et al, 2007, p.4.

[72] Baumgärten, et al. 2009, Quaas, et al. 2008.

[73] Rutter 1985, 1987, Carver 1998, Masten et al. 1990.

[74] Werner 1986, 1993; Masten 1999.

[75] Hamel & Valikangas 2003, Valikangas 2007.

blockbuster product, the sudden departure of the founders, or intense exposure to external scrutiny after an IPO.

In Silicon Valley, successful teams often endure several knot-holes and, in so doing, develop the capacity to manage novel situations spontaneously. They develop a thick skin and the resilience needed to bounce back. The process can help crystallize an enterprise's "purpose" and clarify its core priorities and critical trade-offs. It is during these challenging times that flexibility is at a premium. Paradoxically, these situations are also least likely to be forecasted ahead of time, as is the case in environmental ecology (Brock & Carpenter 2009). This process can result in a firm "shedding its old skin" as if emerging from a chrysalis.[76]

2.2.11 Robustness

Just as the crocodile's digestive system is robust and can accommodate a wide variety of foods, or camels store water in their humps to withstand arid desert conditions, the term "robust" is defined as "not slender or delicate or weak". As such, it is often used interchangeably with flexibility, especially when functioning in extreme conditions. The literature on robustness spans operational research (Rosenhead 1972), computational optimization (Paenke 2006), evolutionary biology (Hagen 2005) and ecosystem management (Kitano 2004).

The concept was introduced in operations research as a decision criterion in addressing complex, uncertain situations. The focus was on a system's ability to endure shocks and perturbations not considered during initial assessments.[77] In this context, the term refers to a system's ability to gain the highest proportion of good, or the lowest proportion of undesirable consequences, within a given "action space".

An enterprise's robustness is proposed as a measure of how much it can withstand shocks if it "hits" obstacles in high-risk, dynamic arenas. It is analogous to having a "force-field" around the enterprise, an "airbag" to absorb a blow, a "Teflon" coating to insulate and protect, or shock absorbers placed in areas of maximum impact. It is argued that robust systems can neutralize, deflect and dissipate the impact of turbulence. Simply put, robustness refers to the ability to remain unscathed.

---

[76] Sybase, Inc. is a good example, evolving as a database company in the 1990's to become a key player in mobile software.

[77] Rosenhead et al. 1972, Rosenhead 1980.

Researchers at the Santa Fe Institute have explored the principles of resilience and robustness in several application domains (Jen 2004). They set up an entire research area devoted to robustness in biological and social systems. Their research focuses on socio-technical systems, biological ecosystems, organizing the Internet, computation, integrated circuit design, molecular neurology and genetics. In genetics, phenotype robustness is defined as *"the reduced sensitivity of a phenotype with respect to perturbations in the parameters that affect its expression"*.[78] In this context, a crucial distinction is made between environmental robustness (buffering against non-inheritable responses to perturbations) in contrast to genetic robustness, viewed as recurrent mutations.

While this phenomenon, encapsulated in the term "perturbations", has received attention at the Santa Fe Institute (Helbing et al. 2009), it is also the focus of research at Stockholm's Beijer Institute of Ecological Economics (Brock & Carpenter 2009). Brock & Carpenter introduce the concepts of "squealing" and "flickering" as nuanced indicators of weak signals of an impending system flip into an alternate state that can be mitigated by robustness. They propose these measures in order to pinpoint which parts of a system need to be robust to prevent a system flip into a catastrophic state. It is a measure of the flexibility inherent in a system to muffle or magnify these signals, thereby providing an early warning system. As they argue *"Flickering may trigger regime shifts...Conditions that increase muffling will decrease the chance of regime shifts caused by shocks. Conversely, conditions that increase magnification will increase the chance of regime shifts caused by shocks."*[79] These innovative concepts have significant implications for developing a dynamic strategy. We will return to this topic in Chapter 5.

The broad swathe of application areas underscores the ubiquity of the concept of robustness. In this body of research, there is frequently an overlap between the terms, robustness and resilience. Although conceptual clarity has been proposed several times (Read 2005), the interchangeable use of the terms obscures a potentially crucial distinction between the two. Resilience refers to the capacity for revival and renewal and the ability to "bounce back", whereas robustness is about the capacity to withstand change by "bouncing off" or repelling undesirable revision-triggers.

---

[78] de Visser et.al. 2003 p. 1960.

[79] Brock & Carpenter 2009 p. 25.

2.2.12 Versatility

The term "versatility" is defined as turning readily from one subject or occupation to another or having the capacity to deal with many subjects, at times simultaneously. The term was first introduced by Bonder in military operations research to conceptualize how various systems can be deployed in different theaters of operations, or utilized to do a variety of different things within a given theater of operations.[80] He argued that versatility is achieved by installing the capability to respond to a wide range of scenarios ahead of time, or by rapidly modifying an approach, once a change has occurred (Bonder 1976).

Tangentially, anthropologists accredit a versatile diet as a driving force for the success of our earliest Homo ancestors. They had *"biological and cultural adaptations for a more flexible, versatile subsistence strategy. This strategy would have put the earliest members of our genus at an advantage given the climatic fluctuation and the mosaic of microhabitats in Africa."*[81] Other anthropologists attribute human mobility as a source of versatility (Devine 1985). The natural world offers other examples of versatility. A chameleon is the most erudite example. Other animals have evolved their behavior to adapt to changing conditions. For example, as a result of global warming, snow melts earlier in parts of the Arctic. This poses a problem for the ptarmigan as the male birds maintain their white plumage (camouflage in the snow) in order to attract breeding partners. It has been observed that male birds, after mating, dirty up their plumage by rolling in the mud to prevent predators from seeing them too readily.[82]

In a business context, versatility is about being able to seamlessly switch between different priorities, for example, from prototyping to production, or from R&D to sales. It is also an essential characteristic of effective entrepreneurial teams, where the need to shift gears and to improvise is at a premium.[83] In addition, it is useful when assessing a knowledge worker's capacity to multi-task, to wear different hats, and to deal with multiple priorities and reporting relationships in complex matrix organizations (Bahrami 1992).

2.3 Integrating Different Senses of Flexibility: A Unifying Framework

The preceding conceptual analysis of related terms illuminates the "family resemblances" between the different senses of flexibility. It also highlights the complex

---

[80] Bonder, 1976, 1979.

[81] Unger et al. 2006, p. 210.

[82] Montgomerie et al, 2001.

[83] Brown & Eisenhardt 1998.

and multi-dimensional nature of the concept. As depicted in Figure 5, in some senses, such as plasticity, malleability or elasticity, the term denotes a degree of pliability, in that the object must yield to some form of pressure. In other senses, such as liquidity, it means that things can be easily modified; for example, assets that can be converted to another form without incurring any switching cost.[84] Other terms, such as agility and versatility, denote an object's capacity to redefine itself as conditions change, or in a proactive sense, to bring about a new state of affairs.

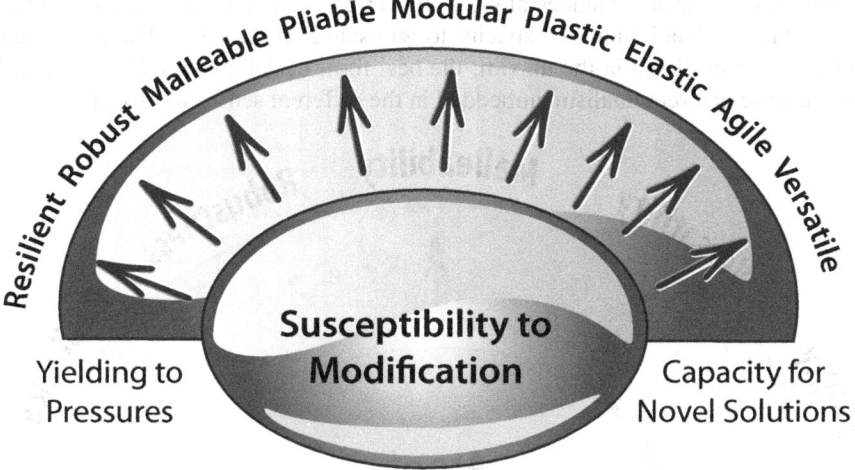

Figure 5. The "polymorphous" nature of flexibility

Our review of the literature leads us to conclude that flexibility is a *polymorphous* concept. The underlying definitional problem that has plagued the topic is one of consistency and transferability, in that those attributes that provide flexibility in one context need not be the same as, or appropriate for, other situations. This, we suggest, is the underlying reason for the conceptual schizophrenia prevalent in the literature. To be truly flexible, all the attributes have to be considered and deployed appropriately in context. An enterprise may have to be agile in entering a new market, versatile in introducing new products, resilient in dealing with setbacks, and robust in protecting intellectual property or brand reputation. Often, multiple capabilities may have to be deployed in parallel.

Several researchers have alluded to a general over arching sense of flexibility, termed "meta" flexibility, "strategic flexibility"[85] or "größer flexibilität".[86]

---

[84] The idea is inherent in computing and the notion of "hot-swapping", when peripheral devices are connected and disconnected during a computer's operation.

[85] Ansoff 1965, Eppink 1978, Volberda 1998.

[86] Meffert 1985.

This "higher order" notion is not only difficult to articulate, but is especially challenging to implement. To build on our conceptual analysis, it is clear that there is an underlying commonality encapsulated in the notion. We synthesize terms with a family resemblance under the umbrella concept of "super-flexibility". Our goal is to provide a conceptual framework that integrate the different senses of flexibility, from agility, versatility, and adaptability, to resilience, robustness and malleability. As depicted in Figure 6, the "arc of super-flexibility" provides a visual construct that incorporates its various nuances along a dialectical spectrum; the ability to transform on the one hand, and the capacity to withstand on the other. The conceptual dualism is encapsulated in the maxim; the best form of defense is offense. Table 3 highlights the inherent dualism embedded in the different senses of flexibility.

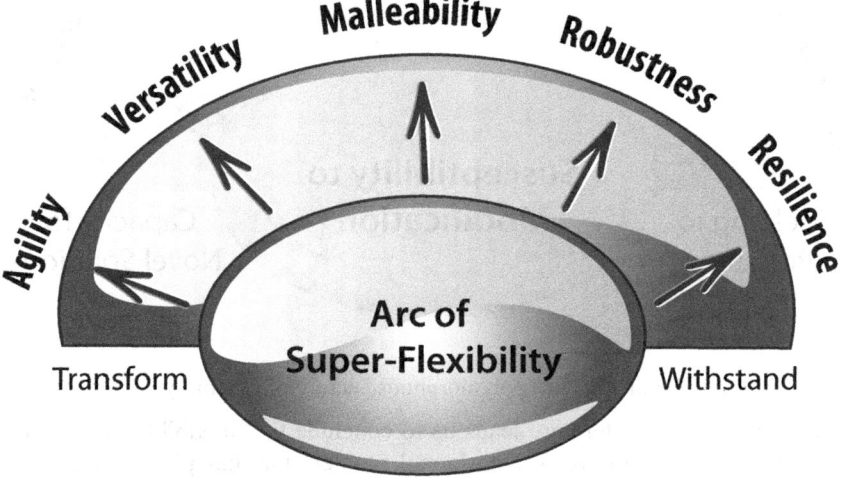

Figure 6. The arc of super-flexibility

In summary, we define the term "super-flexibility" as the ability to dynamically adjust to fluid conditions, at present and in the future. At times this may entail transformation and reinvention. At other times, it may mean staying the course, and hunkering down to withstand unsettled conditions. In certain cases, it may imply the capacity to do both, often simultaneously. In addition, sometimes adjustments may be temporary and ephemeral.

FLEXIBILITY	WITHSTAND	TRANSFORM
AGILITY (Gazelle, Cheetah)	Rapidly switching to a defensive posture (Wellington's squares), rapid turns or reverse, jumping out of the way of an impending disaster.	Swiftly modify existing structure for an ephemeral situation, ephemeral IT user needs, scaling across geographies, re-deploying in a new domain.
ADAPTABILITY (Tadpole to Frog Caterpillar to Butterfly)	Anticipated response to expected triggers, scenarios or planned contingencies.	Capitalizing on the exigencies of a novel situation, responding to new user needs.
(AMBI)DEXTERITY (Orangutang, Amphibians and Marsupials)	Bi-modal direction shift, "explore and exploit".	Simultaneously scaling up or down, dual use technologies, switch between high and low gears.
ELASTICITY (Stork, Flying Fox)	Shrinking back while maintaining composure.	Stretching without breaking.
HEDGING (Squirrel)	Mitigating downside risk.	Skimming upside potential.
LIQUIDITY (Jellyfish)	Moving resources from offense to defense without friction.	Recombining without time or resource friction/penalties, smooth s in product mix/volume.
MALLEABILITY (Octopus)	Easily bent into non-regular shape with the potential to return to its previous state	Bends into new shape, able to be modified for a new situation.
MODULARITY (Bees, Ants, Coral reef)	Downsize without impacting other components	Recombining organization units, product subsystems, IT systems
PLASTICITY (DNA, genetic code)	Phenotype adaptation to environmental conditions, eg an increase in predators.	Phenotype adaptation to environmental conditions eg temperature/ nutrient abundance.
PLIABILITY (Snake)	Molding into shape.	Bend back and forth.
RESILIENCE (Starfish)	Staying power, bouncing back, recoiling from stress to resume previous posture, degrading gracefully.	Returning to good health after trauma, overcoming disadvantage to succeed.

FLEXIBILITY	WITHSTAND	TRANSFORM
ROBUSTNESS (Crocodile, Hippo, Whale)	Ruggedized for hostile environments, bouncing off threats, withstanding pressure.	Teflon coated, air bag safety devices, heat shields feature preservation.
VERSATILITY (Chameleon, Hummingbird)	Horses for courses, fit for different ecosystems, differentiated responses.	Wearing different hats/ multitasking, regroup like a flock of birds.

Table 3. Super-Flexibility and its different nuances

Super-flexibility is the ability to draw on a portfolio of concepts to devise approaches and capabilities in order to adapt to dynamic realities. The goal may be to either withstand and/or to transform as conditions morph. These have to be uniquely configured according to the needs of the situation, the capabilities of those executing the change, and the intent of the endeavor. There is no "silver bullet" or generic formula that can solve the "problem" of flexibility. Actions that may be appropriate one day in a particular set of circumstances may be totally inappropriate in almost identical circumstances on another day. One size does not fit all. Knowledge workers have to select and to deploy the type of flexibility that may be most appropriate in a given context. The different senses of flexibility point to different tools that can be deployed for different purposes. This is why the subtitle of the book is "*A Toolkit for Dynamic Adaptation*".

2.4 Conclusion

This chapter described multi-disciplinary contributions to explore and explain the notion of flexibility. We explored several related concepts with a "family" resemblance. We proposed the umbrella term "super-flexibility" to integrate its various meanings and nuances.

In the multi-disciplinary literature on flexibility, there seems to be an underlying assumption that flexibility is a tangible capability, an attribute of a system, or even a quality of a decision or a strategy. This may be the case but is not the whole story. Being flexible is not just about having the right combination of *capabilities* or assets but also about *lubricating* dysfunctional pressures that build up when adapting to new realities. Its effective deployment, we suggest, depends on the ability to act spontaneously, to be configured for simplicity[87] and to provide lubrication and minimize friction.

---

[87] Also see Davis et al. 2009.

Real-time adaptation is difficult. It takes ingenuity to face a novel situation and true leadership to improvise on the spot. This is why simplicity is critical for real-time adaptation. After extensive research on machine tool scheduling[88] it was concluded that simple machines were easier to modify for novel outputs than those optimized for dealing with predicted contingencies. The latter require complex modifications and were ineffective when they had to adjust to unexpected changes in demand or product mix. Our experience in Silicon Valley bears this out. Simpler things are easier to change, especially when complex "real-time" modifications are needed.

In the following chapters, we transpose the conceptual to the practical application of super-flexibility. Since, we argue, most business situations are unique, we do not intend to propose "best practices" or generic approaches. Instead, we present five "conceptual coat-hangers" as diagnostic frameworks. These should be considered as a menu of options and as food for thought. Entrepreneurs, executives, and knowledge workers should view these as diagnostic tools, core principles, and shared frameworks. They can be used when devising strategies, developing execution roadmaps, reorganizing structures, aligning teams, or recycling assets. The frameworks are derived from our field research and practical experience in Silicon Valley since 1982. Taken collectively, we hope they provide an alternative optic that enable our readers to reflect on their experiences and to devise novel approaches as they address the challenge of perpetual adaptation in an age of transformation, innovation, and discontinuity.

---

[88] Iravani et al. 2003.

3 The Research Laboratory: Silicon Valley's Knowledge Ecosystem

Silicon Valley is an ideal research laboratory for studying super-flexibility. Living on the cutting edge of technology and innovation, nothing stays stable for long. Competitive landscapes habitually transform, almost overnight. New start-ups keep the incumbents on their toes. Multi-cultural entrepreneurs bring in diverse recipes from all over the world. Knowledge workers change jobs and move between assignments. New players create novel solutions; and today's successful "stars" habitually become tomorrow's "black holes".

Although Silicon Valley has endured explosive growth, punctuated by several economic downturns, during the past 30 years, it continues to be a global center for high tech innovation and entrepreneurship. It is the epicenter for global venture capital and attracts entrepreneurial talent from all over the world. Although time will tell whether this trend will continue in the future, Silicon Valley has shown considerable resilience in the face of skepticism about its continued viability. This chapter examines the special features of Silicon Valley, its historic antecedents, its core building blocks, and its relevance as a research laboratory for studying super-flexibility.

There are a number of precedents for studying flexibility in circumscribed settings, bounded by time frames, industries, or societal conditions. As discussed in Chapter 2, the Great Depression of the 1930s unleashed a number of pioneering studies on the notion of flexibility (Hart 1937a, 1937b, McKinsey 1932, Stigler 1939). The focus of these studies was on creating new businesses, and farmers' response to oscillations in the price of agricultural produce (Backman 1940, Mason 1938, Nicholls 1940). Later "strategic-flexibility" was studied from the vantage point of corporate responses in the immediate aftermath of the 1973 Oil Crisis (Eppink 1978a, 1978b). The notion of "resilience" was examined by studying natural ecosystems and the impact of human expansion (Holling 1973). Recently, "strategic resilience" has been proposed as a means of re-inventing large corporations (Hamel and Valikangas 2003).

Silicon Valley has been at the forefront of many contemporary trends in business. For example, the practice of "offshoring" was initiated by the region's disk drive and semiconductor industries during the 1980's. Firms in the Valley are early adopters of new technologies and serve as beta-test sites for local companies. We believe Silicon Valley can provide practical insights on super-flexibility in an age of technological discontinuity, economic uncertainty, and global entrepreneurship.

"Our firms need to be flexible to stay competitive; however, flexibility for firms translates into anxiety for our workers. The new employment environment is characterized by turbulence, uncertainty and the need for adaptability in the following ways: more frequent employer switches, shorter job tenure, required retraining/ skills up-grading, frequent wage gaps and fluctuation, increasing self-employment, and required geographic mobility" (Index, Joint Venture Silicon Valley, 2008).

We characterize Silicon Valley as a "Darwinian", dynamic, knowledge ecosystem. The term "ecosystem" is defined here as a "community of autonomous players, that function interdependently, that feed off, compete and collaborate with one another, and that operate within a common climate". Its core building blocks include:

- **The "knowledge originators"**: including universities and corporate and government research laboratories, nurturing talent, ideas, and emerging technologies.
- **The "knowledge hatcheries"**: the critical mass of seasoned entrepreneurs, "angel" investors, and venture capital firms, providing risk funding to seed start-ups and fuel their growth.
- **The "knowledge generators"**: the cluster of emerging start-ups, mid-sized adolescents, and established giants that produce innovative products and services. They also provide the entrepreneurial talent pools from which many spin-offs are drawn.
- **The "knowledge lubricants"**: the groupings of specialized lawyers, accountants, executive search specialists, consultants, and other service providers that provide a complementary support infrastructure.

Enterprises in Silicon Valley are embedded in symbiotic and interdependent relationships with the broader ecosystem. Buyers become suppliers; customers turn into competitors; partners become vendors. The close physical proximity between firms, and the incessant movement of people, ideas and information create a setting that is analogous to a biological ecosystem. The walls between the "enterprise" and the ecosystem are not solid but opaque and decidedly permeable.

3.1 Conceptual Underpinnings

The ecosystem concept is not new or limited to Silicon Valley. Indeed, clusters of firms in related industries have historically coalesced around a critical mass of business activity (Porter 1990). During the 19th century, for example, many firms in Birmingham, UK, clustered around the critical mass of expertise in, what is known in the vernacular as, "metal bashing".

The automobile sector amassed around Birmingham (U.K.), Detroit (U.S.A.), and Stuttgart (Germany) during the 1900s. In the City of London, financial industries have evolved around the famous "Square Mile". Similarly, Italy's textile industry has coalesced around the city of Prato. High technology industries of the information era also conform to this clustering tendency.

Several regional technology clusters have sprouted around the U.S. during the past two decades, including Boston's "Route 128", Austin's "Silicon Hills", Seattle's "Technology Corridor", Illinois' "Silicon Prairie", New Jersey's "Princeton Corridor", San Diego's "Golden Triangle", and Utah's "Software Valley". Scotland's "Silicon Glen" and Cambridge's "Silicon Fen" have also attracted many technology-based companies. During the 1980s and early 90s, Singapore, and later Bangkok, became centers for disk drive and computer sub-systems manufacturing. India's Bangalore region, today the hotbed of entrepreneurial companies, built its reputation in Unix programming. Additionally, a number of government sponsored science park initiatives, such as France's Sofia Antipolis, and Taiwan's Hsinchu, have also induced a critical mass of technology companies. By far, the best-known cluster of high technology firms is located in California's Silicon Valley.

According to the "2008 Index of Joint Venture Silicon Valley", the region covers an area of 1,854 square miles in the San Francisco Bay area, has a population of 2.52 million, and is home to 393 public companies and more than 22,000 high tech establishments. Its economy has evolved during the past 30 years, triggered by periodic emergence of disruptive innovations. Initially boosted by defense spending during the 1960s, the epicenter of innovation shifted to semiconductors and integrated circuits in the 1970s, evolved to personal computers, disk drives and peripherals during the 1980s, was dominated by software, search engines, Internet services, and disk archiving in the late 1990s, and has gravitated towards clean tech, social networking, and life sciences during the last five years.

3.2 The Evolution of Silicon Valley

There was no singular event or grand plan which led to the meteoric rise of "Silicon Valley".[1] Instead, a series of independent events, coupled with fortuitous timing, transformed a regional agricultural community into a global engine for technological innovation and entrepreneurship. The region evolved organically over time, when several complementary forces gelled together and resulted in the formation of a critical mass of high technology firms.

From a technological perspective, the parallel development of two major innovations forged the foundational building blocks that underpinned the rapid growth of Silicon Valley during the 1960's and 1970's. The first, and the best-known of these, was the commercial development of the transistor at AT&T's Bell Labs in 1948. The second was the development of disk drives or information storage technology using magnetic recording techniques. Using tape in 1953 and magnetic disks by 1957, the technology was developed at IBM's Santa Theresa Research Laboratory (Harker et al. 1981).

William Shockley invented the transistor at Bell Laboratories in New Jersey in 1947. He moved to Palo Alto, his home town, in 1954 and set up Shockley Semiconductor Laboratories. His core tem of eight scientists became the founding nucleus for the growing West Coast semiconductor industry.

---

[1] Addressing a meeting of the Churchill Club (October 1992), Bill Hewlett suggested that the origins of Silicon Valley, in his opinion, almost date back to the development of ship-to-shore radio and the early days of television, before RCA moved its R&D labs to the East coast.

They left Shockley Lab in 1957 and founded Fairchild Semiconductor. Further advances in semiconductor technology and the emergence of a major market in the defense industry helped launch many spin-offs, largely out of Fairchild, during the 1960's; among them National Semiconductor, AMI, Advanced Micro Devices and Intel.

During the same period, IBM set up its "skunk works" in Los Gatos with the aim of producing technical breakthroughs and innovative products. The development of Winchester disk drive technology[2] later led to the formation of a multi-billion dollar industry in Silicon Valley (Mulvany et al. 1975, Stevens 1981). Several members of the IBM team were later responsible for the founding of Memorex, Shugart, Seagate, Conner Peripherals, Adaptec, Auspex, Maxtor, and Quantum. The disk drive industry has been a major source of innovation and international dominance for US companies.[3] Chapter 4 reflects on the early evolution of this defining sector in Silicon Valley.

Stanford University's Dean of Engineering, Frederick Terman, played a crucial role during the early years by forging a close working relationship between the Engineering School and the emerging local firms. The formation of the Stanford Industrial Park in 1951 was an additional catalyst. It became a mechanism for transferring technology from the university to the nearby firms.[4] During the 1960's, the Park became an attractive location for the growing electronics companies. Their number expanded steadily, from 32 in 1960, to almost 70 by 1970 (Rogers & Larsen 1984).

Boosted by California's unique pioneering spirit, these building blocks became the foundation of Silicon Valley. Since the days of the Gold Rush in the 1850s, and later the "Dust Bowl" migration during the 1930s, California, the frontier land, had attracted the risk-takers, the innovative and the ambitious (Kotkin & Grabowicz 1982). It is hardly surprising that many entrepreneurs, who felt the need to challenge the status quo and to break with tradition, found a conducive home in Northern California. By the mid 1960's, a critical mass of technology companies had been established in the San Francisco Bay Area. Santa Clara Valley was transformed from prune yards and orchards into a large Petri dish for creating entrepreneurial ventures and knowledge-based enterprises.

---

[2] The team included L.D. Stevens and Ken Houghton, who later became the Dean of Engineering at Santa Clara University.

[3] The US disk drive industry is dominant in merchant production, although much of its manufacturing is offshore, or in partnership with Japanese companies. The industry remains vibrant, as attested by the sustained growth rates and the pace of new product development (McKendrick et al. 2000).

[4] The first tenant was Varian Associates, a spin-off from Stanford University's Physics department. Hewlett Packard followed in 1954. David Packard and Bill Hewlett, Terman's former students, had co-founded Hewlett Packard in 1939.

During the past 30 years, Silicon Valley has nurtured the growth of many global technology companies. Well-known examples include Intel, Apple, Seagate, Adobe, Cisco, Oracle, Symantec, E-bay, Intuit, National Semiconductors, Electronic Arts, Yahoo, Google, and Sun Microsystems. In addition, Silicon Valley is home to several thousand start-ups and mid-sized technology enterprises. As indicated in Table 3, dominant industry clusters include information products & services, life sciences, innovation services, and business/ community infrastructure.

Sector	Number of Employees	Percentage of total Silicon Valley employment
Information products & services	285,614	20.5
Life sciences	33,311	2.4
Innovation & specialized services	152,218	10.9
Business infrastructure	64,187	4.6
Community infrastructure	790,534	56.8
Other manufacturing	66,381	4.8

Table 4. Silicon Valley's major areas of economic activity 2007
(Source 2009 Index, Joint Venture Silicon Valley)

3.3 The Building Blocks

Several specialized building blocks, each playing different yet complementary roles, have turned Silicon Valley into an interdependent knowledge ecosystem. There are several major groupings. These range from universities and research labs, to angel investors and venture capital, support services, and core enterprises. Based on their unique contribution, we characterize these as "originators", "hatcheries", "generators", and "lubricants". This classification is somewhat rudimentary and is not meant to be a comprehensive taxonomy of the various "species" in the ecosystem. Without extending the parallels with the biological analogy too far, the remainder of this chapter describes the core building blocks and the "climate" of this ecosystem. We conclude by reflecting on why Silicon Valley has been an effective learning laboratory for studying dynamic adaptation.

3.3.1 The Knowledge Originators

A knowledge ecosystem incubates new ideas and nurtures their practical development into innovative products and services. In Silicon Valley, innovations are largely based on technological breakthroughs. In this context, universities and research institutes are the ecosystem's most visible building block. They are a critical source of early stage technologies and train technical professionals who become entrepreneurs and knowledge workers. In a nutshell, they are the ecosystem's "originators".

Silicon Valley is a magnet for multi-cultural knowledge workers from different parts of the world. Many come to attend the region's universities and remain in the area; others are recruited to work for Valley-based companies overseas and may transfer back to the home base. Since high technology firms are global from their inception, multi-cultural knowledge workers facilitate rapid development of global operations. Based on 2008 data from the non-profit organization, Joint Venture Silicon Valley, 36% of Silicon Valley's population was born outside the US.

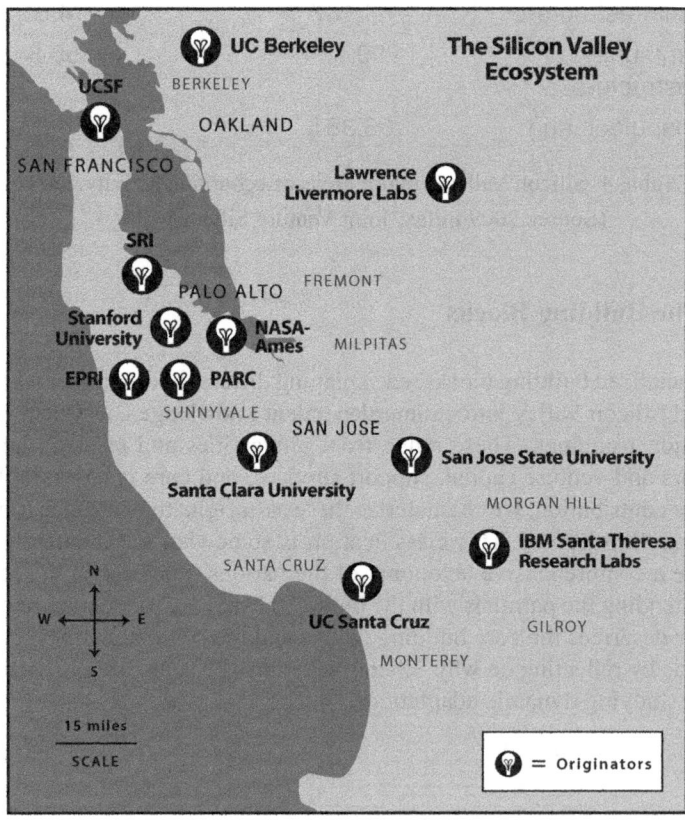

Figure 7. Silicon Valley's knowledge originators

Universities also catalyze networking and relationship building among future entrepreneurs. Social links and collegial relationships play a crucial role during the process of venture creation and enterprise formation. For example, two IT professionals from the Stanford Business School and the Computer Science Department co-founded Cisco Systems in the mid-1980s. Sun Microsystem's co-founders included two Stanford MBA students, a graduate student from the Stanford Engineering School, and a PhD student from Berkeley's Computer Science Department. All four founders of ROLM were graduate students at the Stanford Engineering School, as were Yahoo's co-founders, Jerry Yang and David Filo. "Google" was founded by student friends Sergey Brin and Larry Page, who according to the official history of the firm "were not terribly fond of each other when they first met at Stanford University as graduate students in Computer Science in 1995". [5]

From time to time, faculty members also start companies. For example, Bill New, a professor at the Stanford Medical School, co-founded Nellcor in 1981, a medical electronics company that developed the oximeter as an indispensable aid for anesthesiologists. John Hennesy, who later became the President of Stanford University, was a co-founder of MIPS during the early 1980s. Silicon Graphics was founded by Jim Clark of Stanford's Computer Science Department. He later co-founded Netscape with a young research student, Marc Andresson, from the University of Illinois. Apart from SGI and Netscape, Clark was also a co-founder of MyCFO and Healtheon during the Internet boom years. He later funded the Bio-X facility at Stanford. The goal is to cross-fertilize medicine and biology with computer science and engineering. Ed Penhoet, Dean of the School of Public Health at the University of California, Berkeley, was a co-founder of Chiron. Many faculty members are also advisors, consultants, and board members of growing companies.

Corporate research institutes have also played a crucial role in generating technological expertise. Sometimes, as is the case with IBM's storage research center in San Jose, the pioneer of the Winchester disk drive, the parent can benefit from the R&D innovations. Other times, the technical breakthroughs may not pay off for the parent but can benefit the ecosystem as a whole. A case in point is Xerox's Palo Alto Research Center or PARC. Bob Metcalfe, a research scientist at PARC, developed the Ethernet, the foundation of local area network technology (LAN). He left Xerox in 1980 to form 3Com and went on to commercialize the technology. Similarly, Chuck Greschke and John Warnock developed the Postscript technology at Xerox PARC, but later spun-off to form Adobe Systems during the early 1980s.

Local research institutes have also been responsible for several pioneering technologies. Optical disk drives, the mouse pointing device, and the magnetic ink character system for bank checks, for example, were all initially developed at the Stanford Research Institute (SRI International); Funding from public institutions, such as DARPA (Defense Advanced Project Research Agency) and NSF (National Sci-

---

[5] Source: www.google.com/corporate/history.html.

ence Foundation), or from private foundations, have also been critical in promoting basic research and its targeted application.

A distinguishing feature of local universities is their open attitude towards information exchange, and the opportunities they provide for cross-fertilization between business and academia. Collaboration may take the form of joint research projects, exchange of staff, or hosting of conferences and networking forums. During the early 1990s, for example, UC Berkeley's Haas School of Business started the first entrepreneurial incubator. The initial goal was to provide facilities for graduating students to start their own ventures. Haas' Lester Center for Entrepreneurship provides the students with contacts in the legal, accounting and venture communities. Both Stanford and Berkeley leverage a broad range of adjunct faculty in their medical, business, computer science, and engineering schools. These experienced entrepreneurs and professionals bring in experience, expertise and valuable connections.

The interlinked processes of cross-fertilization, collaboration, networking, and information exchange are critical in the formation of new entrepreneurial ventures. Some involve formal exchanges, job transfers, or temporary internships. Others include collaborative research or R&D funding. This emphasis on nurturing "open borders" between universities and other building blocks of the ecosystem has been a critical success factor in nurturing innovation, commercializing new technologies and creating new ventures.

3.3.2 The Knowledge Hatcheries

In order to commercialize new breakthroughs, entrepreneurs need catalysts who can incubate and "hatch" their ideas by providing risk capital, relevant contacts and early feedback. Angel investors and venture capitalists are the crucial catalysts in this context. They provide the capital, the expertise, the discipline, the network, and ultimately the "runway", to help fuel the growth of new entities.

Risk capital providers are a crucial component of the Silicon Valley ecosystem (Kenney & Florida 2000). Although one can overstate the importance of venture capital, the community is responsible for accelerating the growth of new ventures by providing funding, management know-how and market feedback during the crucial early stages. Armed with networks of relevant contacts, they augment founding teams, especially as a venture evolves through different stages of development.

Silicon Valley accounts for 30% of all US venture funding and has the world's largest venture capital cluster.[6] The vast majority of venture capitalists are, in the main, responsible for funding new ventures after the initial "seed" stage. Typically, co-founders and private investors provide the initial seed funding. This enables

---

[6] Source: Joint Venture Silicon Valley Index 2008, P. 14.

a start-up to develop a prototype, although several rounds of financing are typically needed to ramp up its growth. Critical activities include forging distribution channels, generating reference accounts, developing product enhancements, and engaging in global expansion. The principal role of the venture capitalists is to provide the funds necessary to "ramp" the enterprise into a sizable business by providing the "runway" so it can take off.[7]

Start-ups need several rounds of financing before they are in a position to generate sufficient revenue and earnings growth to embark on a liquidity event, such as an initial public offering, or an acquisition by another company. The "lead" investor may help with follow-on financing and the IPO or the acquisition process.[8] Moreover, forged relationships between entrepreneurs and venture capitalists may endure over and above any one venture. They may fund the entrepreneurs' next start-up, or invite them to join their venture firm as limited partners, general partners or venture partners. A number of established venture capital firms have "entrepreneurs in residence" programs, an opportunity to leverage the knowledge, the capabilities, and the experience of seasoned entrepreneurs who may be in-between assignments. They may be enlisted to review deals, to jump-start a portfolio company, or to provide ideas for hatching a new start-up.

3.3.3 The Knowledge Generators

Silicon Valley is well known for its track record in generating a critical mass of technology companies. By far, the most significant building block of the ecosystem is the broad variety of fledgling start-ups, mid-sized adolescents, and agile giants that make up the diverse pool of knowledge "generators". They bring together the talent pools, the ideas, and the technical breakthroughs in order to create new products and innovative services for global markets.

Successful ventures experience rapid growth and evolve through various stages of development in quick succession. The embryonic phase spans the time that the business idea is first conceived to the time that the prototype is developed. This stage is characterized by formation of the founding team, development of a plan of action to capitalize on a new idea, a market opportunity or a technological break-

---

[7] One of the driving forces behind the historically high growth rates is the structure of venture capital limited partnerships that in the past have typically lasted for 7-10 years. In order to show a return to the shareholders, investors need to liquidate their positions within the time frame specified by the limited partnership. Therefore, the exit strategy of a portfolio company has to be orchestrated within this time frame, so the proceeds can be shared among the partners and the investors. Venture capitalist's often hedge their bets by investing in several firms vying for dominance in a given arena. Even the most seasoned venture capitalists may be unable to spot winners early on, as witnessed by their initially unfavorable reactions to ROLM, Seagate, and Adaptec, among many other successful ventures.

[8] Venture capitalists rarely invest alone in a deal, but with a group of other venture capital firms. A historical description of the role of venture capital in Silicon Valley is in Hambrecht (1984).

through, raising capital from "angels", seed investors, family and friends, and developing the first prototype. Typically, there is a high level of optimism, focus on funding and prototype development, formation of a core team with complementary capabilities, and informal interactions. Many ventures are terminated during this phase, if they fail to get sufficient market traction.

During the emergent phase, successful firms experience "lead user" acceptance to signal future viability. Critical tasks include validating the business proposition, improving the prototype, forging collaborative partnerships and stimulating market demand. The organization may expand rapidly, and begins to outgrow its informal procedures and face-to-face interactions.

Ventures that do not experience market growth face a different reality. Some recalibrate their business trajectory and target different market segments. Others seek partners that augment their own capabilities. Some may sell their core technology to an established player. There are also many instances of the "living dead" (Bourgeois & Eisenhardt 1987); companies that would not survive without an artificial life support system; venture backers or angel investors who continue to fund their operations.

The ability to introduce strategic change and to redirect priorities may be relatively uncomplicated for a single-product company. The situation becomes more complex when a start-up reaches "adolescence". By this phase, a company may have introduced a second product line and would have typically broadened its sales efforts to cover additional market segments. It faces competition from both, new start-ups (at times its own spin-offs), as well as established companies that may be lured by growing market acceptance for pioneering products and demystification of new technologies. This competitive "pincer envelopment" can result in a loss of strategic focus and fragmentation of management attention.

Depending on the prevailing market and economic conditions, by this stage the typical adolescent company would have typically gone through a "liquidity event". This may be an Initial Public Offering (IPO) or an acquisition by another company. Organizationally, it has to digest its growth and instill a sense of uniformity and discipline. Informal procedures give way to more formal processes. The founding team may have been augmented or replaced by professional managers. While some members of the original team may choose to stay, it is unlikely that they retain their original power and influence. Some may have "burnt out" from the earlier years of "100 hour weeks"; others may simply be unable to cope with new managerial (rather than technical) challenges, or may want to pursue other interests, especially when their financial goals have been realized.

When it reaches the established phase of an "agile giant", a technology firm would have consolidated its position, and diversified into related businesses. This does not mean that it has a guaranteed future. Many have to reposition and reinvent themselves to address emerging market needs, as indicated by the

HP-Compaq merger, Adobe's acquisition of Macromedia, Apple's reinvention as a consumer electronics company, or Intel's exit from the memory business. However, in general, established technology firms are viewed as significant industry players.

Evolution through each stage depends on several factors: industry growth rates, market acceptance of new technologies, managerial competence, luck, and timing. The challenge is especially complex because of compressed time frames, steep oscillation in growth rates, quick emergence of global customers and competitors, rapid evolution of technological know-how, short product and market life cycles, and high expectations of knowledge workers.

Close physical proximity between different high tech companies is a critical success factor in Silicon Valley. It provides opportunities for spin-offs, cross-fertilization, and the creation of flexible partnering arrangements. Moreover, pioneering products and services do not develop in a vacuum, or in isolation from the user community. The diverse range of technology companies and the presence of various industry clusters means that the ecosystem hosts early adopters and lead users of new products and services. These players provide the crucial early feedback and help recalibrate the design features and market positioning of new products and services. They test product feasibility and usability so that engineering and marketing plans can be fine-tuned for later introduction into the broader mainstream market.

3.3.4 The Knowledge Lubricants

Hatching a technology venture is a complex process requiring the contribution of several specialists. However, a young start-up cannot afford to recruit all the experts, even when their expertise is needed urgently. In many technology sectors, product life cycles are short and windows of market opportunity are narrow. A crucial feature of the Silicon Valley ecosystem is the presence of a sophisticated service infrastructure of complementary specialists. They provide the necessary "lubrication" to get a new venture off the ground. They enable startups to focus on their chosen steeple of expertise, rather than dissipate their energies across a broad range of support activities. Lawyers, accountants, market researchers, headhunters, real estate brokers, technical advisors, among others, provide variable, specialist expertise, as and when needed.

Contract manufacturing services are available to develop prototypes, or to engage in high volume or "peak load" manufacturing of sub-systems and finished goods. Specialized public relations firms provide assistance with strategic marketing, product packaging, trade shows, company logos and other collateral. Accounting and law firms have specialized technology practices. Executive search firms scan for new talent and help augment management teams of growing ventures.

Real-estate firms have expertise in the provision of facilities, especially designed for high technology firms. For example, some may require clean rooms or highly purified water supplies.

Law firms play a crucial role in the creation of new ventures.[9] A handful of prominent law partnerships have grown in Silicon Valley by specializing in high technology services. They undertake several tasks, including initial incorporation and company name search, stock allocations, patent filings, alliance and acquisition agreements, preparation of public offering prospectus, SEC filings, and litigation support.

Typically, investors collaborate closely with law firms during several rounds of financing. A new start-up may be offered favorable fee structures, in the hope that as it grows, it would need substantial legal assistance and can pay accordingly. Senior partners typically forge long-standing relationships with the venture capital community and refer entrepreneurs to venture capitalists who have expertise or prior experience with a specific type of venture, a business category, or a vertical industry.

In summary, the "lubricants" are a critical component of the ecosystem and provide a broad range of complementary services. If a start-up needs to prototype an integrated circuit to test a new design, it can be fabricated in a matter of days; if it needs a booth for a trade show, it can be put together over a weekend; if it requires specialized advice, it can be provided by a phone call.

3.4   The Ecosystem's "Climate"

Just as species in a biological ecosystem share a common climate, so do the various building blocks of the Silicon Valley ecosystem. We use the term "climate" to refer to operating norms and ground rules that characterize common practices within the ecosystem. Whereas the building blocks described earlier are analogous to the "anatomy" of the ecosystem, the "climate" reflects its "personality". A cumulative result of historical precedents, successful business recipes, and legendary role models, these norms are about the business of technology venturing and the rules by which the game is played.

The ecosystem's climatic conditions are critical in understanding core processes that enable the ecosystem to adapt to new realities. As is the case with changing seasons in a natural ecosystem, Silicon Valley's climate is subject to continuous ebbs and flows; sometimes weather patterns can be predicted; other times they evolve unexpectedly. The following section describes broad "climatic conditions" that we have observed over time and that we believe characterize the ecosystem's modus operandi.

---

[9] For additional details, see Suchman (2000).

3.4.1 Goal-Driven Work Ethic and Eternal Optimism

A critical ingredient of the Silicon Valley ecosystem is the pioneering spirit and the relentless work ethic. The entrepreneurial culture was initially born out of a Californian history of pioneers making the perilous journey over the Rocky Mountains, coupled with the legacy of the Gold Rush.[10] As a result, Silicon Valley's cultural DNA is characterized by hard work, goal-driven action, and focused specialization.

After World War II, many ex-servicemen moved to the Bay area, encouraged and subsidized to attend local universities and to undertake further education. This development provided an educated and disciplined workforce for the early-generation companies, such as Hewlett Packard, Varian, Fairchild, Watkins Johnson and Lockheed. With the growing strategic importance of the Pacific Rim and the increasing technological intensity of the "Cold War", the educated GI's provided a disciplined and eager workforce that helped build many Valley companies during the 1950's and the 1960s. As this talent pool matured and rose to executive positions, the culture of many of the early pioneers was infused with strong work ethic, coupled with discipline and integrity.

This generation was later augmented by troops returning first from Korea, and later from Vietnam. Ironically the contrast between this "work hard/play hard" lifestyle was brought into sharp focus when contrasted with the rise of the "Hippy" movement in San Francisco during the late 60s and the 70s. Initially, the two worlds collided, but, over time, the two ends of the generational spectrum gradually coalesced.[11] We suggest that the fusion of the two worlds has played a critical role in forging the disciplined, yet creative, spirit of Silicon Valley.[12]

Historically, Silicon Valley entrepreneurs have exhibited many of the qualities of the early pioneers. They have taken enormous risks, innovated in areas that many said could not be done, worked long hours over extended time frames, showed passionate commitment to their ventures, and even suffered personal problems, while developing a product or building an enterprise.

This is not to suggest that all entrepreneurs in Silicon Valley are so passionate about their ventures that generating wealth is not on their radar screen. Indeed, attitudes towards wealth generation changed considerably during the Internet boom years, with the influx of a younger generation into the area. Financial targets and a quick "exit strategy" became the critical motivational drivers. However, if financial rewards were the only or the ultimate goal, it would be difficult to explain the

---

[10] See Kotkin and Grabowicz (1982)
[11] When Remedy, an enterprise software company in the helpdesk business, took its public offering road show to Wall Street and the City of London, the theme from Led Zeppelin song "Stairway to Heaven" was used as incidental music.
[12] This blending of dual cultures is underscored by some of the anecdotal observations we have heard from long-standing Valley entrepreneurs. They describe effective teams as a combination of the "suits" and the "cowboys".

phenomenon of "serial entrepreneurs". It does suggest, however, that those who have become legends in Silicon Valley, or who are inspirational role models, do exhibit "passionate" qualities. Their primary goal is not simply financial gain. There are strong emotional and intellectual drivers as well.

3.4.2 Limited "Safety Net" and Minimal "Life Support System"

Silicon Valley is truly a Darwinian ecosystem. There are no safety nets in that "only the fit survive". In this context, fitness is about competence, intelligence, adaptability and initiative, as well as prudent timing and luck. Fitness applies to both, individuals as well as enterprises, and can be assessed in terms of how well individual skills and capabilities, as well as enterprise products and services, match emerging opportunities.

A limited life support system means that nothing can be sustained artificially for long. This climatic condition, while brutal at times, can also facilitate rapid adaptation. For example, the high cost of living in the area has led many companies to move, initially low-skilled jobs, out of Silicon Valley to other locations and countries. In recent years, even core activities have moved offshore to countries such as India, China and Eastern Europe, where technical talent is cheaper and readily available.

There has also been a major shift in patterns of "cluster employment", reflecting market realities and changing conditions. According to 2003 Index of Joint Venture Silicon Valley, during 1992-2001, employment in defense and aerospace fell by 8%, reflecting reduced levels of defense expenditure after the end of the Cold War, while employment in software increased from 7% to 21%. By contrast, the number of jobs in clean tech and "green' businesses grew by 23% during 2005-2007.[13]

Another feature of the adaptation process, boosted by a limited life support system, is the "swarm effect". Just like bees around honey, investors and entrepreneurs throng around the latest new "category". This swarm effect ramps up experimentation rather quickly. However, since there are no safety nets, entrepreneurs and investors also "stampede" away from failed concepts and recipes. So if an idea goes out of favor, or does not pay off as initially promised, its demise is rather swift.

The same principle also applies to new ventures. If a venture is no longer viable, disengagement can be measured in terms of weeks, not months or years. By the same token, if something happens to change the prospects of an out-of-favor technology or a business concept, especially if justified by tangible market evidence, investors move back into the field rather quickly. The emphasis is on pragmatism or on "what works", rather than on idealism or "what should work".

---

[13] Source: Joint Venture Silicon Valley 2008 Index.

A limited "life support system", combined with pragmatism, is a critical catalyst for adaptation. This spirit is further reinforced by the success of "Davids" versus "Goliaths", the collapse of over-funded start-ups that have a great deal of initial credibility. It is also reflected in the dynamic evolution of "large companies". For example, as indicated in Table 5, approximately half the entities listed as the "forty largest technology" firms twenty years ago, no longer exist. Indeed "only four firms on the 2002 list are survivors from the 1982 list. More than half of the 2002 top firms were not even founded in 1982. Each year's list, on average, includes 23 new firms."[14]

1982	2002	2007
Hewlett Packard	Hewlett Packard	Hewlett Packard
National Semiconductor	Intel	Intel
Intel	Cisco	Cisco
Memorex	Sun	Apple
Varian	Solectron	Oracle
Environtech	Oracle	Google
Ampex	Agilent	Sun Microsystems
Raychem	Applied Materials	Sanmina-SCI
Amdahl	Apple	Applied Materials
Tymshare	Seagate	Calpine
AMD	AMD	eBay
Rolm	Sanmina-SCI	Synnex
Four Phase Systems	JDS Uniphase	Yahoo
Cooper Labs	3Com	Franklin Resources
Intersil	LSI Logic	AMD
SRI International	Maxtor	Symantec
Spectraphysics	National Semiconductor	Agilent
American Microsystems	KLA Tencor	Robert Half Int'l
Watkins Johnson	Atmel	Con-Way
Qume	SGI	Gilead Sciences
Measurex	Bell Microproducts	Nvidia
Tandem	Siebel	Bell Microproducts

---

[14] Source: Zhang 2003, P. 6: 1982 & 2002 data, Zhang 2003; 2007 Data from The San Jose Mercury News, Silicon Valley 150, April 11, 2008.

1982	2002	2007
Plantronics	Xilinx	SanDisk
Monolithic	Maxim Integrated	Adobe Systems
URS	Palm	Network Appliance
Tab Products	Lam Research	Electronic Arts
Siliconix	Quantum	Intuit
Dysan	Altera	Juniper Networks
Racal-Vadic	Electronic Arts	KLA-Tencor
Triad Systems	Cypress Semiconductor	Granite Construction
Xidex	Cadence Design	Lam Research
Avantek	Adobe Systems	LSI
Siltec	Intuit	Spansion
Quadrrex	Veritas Software	Maxim Integrated
Coherent	Novellus Systems	National Semiconductor
Verbatim	Yahoo	Varian Medical Systems
Anderson-Jacobson	Network Appliance	Xilinx

Table 5. Top twenty firms in Silicon Valley, 1982 and 2002 (Source Zhang 2003); 2007 Data from The San Jose Mercury News, Silicon Valley 150, April 11, 2008

3.4.3 Collaborative Partnerships and Recombinant Innovations

The Silicon Valley ecosystem nurtures collaborative relationships amongst specialized enterprises. Collectively, the groupings of knowledge originators, hatcheries, lubricants, and generators, provide "meta" flexibility at the level of the ecosystem. This is largely achieved through a process of "interlinked specialization and complementary collaboration"[15], Each firm focuses on what it does best and leverages others' for complementary activities. For example, a start-up can focus on technical design, and use other entities for prototype development, market research, public relations, advertising, and staffing. Established firms acquire young companies with breakthrough innovations, as indicated by Cisco's growth-by-acquisition strategy during the 1990s. Mid-sized adolescents become a distribution channel for emerging start-ups.

---

[15] The notion of "diverse specialization" was first discussed by Piore and Sabel (1984).

Collaborative partnerships are the lifeblood of the ecosystem. They are forged between individuals when they coalesce into entrepreneurial founding teams; venture capitalists forge alliances, in the form of a syndicate, to co-invest in new ventures. Alliances are forged between established and emerging firms for manufacturing, development, or distribution purposes, and with contractors, vendors, and outsourcers for providing complementary capabilities.[16] These arrangements are helpful for small start-ups, hoping to penetrate challenging markets, or for larger firms, intending to fill their pipelines and maintain the flow of innovative products.

The innovation process reflects this emphasis on collaboration and complementaries. It is as much about blending and combining, through collaborative processes, as it is about breakthroughs in new fields. Often an end-of-life technology can be refreshed and augmented by the addition of something new. Or something that was only possible to do in a given domain can be applied to another.

Consider, for example, how removable Winchester disk drives leveraged the technology used in floppy disk drives and enhanced input/output controllers in order to upgrade to non-sealed units, first with Syquest cartridges, and later with Zip drives; how Google's founders used data mining technology to develop a search engine; or how ROLM's founding team pioneered the digital PBX by applying minicomputer technology to the telecommunications equipment business.

3.5 Super-Flexibility and the Ecosystem

Silicon Valley's operating norms and entrepreneurial "climate" impacts the dynamics of the adaptation process. It is not sufficient to create the anatomical building blocks, without considering the climate's impact on the ecosystem. Having venture capital, without the ability to "pull the plug" at the right time, is not conducive to creating viable, new ventures. Similarly, having world-class universities and research laboratories, without developing an open attitude to partnering and information sharing, does not lead to the generation of a critical mass of innovative ventures. Silicon Valley should be understood in the context of both, its anatomy as well as its personality. Taken as a whole, it provides an innovative laboratory for studying the process of dynamic adaptation.

---

[16] Global alliances have been a historic feature of Silicon Valley. For example, The now-defunct personal communications start-up, EO, had a number of global partners, including AT&T, Matsushita, Marubeni, amongst others, only 18 months into the venture's life-cycle, before being acquired by AT&T. 3DO, a multimedia firm founded by Trip Hawkins, the founder of Electronic Arts, was initially a joint venture between Time Warner, Matsushita and Electronic Arts. Similarly, General Magic, the personal communications software company and an Apple spin-off, was initially forged through an alliance between Apple, AT&T, Philips and Sony. Quantum Corporation, the disk drive firm, allied itself with Matsushita, as its manufacturing partner, during the 1980s. Auspex Systems, the file server company, forged an alliance with Fuji-Xerox in its formative years, involving both investments and distribution agreements.

The constellation of knowledge originators, hatcheries, generators and lubricants in Silicon Valley, characterize a dynamic ecosystem of independent, yet complementary, entities, communities, and cultures. The ecosystem is super-flexible by being robust as well as versatile. It is able to withstand turbulence, but can also transform and adapt itself. Since each building block is modular and autonomous, the ecosystem can withstand shocks and perturbations. If a venture fails, or a "category" goes out of favor, it is not necessarily detrimental for the entire ecosystem. The ecosystem is versatile in that new competencies can be quickly generated through the process of collaboration and cross-fertilization.

Silicon Valley's knowledge enterprises operate in a fluid, loosely-coupled, dynamic ecosystem. The ecosystem has specialized, modular building blocks, and a shared, common climate. Its distinctive "macro-climate" is characterized by "meritocratic norms", limited safety nets, transparent *de facto* standards, open feedback loops, interdependent relationships, and a dual focus on competition and collaboration. Distinctive "micro-climates" coexist within the broader "macro-climate", providing additional stimuli to adapt to unique industry and enterprise norms. The ecosystem, we argue, provides the "meta" context within which entrepreneurial firms can dynamically adapt to new realities.

Silicon Valley has generated a critical mass of knowledge enterprises, whose innovative products and solutions have transformed the global economy. The ecosystem provides an anchor of stability within which incumbent firms and new start-ups can flourish and become a source of innovation and employment. Yet it adapts to new realities through a process of "recycling" where failed ventures and terminated initiatives are re-configured, re-blended, and ultimately re-packaged in order to adapt to emerging challenges and new opportunities. The dynamic concept of "recycling", our first action principle, will be explored in Chapter 4.

4 Super-Flexible Ecosystems: Innovating by Recycling

How does the Silicon Valley ecosystem maintain the pace of innovation and entrepreneurial creativity? How does it adapt to the ups and downs of business cycles and innovation loops? How does it nurture the relentless entrepreneurial spirit? How does it remain super-flexible? The principle of "recycling" may be one piece of this complex puzzle. It describes how talent, ideas, products, and technologies are re-blended, reconfigured, re-packaged, re-purposed, and ultimately "recycled". Recycling, we propose, is the cornerstone of the adaptation process in Silicon Valley. It enables the ecosystem to harness "failures", to learn from setbacks, and to become re-vitalized in the process. The "recycling" lessons of Silicon Valley may be useful for other entrepreneurial hubs around the world, and for established global corporations that have to continuously innovate by introducing new products and services.

Recycling is a critical feature of Silicon Valley's ecosystem dynamics. It provides the adaptive capacity for innovation and venture creation (Bahrami & Evans 1995). During periods of rapid growth, there is a need to capitalize on market opportunities and technological innovations with agility and versatility. During economic downturns, the "froth" evaporates, clearing the field for the dominant players to consolidate, and for marginal ventures to degrade gracefully. It is typically during these down times that entrepreneurial teams leverage failed initiatives and learn from setbacks. This chapter focuses on how recycling works in the Silicon Valley ecosystem. We describe enabling mechanisms that operate at the meta level of the "ecosystem". It is a precursor to our discussion of the action principles of maneuvering, recalibrating, orgitechting and aligning, discussed in chapters 5 through 8, that facilitate adaptation at the level of the enterprise.

The rationale behind "recycling" is easy to understand. Operating in knowledge-based arenas is like being a pioneer. Relevant information is in a state of flux; it continuously morphs and evolves. There are few recipes and blueprints for success. Ultimately, business propositions have to be tested "on the ground", pass the market traction test, and respond to lead-user feedback. Just as pioneers may go down "blind alleys", entrepreneurs often pursue business propositions that may not succeed and become branded as "failures". This situation presents a dilemma: How to nurture, encourage, and facilitate rapid experimentation and prototyping, and minimize the negative stigma and the waste of resources typically associated with failed ventures.

We propose that "recycling" is a critical enabler in this context. It allows learning from setbacks and makes it possible to reconfigure knowledge, talent, technologies, and resources. The process enables new ventures and innovative products to rise from the ashes of "failed" initiatives. Failure is a necessary feature of the entrepreneurial, risk-taking process, and there is a high mortality rate associated with new ventures. However, this is also a crucial part of adaptation. Just as plants and animals adapt to their surroundings through evolutionary processes by way of "phenotype plasticity", so do entrepreneurs and knowledge workers. There is life after death in this ecosystem in that the demise of a firm, or the failure of a product, may lead to the formation of other entities, and the development of innovative products and services. This chapter describes the different recycling mechanisms and illustrates their use in the context of the Silicon Valley ecosystem.

4.1 Recycling Catalysts

This section explains how recycling takes place in Silicon Valley and discusses why it is a catalyst for innovation and adaptation. We have aggregated recycling catalysts into four distinctive categories. As depicted in Figure 8, these include: recycling by "re-creating", inducing high birth rates for new ventures; recycling by "cross-pollinating" through talent mobility and "information diffusion"; recycling by "recursive learning" through exploring, prototyping, and failing; and recycling by "re-inventing" through re-financing, re-purposing, re-combining and re-packaging. The important point to note is that "recycling" applies to products, technologies, and resources, as well as to talent, information, and know-how.

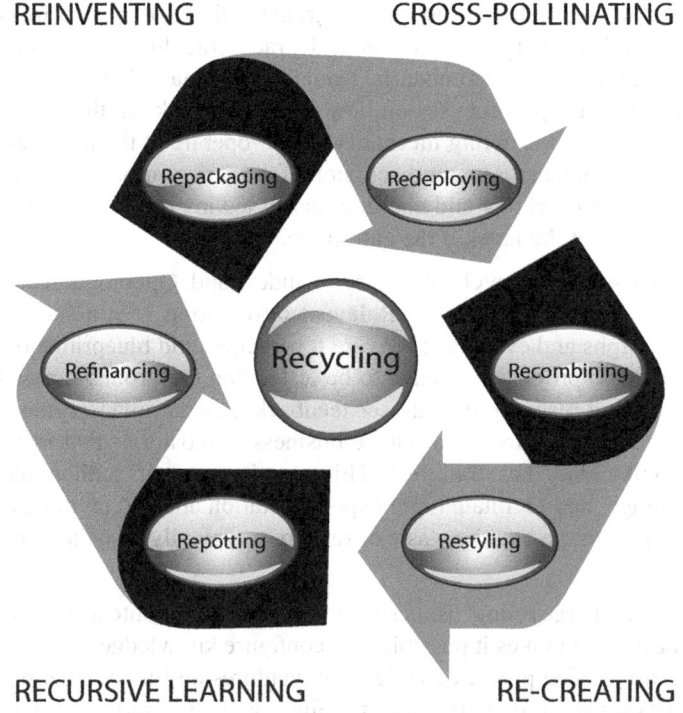

Figure 8. Recycling mechanisms

4.1.1 Recycling by Re-Creating: High Birth Rates for New Ventures

A striking feature of Silicon Valley is the high birth rate for new ventures. According to Zhang (2003), 29,000 high tech companies were founded in Silicon Valley from 1990-2000. As seen in Table 6, there were 1226 new venture-backed start-ups funded in Silicon Valley in 2007, compared with 488 in New England and Route 128. During the same time frame, new ventures, or those started after 1990, accounted for most of the employment growth in the area.[1] We suggest that high birth rates facilitate recycling; the most successful elements of failed ventures can be blended into new ones.

New ventures are founded in several ways. They may be induced by venture capitalists, recognizing growth opportunities presented by emerging technologies. New ventures may start accidentally, through efforts of enthusiasts and hobbyists. Venture formation may be triggered by collaborative research programs, or by graduate students' doctoral studies. Some are formed by intact teams, spinning off from existing companies, by "serial" entrepreneurs, or by complementary experts from different entities.[2]

As indicated in Chapter 3, the Silicon Valley ecosystem is a catalyst for networking among founding teams. Many get to know one another at universities, or are introduced to each other by early investors; or as is often the case, they may have forged collaborative relationships in their previous relationships as customers, vendors, colleagues, or even competitors.

---

[1] In 2001, start-ups less than five years old employed 159,300 people in the area (Zhang 2003, p.11).
[2] Every year, venture capital firms fund many new ventures in Silicon Valley (see table 6). However, this is only a fraction of new ventures. Many are "boot-strapped", self-funded, or kick-started through financial assistance from family, friends, and business "angels".

Year	New England	Silicon Valley
1995	233	500
1996	332	762
1997	380	869
1998	460	1042
1999	649	1701
2000	871	2161
2001	573	1103
2002	437	803
2003	442	855
2004	420	946
2005	413	985
2006	436	1184
2007	488	1226
Total	**6134**	**14137**

Table 6. Annual number of venture-funded start-ups
Source: PriceWaterhouseCoopers MoneyTree™ Report 2008

Historically, the birth of many well-known technology companies has been linked to technology enthusiasts. They may have developed the initial prototype for their own use, or because of their personal interest. Well-known examples include Hewlett Packard and Apple Computer. Yahoo is a more recent example. The business idea started as a "hobby" for Jerry Yang and David Filo, its two founders, while they were graduate students at Stanford. Called "Jerry's Guide to the World Wide Web", it was an informal tool for Jerry, David and their friends to navigate the net: *"In the early days, it was clearly something for our own use...then after other people started using it, it became something for them to use...nothing more than just kind of a hobby."*[3]

"Serial" entrepreneurs also contribute to high venture birth rates. As depicted in Figure 10, and discussed later in the chapter, Alan Shugart parted company with Shugart Associates during the mid-1970s. He went on to co-found Seagate Technology in 1979 with another Shugart co-founder, Finis Conner. Conner and Seagate co-founder Tom Mitchell left to found Conner Peripherals. At the time, it became the fastest growing company in the US business history Similarly, Lar-

---

[3] Source: Video case study "Yahoo: Jerry and Dave's Excellent Venture", Stanford University, October 1997.

ry Boucher, left his first entrepreneurial venture, Adaptec, to co-found Auspex Systems in 1987. He moved on to start a new company, Alacritech, in 1997. Other well known "serial" entrepreneurs include Jim Clark (SGI, Netscape, Healtheon, My-CFO), Steve Jobs (Apple, Next, Pixar), Trip Hawkins (Electronic Arts, 3DO, Digital Chocolate), and Tom Siebel (Gain Technology and Siebel Systems).

Another source of new ventures can be best described as "re-starts". These refer to ventures that are acquired by larger firms but later flounder. They can also be venture-backed start-ups that do not get follow-on funding; or ventures where the original founders and investors are "washed out" during the later rounds of financing. Some are able to rise from the ashes of the failing parent or may be bought out.

Re-starts are an important source of new venture formation. It is rare to get a start up right the first time. Innovations often take time to mature or they may be too early for the target market. As we argue in chapter 6, a critical entrepreneurial skill is the willingness and the ability to recalibrate product features and marketing recipes until they address user needs. Re-starts are a good illustration of the recalibration process at work.

The desire to commercialize scientific breakthroughs are yet another form of venture formation, especially in biotechnology and life sciences. Well-known examples are Boyer and Cohen, the co-founders of Genentech, and Tom Fogarty, the inventor of the catheter. He commercialized his invention and later founded a venture capital firm, specializing in life sciences. Bill New left Stanford Medical School during the late 1980s to found Nelcor, commercializing the oxymeter, to help anesthesiologists. Carver Mead, a professor at Cal Tech, and a pioneer in the field of neural processors, joined forces with Frederico Fagin, founder of Zilog, to start Synaptics. Syntex commercialized Carl Dersai's Nobel Prize winning discovery of the contraceptive pill. William Sharpe, the Noble Prize winner and Stanford professor, co-founded Financial Engines, during the late 1990s.

Spin-offs from existing firms are also a significant source of new venture formation. A recent study (Zhang 2003, Table 4.1) confirms Silicon Valley's relatively high birth rates, in terms of venture-backed spin-offs from established companies: "...*leading firms in Silicon Valley significantly outperformed their counterparts in the Boston area in terms of producing entrepreneurs ... together DEC and Raytheon spun off 48 venture-backed start-ups ... about half of the 99 spin-offs from HP... Apple has spun off 71 venture-backed start-ups, whereas Lotus in the Boston area (has) 26 spin-offs... Even IBM ... with a presence in both areas, has 77 spin-offs in Silicon Valley, compared to 23 in the Boston area.*" (Zhang, p.50-51).

The point to note is that irrespective of their origin or financial backing, high birth rates, coupled with the infusion of talent from "failed" ventures, boosts the innovation process, leverages existing know-how, generates new insights, and creates an environment that is conducive to enterprise creation.

Silicon Valley	Employee Founders	Venture Capital backed Spin-off Start-ups	Boston Area	Employee Founders	Venture Capital backed Spin-off Start-ups
Apple	94	71	Data General	13	13
Cisco	41	35	DEC	52	41
HP	117	99	EMC	9	6
Intel	76	68	Lotus	29	26
Oracle	73	57	Prime	5	5
SGI	50	37	Raytheon	7	7
Sun	101	79	Wang	11	11
IBM	82	77	IBM	23	23

Table 7. Spin-offs from leading firms in Silicon Valley and the Boston area
(Source: Zhang, 2003, p.50)

4.1.2 Recycling by Cross-Pollinating: Talent Re-Deployment and Information Diffusion

As Saxenian (1994) has noted, Silicon Valley enjoys a "regional advantage" partly because its culture encourages knowledge workers to move between entities. Indeed, talent mobility is a crucial feature of Silicon Valley's employment dynamic. Executives move from high tech companies into venture capital and consulting. Engineers change jobs by moving just "down the road". Consultants take on new roles as investors and executives. Many leave the relative security of an established firm to join a small venture, or to start their own companies.

There are many examples of talent mobility in Silicon Valley, dating back to its pioneering days. For example, Gene Kleiner, founding partner of Kleiner Perkins, Caufield & Byers (KPCB), one of the Valley's leading venture capital firms, was previously at Fairchild Semiconductor. Tom Jermoluk, the former CEO of Silicon Graphics, moved to Excite@home, the venture-backed start-up during the early 1990s, and went on to become a partner with KPCB. He joined other entrepreneurs, @Home's co-founder Will Hearst, Oracle's former COO, Ray Lane, and Sun's co-founder, Vinod Khosla, who also joined Kleiner during the 1990s. George Sollman, the former President of the American Electronics Association, moved from Shugart, the disk drive company, to the venture community, and later became the turnaround CEO of a voice-messaging firm, Centigram, before starting his own venture, At Motion, in 1997.

Talent mobility is not limited to the venture community. For example, Stig Hagstrom, who was responsible for one of the research labs at Xerox PARC, moved to Stanford University's Material Science Department and later founded the Center for Innovations in Learning at Stanford in 2002. Mario Rosati, the co-founder of the technology law practice, Wilson Sonsini Goodrich & Rosati, became an adjunct professor at the Haas School of Business, University of California, Berkeley.

Mobility is just as common among executives who may work for competing firms. For example, after stepping down as the Chief Operating Officer of Seagate Technology, Tom Mitchell became a co-founder of the competing disk drive firm, Conner Peripherals, and returned to Seagate, after it acquired Conner. Jim Bagley and Steve Newberry, the Chairman and CEO of Lam Research, were members of the top executive team at Lam's competitor, Applied Materials.

At its core, the ecosystem operates through an inter-connected network of personal relationships, a long-standing feature of Silicon Valley. Shugart, the pioneering disk drive company, was co-founded by eleven former colleagues. They had worked together for IBM and Memorex. Shockley Laboratories was the initial setting that brought together Fairchild's founding team. Intel founding team had also worked together at Fairchild.

As indicated in Figure 9, informal networks are formed in several ways. They may be forged accidentally, among those with the same hobby or even those using the same sports or social clubs. Universities, research labs, and established firms, like HP, Intel, or Oracle, may be the initial setting for bringing entrepreneurial teams together. Relationships may be forged deliberately through referrals from lawyers, accountants, and venture capitalists. Overall, personal and professional networks are the fulcrum of activity in Silicon Valley.

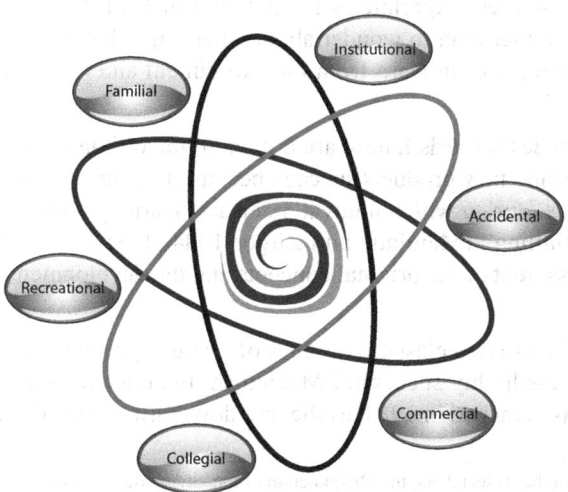

Figure 9. Categories of personal and professional networks

Cross-pollination is not limited to talent mobility. It also applies to rapid diffusion of information. It is difficult to keep secrets in Silicon Valley for several reasons. These include close physical proximity between companies, early adoption of e-tools, fast moving nature of high tech industries, inter-firm mobility of knowledge workers, and extensive reliance on contractors, partners and vendors. Ideas can be quickly picked up, transferred and bounced around in formal as well as informal exchanges. The center of gravity is not about knowing what to do, but about how and when to do it.

In addition, information has a short "half-life". New products are alpha and beta-tested by early adopters. Pioneering firms have to release technical information to their vendors, contractors and partners. Moreover, due to the rapid pace of change, information about products, markets, and competitors quickly become obsolete.

Formal and informal exchanges among "techno-evangelists" are another source of information diffusion. These individuals have a passion for their interests and interact on the net, at user group meetings, conferences, trade shows, and other forums. The ecosystem provides a broad framework within which knowledge workers can exchange ideas. An idea that may have failed at one time in a particular context may be re-used later in a different setting and eventually pay off.

4.1.3 Recycling by Recursive Learning: Exploring, Prototyping, and Failing

In Silicon Valley there is no stigma attached to honest failure. Entrepreneurs are measured by what they do today, not by what they did in the past. This means that they can engage in novel experiments in the belief that it is better to try something risky and to fail, rather than to wonder about what might have been. Even if a venture fails, entrepreneurs can learn from the experiment and move on to start a successful entity.

Tolerant attitudes towards failure are critical to the ultimate success of the recycling process.[4] Many new products succeed because they are refined as the result of a learning process, during which innovators clearly learn by "doing"; but they learn even more by "failing" (Maidique and Zirger 1984, 1985). These "failures" may lead to a re-assessment of the original concepts and the development of new alternatives.

Apple III and Lisa are two classic examples of "failed" products that eventually led to the launch of the highly successful Macintosh. Intended to be a successor to the Apple2, Lisa was launched in 1983, as the first downturn of the PC era began to bite.

---

[4] As pointed out by other researchers, the phenomenon of the "living dead" illustrates the futility of maintaining a high technology firm, without any demonstrable success, on an expensive life support system. See Bourgeois and Eisenhardt (1987).

Although it was a technologically sophisticated computer, it was too expensive and did not sell well. The design was later recalibrated and the technology was recycled into a smaller, simpler, and cheaper product. The new product, called Macintosh, was introduced in 1984 and has been a major industry success, as was its later successor, the iMac. Similarly, after Handspring merged with its competitor, Palm, in 2003, the combined teams rapidly repackaged the Treo communicator/organizer as a Palm product and relaunched it.

The ability of the ecosystem to recycle know how is closely linked to a tolerant attitude towards failure. Many entrepreneurs do not use the word "failure" as part of their vocabulary. Instead failures are viewed as "set-backs", temporary challenges to be solved, and critical learning opportunities. Today's failure becomes the crucial ingredient for tomorrow's successful recipe. Knowledge workers who have experienced failed start-ups, learn from their setbacks and apply the lessons to their later assignments. Many seasoned venture capitalists prefer to fund entrepreneurs who have had the "scar tissue" of previous "failures". The assumption is that it is unlikely that they would repeat the same mistakes twice. Past success, on the other hand, can breed arrogance and over-confidence. It can limit an entrepreneur's ability to learn from diverse input and tangible feedback.

The essence of recursive learning is exploring, prototyping, generating feedback, experiencing setbacks, and recalibrating. Attitudes towards failure are especially critical when there are no historical precedents or success recipes. Even with the most elaborate planning, it may not be clear, ahead of time, how customers are likely to react to a new class of product. The related principle of "recalibration" will be discussed in Chapter 6.

4.1.4 Recycling by Re-Inventing: Re-Financing, Re-Packaging, and Re-Purposing

Another approach to recycling is through reinvention. The process entails selecting effective features of a failed product, or an unsuccessful venture, combining these with novel ingredients, and reintroducing it in a new form. Several enablers boost the reinvention process. These include re-financing a venture with new investors and revised valuations, re-packaging a product with new features, a new name and a new logo, and combining a number of ventures in the same arena, under a new corporate umbrella, giving it a new identity and a new focus.

The move to repackage is most evident during downturns in the Valley. It is also a low cost method of developing new products. An early example was the development of hard cards by Quantum during the 1980's. This was a time when PC users increased their storage capacity by adding disk drives and an I/O controller card. Another example was the fusion of Winchester technology into a removable disk storage device. The product that won at the end was the Zip drive from Iomega. It evolved from the Bernoulli drive and removable Winchester, fused together with I/O controller technology.

Other well-known examples of product reinvention are the repackaging of the Macintosh as the new iMac during the late 1990s, and the evolution of the PalmPilot, first developed as a handheld game console called the "Zoomer". Due to cost constraints, the developers adapted the device and turned it into what later became the "PalmPilot". US Robotics bought the company just as the product began to take off. It was acquired by 3Com for its networking technology. Palm was later spun off by 3Com as an independent company. The original developers of "PalmPilot" left to start Handspring, and developed the "Visor". Palm merged with Handspring in 2003.

Reinvention can also be the result of combining ventures that compete in the same arena. Venture capitalists, for example, often combine several ventures in order to get "critical mass", to gain credibility, to reduce overhead, to expand product portfolios, to put together an effective marketing team with a solid technical team, or to combine balance sheets in preparation for a public offering or an acquisition. The inverse can also occur during downturns in that the rationale behind re-combining may be sheer survival. A case in point is the merger between Palm and Handspring in 2003, or the merger between Macromind and Authorware, into Macromedia, during the early 1990s.

This trend was further amplified during the downturn of 2002/3 for ventures with common investors. A good example was the merger between Cross-Weave and AmberPoint, funded by Sutter Hill Ventures and Norwest Venture Partners.[5] Cross-Weave had received $10.6 million in 1999 in two rounds of financing. AmberPoint raised $9.1 million in 2001 and a second round of $13.6 million in November 2002. While in some senses this could be seen as an acquisition, in that only a handful of CrossWeave's employees joined AmberPoint, the benefits for the investors were substantial.

Re-packaging often requires a new management team, new investors, and new valuations to kick-start languishing ventures. During growth cycles, a venture firm's portfolio typically expands, either by focusing on early stage deals or by accelerating Series B & C stage companies ready for IPOs. During downturns, the situation changes considerably. Venture firms can not fund all the ventures in their portfolios. The poorer performers, or those with limited prospects, are discontinued. Even those that receive follow-on funding are often "washed out" through re-valuations of previous equity distributions. The objective is to take a fresh "objective" look at the portfolio. This minimizes the emotional commitment that existing investors may have to the "original" value proposition.

---

[5] Source: The Venture Capital Analyst, Venture One April 2003 , p.7.

New investors are brought on board, and a "refreshed" trajectory typically follows. The challenge is to ensure that re-valuation does not negatively impact early employees who may be critical to its eventual success. This is yet another mechanism for adaptation.

4.2. Case History

The following case vignette illustrates the recycling process in practice. Our intention is to show how the demise of a company is not necessarily wasteful; how its talent pool, technologies and products can be recycled into the broader ecosystem and give rise to new ventures and novel innovations. Our focus is on a pioneering company in the disk drive industry that no longer exists. Its demise led to the formation of other disk drive entities and the formation of a critical sector in Silicon Valley.

Shugart Associates was a pioneering disk drive company during the mid-1970s and early 1980s. Its eleven co-founders had worked together at IBM and Memorex. Each co-founder invested $5000 to start the business in 1973. They later received venture capital backing from Bill Hambrecht of the venture firm Hambrecht &Quist, and John Friedenrich at Donaldson Lufkin and Jenerette.

At first, Shugart was engaged in the parallel development of three products: an OEM disk drive, an OEM printer and a desktop computer. The founding CEO, Alan Shugart, left the company shortly afterwards and was succeeded by another co-founder, Don Massaro, who refocused the business on disk drives.[6]

Shugart's first product, an 8-inch floppy disk drive, was introduced in May 1973 with volume shipments beginning in July 1973. It introduced the double-density 8-inch floppy disk drives in April 1975. This was followed by another innovation that has become part of Silicon Valley folklore. As discussed in chapter 5, the SA400, 5.25-inch floppy disk drive was introduced in September 1976 and became a major success. It accelerated the company's growth, with revenues rising to $18.14 million by 1977. Shugart augmented its product line by developing an 8 inch Winchester disk drive. Much like the earlier SA-400, its development was funded by two of its customers.

As recounted in Chapter 5, the 5.25 inch floppy disk drive became an industry standard, fueling the meteoric growth of word processors during the late 1970's and early 1980's. Shugart was ideally positioned to exploit the soon-to-emerge personal computer market. At this time, market conditions precluded a public offering so it was not a favored "liquidity event".

---

[6] Interestingly, Don Massaro, who replaced Alan Shugart as President of Shugart, became CEO of Xerox Printing Division. He left Xerox to co-found Metaphor Computers with Dave Liddell, the coinventor of Ethernet at Xerox PARC. Massaro later became VP of Marketing at Conner Peripherals and then spun off with a Conner co-founder, Bill Schraeder, to start Diamond Multimedia.

Xerox acquired Shugart in 1978, together with printing pioneers, Diablo and Versatec. At the time, these acquisitions were an important element of Xerox's strategic focus on office automation. Fueled by increasing demand for the 5.25-inch floppy and other products, Shugart's revenues continued to grow rapidly. However, even before the acquisition, several members of its management and technical team had left the company; some to form "niche" disk drive start-ups, others to join competing firms. For example, two members of Shugart's core team, Jim McCoy and David Brown, joined forces with System Industries' Jim Patterson, to co-found Quantum in 1980.

In 1981, not yet weakened by these spin-offs and Japanese competition, Shugart continued to innovate and prosper. It pioneered, among others, the Shugart Associates Standard Interface or SASI. The goal was to help systems integrators develop the microcode and allow Winchester disk drives meet the unique operating systems requirements of different manufacturers. Eventually, this product became an industry standard, enabling disk drives to be interchanged between previously incompatible computers.

SASI was the forerunner of what became the widely accepted SCSI standard, "controlling" both, IBM PCs (along with PC-compatibles) and the Apple Macintosh. Ironically, the team who pioneered the SASI innovation, had proposed creating a disk drive controller business as part of Xerox's efforts to stimulate internal ventures. However, at the time the business proposition was rejected. The "controller" team, led by Larry Boucher, left Shugart and founded Adaptec in 1981.

During this period, Shugart was also engaged in other product development initiatives, including the optical disk drive technology. In this case, a subsidiary unit, Optimem, was established as an international strategic alliance between Xerox and SGS Thomson of France. Another venture unit was created to develop the 3.5-inch floppy disk drive, destined for portable computers.

Between 1981 and 1983, Shugart's revenues grew considerably; at the same time, industry and competitive dynamics were transformed. Several niche spin-offs, together with other start-ups, began to erode selected parts of its business. Japanese manufacturers made aggressive inroads into the low-end floppy disk drive market by competing on the basis of low price and high quality. IBM sourced the floppy disk drive for its new PC from Tandon, whose Indian founder had established low cost manufacturing operations in India. Yet Shugart was still, at this stage, the leading "across-the-board" supplier of rotating memory products. Cost reduction strategies, especially related to "offshore manufacturing", would become the decisive competitive battle.

Following an abrupt industry downturn that resulted in two years of consecutive losses, Xerox divested Shugart. By this time, Xerox was facing the cash needs of its new acquisition in the insurance industry, Crum and Forster. The floppy disk business, accounting for about one third of Shugart's revenues, was sold off to its

Japanese joint venture partner, Matsushita. Its Winchester disk drive division was discontinued, and its optical disk drive unit, Optimem, was sold to Cipher Data, itself later acquired by Archive. The much paired down Shugart, stripped of its 5.25-inch and pioneering 3.5-inch floppy and Winchester lines, was sold off to a group of investors. It continued to operate for some time as a service and distribution center in Los Angeles, focusing on drive-refurbishing and end-of-life products.

Studies of Shugart would typically end with its disengagement. Using our traditional optic, the company would be viewed as a failure, a star that shone brightly for a while and then disappeared. However, although it ceased to exist in its original form by 1986, its people, know-how, intellectual capital, and market relationships have since been recycled. It gave birth to a new generation of entrepreneurial companies, even before it floundered. In Silicon Valley, the firm's legacy continues to this day.

In view of the knowledge-intensive nature of technology businesses, a firm's technical demise, we suggest, is not necessarily detrimental as long as the ecosystem can flexibly recycle its critical know-how and human assets. Shugart's demise resulted in the re-configuration and recycling of its people, their know-how, and their capabilities. As indicated in Figure 10, many of Shugart's employees joined its spinoffs, started new companies, and in some cases, revitalized other entities.

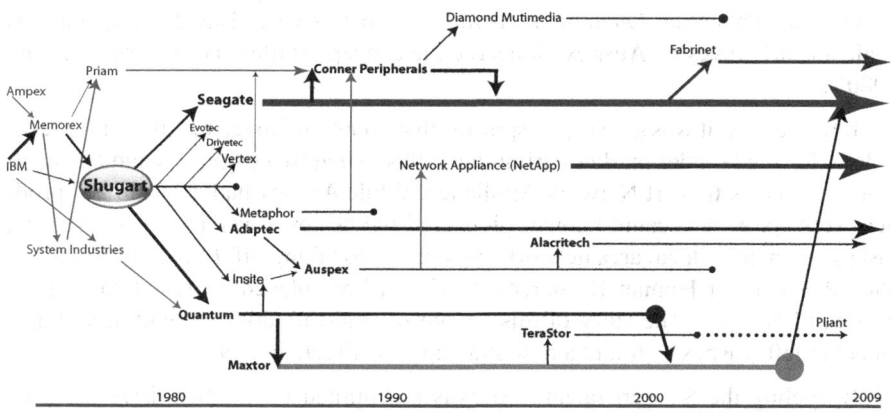

Figure 10. Spinoffs from Shugart in the disk drive industry

Its co-founder, Alan Shugart, left the company early on, and moved to Santa Cruz to pursue other interests. Meanwhile, one of his former IBM colleagues and Shugart co-founder, Finis Conner, left Shugart some time later, to co-found Seagate Technologies, together with Alan Shugart. In 1980, another disk drive company, Quantum, was co-founded by an ex-IBM'er from System Industries, Jim Patterson, and several Shugart engineers, including Jim McCoy and David Brown, who later became Quantum's president and CEO. Both had played major roles in product development at Shugart. Quantum focused on developing 8-inch Winchester disk drives. Jim McCoy later left Quantum and went on to found Maxtor, a leading disk drive company.

Former Shugart employees also started the disk drive controller industry. A team of three, under the leadership of Larry Boucher, left Shugart in 1981 to found Adaptec, pioneering the SCSI Interface. Adaptec's first product was a SCSI interface chipset that was initially developed by Larry Boucher and two colleagues while still at Shugart. At first, they presented an internal business plan to Shugart's executive team to get funding for their internal venture. When their proposal was rejected by Shugart's management, Boucher and his two colleagues left to found Adaptec, focusing on input-output controllers. The founders mortgaged their homes to pay for prototype development. Later, the venture capital firm, TVI's General Partner, David Marquadt, a former employee of Shugart's sister company, Diablo, invested in the first round of Adaptec's venture funding. TVI had been co-founded by Jim Bochnowski, who was DLJ's representative on Shugart's board and later became Shugart's President for about a year. Marquadt was also an early investor in Microsoft and Seagate. Today, Adaptec is a successful public company, specializing in storage infrastructure solutions.

The recycling story is even more intricate. Following a downturn and a spell as Adaptec's Chairman, Larry Boucher co-founded Auspex Systems in 1987, together with Jim Patterson, Quantum's co-founder. In this case, David Marquadt was again an early investor. Auspex pioneered the concept of file servers during the late 1980's.

Interestingly, it was an Auspex spin-off that commercialized the file-server technology for the broader market during the 1990s, when two engineers and a consultant left Auspex to start Network Appliance. While Auspex had a "Cadillac" product, NetApp, as it became known, pioneered the "Chevy" version of file servers, just as the internet/local area network explosion was taking off. Ironically, Shugart's Vice President of Human Resources, Chris Carlton, played a pivotal role in the growth of NetApp. The story of this stream of spin-offs does not end here. Larry Boucher left Auspex to found a new start-up, Alacritech, in 1997.

Recycling the Shugart talent pool was not limited to the disk drive industry. George Sollman, who joined Shugart from Control Data in 1976, as the Product Manager of the 5.25 inch floppy disk drive, later became Shugart's Vice President of Sales and Marketing. In 1984 he moved on to the venture community and later joined a "re-start", Centigram, at the time, a languishing voice-messaging company. In an ironic twist of fate that displays the ethos of Silicon Valley, Sollman was previously responsible for reviewing and rejecting the internal business plan that Larry Boucher had submitted, while at Shugart. Notwithstanding, Boucher became Sollman's first customer at Centigram. He placed an order for a voice messaging system for use at Adaptec.

The voice messaging system at this time was a PC with a number of disk drives, so Sollman's knowledge and contacts were major assets. For example, he invited Jim McCoy, Quantum and Maxtor co-founder, to join Centigram's Board of Directors as Centigram. Their relationship had been forged earlier at Shugart. Sollman took Centigram public and after a spell as the President of the American Electronics Association, he founded Arabesque, later renamed At Motion, a wireless telecommunications company, in 1997. Phone.com acquired At Motion in 2000.

Similar anecdotes could be written about other entrepreneurs and enterprises in Silicon Valley. For example, Tom Siebel was at Oracle before leaving to found Gain Technologies. Although Gain did not succeed, he went on to start Siebel Systems. Eli Harrari, who founded SanDisk, initially worked on solid-state memory at Intel, until the program was famously discontinued.

4.3 Recycling and Super-Flexibility

As illustrated by Shugart's case history, the Silicon Valley ecosystem thrives on the process of recycling, as start-ups and spin-offs are formed, and as "failures" are constantly blended and reconfigured into new ventures. The Shugart case illustrates the dynamic forces that drive the recycling process. Recycling occurs by creating new firms, moving people between entities, cross-pollinating information and know-how, recursive learning by doing and failing, and reinventing a venture in a new form. The recycling process is especially effective during the Valley's down cycle. The ecosystem experiences what we characterize as the "wash effect", whereby the "beach" is cleared of "flotsam and jetsam" and the nutrients are recycled for the next generation of firms to grow. The recycling process, we suggest, extends Schumpeter's (1934) notion of "creative destruction", and provides a practical framework for benefiting from setbacks and failures in contemporary knowledge-based arenas.

The recycling process is enhanced in the absence of the typical stigma associated with failure.[6] Indeed, the high failure rate associated with start-ups increases experimentation and the speed of recycling. In the Popperian sense of "falsifiability" (Popper 1972), entrepreneurs learn, just as scientists do, much from failed experiments. Since organizational death is not viewed as a finite expression of failure, entrepreneurs are able to entertain, what would normally be considered, "outlandish" risks. Prospects of failure and mortality can also reduce feelings of over-confidence and invulnerability among successful incumbents and keep them on their toes. In such a setting, incumbent firms strive to become "agile giants", capable of rapid maneuvering and recalibrating. Operating in conditions of kaleidoscopic change,

---

[6] A rule of thumb in the venture community is that the number of successful start-ups is around 1 in 30, as a "ball park" figure.

a firm's technical demise, we suggest, is not necessarily detrimental as long as the ecosystem can re-cycle its critical know-how and human assets.[7]

The short life cycle of many high-technology firms may also be helpful for sustaining the long-term innovative capability of a knowledge ecosystem. In addition to maintaining the stream of new firms, that in turn provide job opportunities and create new products and services, ephemeral firms increase the variety of experiments, and, when acquired, can help rejuvenate other entities, or become reconfigured in the form of new entities. Recursive learning is crucial, given that it is difficult, if not impossible, to know the "winning formula" ahead of time.

Recycling, we suggest, is critical for understanding the adaptive capabilities of dynamic, knowledge-based, ecosystems. Fundamentally, it enables continuity and change to coexist. The ecosystem provides a stable anchor within which talent pools, ventures, ideas, products, know-how, and relationships can be recycled and redeployed. The process maintains the high birth rates for new ventures. These, in turn, create new jobs, and new products and services. Taken together, the recycling mechanisms described in this chapter provide the broader context within which business entities can strive to become super-flexible.

---

[7] Another illustration of recycling is the story of ROLM Corporation, the pioneer of the digital PBX, acquired by IBM in 1984. Ken Oshman, its co-founder and Chief Executive, moved on to lead Echelon, a pioneer in the networking field. A number of former employees of its Mil-Spec Division founded Ultra, a firm working on high-speed local area networks. Richard Moley, its former Vice President of Marketing and its first PBX product manager, became the CEO of Stratacom. He orchestrated Stratacom's turn-around and its eventual sale to Cisco during the 1990s.

5 Super-Flexible Strategies:
Shifting Gears and Maneuvering Swift Turns

How can leadership teams develop effective strategies in dynamic ecosystems? How should they balance short-term expediency against long-term prudence? How do they change direction and make sudden left turns in their trajectories? How can they surf successive waves of innovation? This chapter is about how technology firms develop their strategies, maintain momentum, and revise their approach as conditions change, in other words how they navigate their dynamic strategic trajectory real-time.

Super-flexibility is the hallmark of adaptive strategies in high tech ecosystems. It provides the capacity to modify strategies "on the fly". This capability is equally critical during times of rapid growth as well as during recessions and downturns. Knowledge-based entities need to develop super-flexible strategies because products rapidly become obsolete, new markets open up quickly, and technological breakthroughs create unexpected opportunities. As we have seen during the recent global recession, even long-established entities, are not immune from changes in the business environment. In the dynamic ecosystem of Silicon Valley, super-flexibility is intuitively valued, even if it cannot be quantified ahead of time.

Successful companies we have observed over the years maintain their momentum and navigate their trajectory by "maneuvering", rather like a school of dolphins, a flock of pigeons, or a herd of antelopes. Maneuvering is about developing a portfolio of initiatives, deploying parallel approaches, not putting all eggs in one basket, and the willingness to shift gears real-time. It encompasses offensive and defensive moves, aimed at the present and the future. Maneuvering is analogous to steering a ship in unchartered waters, where weather conditions and ocean currents can suddenly change with little warning. Effective maneuvering allows an entity to enter novel domains and create new rules of engagement; in essence, it enables them to adapt to new circumstances. A major challenge is overriding active inertia and being willing and ready to make 'sudden left turns". Knowledge enterprises without the capability or the willingness to maneuver are typically unable to overcome inertial forces and can rapidly become 'extinct". This phenomenon is analogous to "phenotype plasticity" in evolutionary biology, as discussed in Chapter 2.

5.1 Conceptual Underpinnings

The term "maneuver" is derived from military strategy and refers to the dynamic configuration and deployment of assets, capabilities and resources, targeted towards the shifting fortunes of war. Historically defined as the means of executing strategy in the midst of an engagement, we use the term to describe how to harness (sometimes instantaneous) kaleidoscopic changes that punctuate a prevailing equilibrium and drive the need to make sudden left turns. We suggest knowledge enterprises need super-flexibility in order to instigate, lubricate, and extend their scope of maneuvers.

Military thinking about flexible maneuvering developed over many centuries and, until the 19th century, largely consisted of the insights of a few pioneering figures. In classical warfare, enemies lined up facing each other and the larger force typically prevailed. The status quo was ruptured by Napoleon who fused together two innovations. In 1760, the French noble-man, Bourcet (1888), implemented a divisional structure in the monolithic, pre-revolutionary French army. This was later augmented by the innovation of drilling troops on a functional, rather than a ceremonial, basis. Instituted by Compte de Guibert, he increased the pace of marching from 70 to 110 paces per minute, preparing the troops for real battle.

With these changes in place, Napoleon (supported by many of his friends as field commanders) was able to put together a military force that relished in the art of maneuver. Even Carl von Clausewitz, the grand father of military strategy, could only marvel at the skill deployed by Napoleon (von Guyczy et al. 2003). Ironically he became bogged down in marshes en route to Waterloo and was unable to join his commander, Blücher, in tipping the balance during the final stages of the battle.[1] Parallels between military and business strategy are succinctly summed up by Clausewitz when he remarked in a letter to Scharnhorst: *"Battle is money and property, strategy is commerce; it is through the former that the latter becomes significant"* (Hahlway 1966, p. 647).

Decades later, during the American Civil War, General Sherman (1875) deployed the art of maneuver with devastating impact. By lessening the load of his troops to a bare minimum, and deploying scouts to act as foragers for food, he was able to move fast and outflank his opponents. With the onset of mechanized warfare, the situation changed yet again.

Fuller, who oversaw the development of the tank, described some of these impacts and extended the idea of maneuver through his dictum of "strike, dislocate and consolidate" (1954). The notion of flexibility was further developed by Liddell-Hart (1929, 1948) as a fundamental principle of warfare. He emphasized the value of the "indirect approach" as the essence of flexibility.

As Foch observed we "should give up talking about maneuvers a priori...it can only be valuable if it leads to fighting under advantageous tactical conditions, if it permits the most favorable utilization of our forces" (1921, p. 42). In the same vein, it is in the execution of maneuvers that super-flexibility is required. Initial efforts to build in flexibility can only be effective when deployed in the heat of the battle. Similarly, in warfare, attempts to develop flexibility for *future* eventualities may or may not work, as warfare is not a static activity.

The objective is to continuously juxtapose several actions and to deploy a combination of assets and capabilities to deal with complex and evolving situations.

---

[1] Marshall Ney, together with his revered Swiss strategist, Jomini, attacked the center of Wellington's forces, misreading Napoleon's order to strike the left flank. Even the grandfathers of strategy, Clausewitz and Jomini, made mistakes.

As Jomini argued: *"the more simple a decisive maneuver, the more certain will be its success."* (Hittle 1947, p.15). Simplicity, as discussed in chapter 2, is a critical cornerstone of super-flexibility. Metamorphic events cannot be predicted or totally planned for.

Recently, management scholars have invoked maneuvers as a conceptual construct to help understand the dynamics of business (Evans 1991, D'Aveni and Gunther 1994, Clemons and Santamaria 2002, von Guyczy, Bassford & von Oetinger 2003). The focus has been on strategic management in hyper-competitive and fast-moving industries, where business leaders have to balance the need to act and respond real-time, in the context of broad strategic guidelines and long-term intentions.

5.2   Revision-Triggers

While engaging in maneuvers, leadership teams must respond to, and inflict, change. As is the case with phenotype plasticity in evolutionary biology, sudden changes in natural ecosystems make it necessary to make adjustments at the level of the individual organism, often without recourse to historical precedent. Change comes in many shapes and guises. Sometimes it follows a stable linear course, other-times it is stochastic or even "kaleidoscopic", where small insignificant changes coagulate into an unpredictable, paradigm-breaking shift. Several categories of stimuli might cause a firm to instigate a maneuver, to modify a maneuver during its execution, to abandon it, or to start over.

As discussed in chapter 1, we term these metamorphic stimuli "revision-triggers". The term is used to describe forces that precipitate a transformation. They encompass monumental events, such as radical innovations, financial crises, geopolitical developments, and wars and revolutions. Consider the magnitude and the impact of the 1979 revolution in Iran, the fall of the Berlin Wall, the tragedy of September 11, and the wars in Afghanistan and Iraq. Micro forces, such as competitive moves, stakeholder expectations, supply disruptions, or leadership disagreements, can also trigger the need to adapt. Serendipitous events, such as windfalls, luck, timing, and even fashion, can also make it necessary to change gears and to make swift turns.

Natural disasters, such as extreme weather, earthquakes, or medical epidemics, also require the deployment of rapid maneuvers. This is clearly illustrated by the SARS crisis during 2003. It seriously impeded the ability of many Silicon Valley companies, with extensive manufacturing facilities in China, to get new products out of engineering and R&D into production. High profile examples of other major disasters include Exxon Valdez, Bhopal, and Chernobyl.

Ground breaking innovations, such as the rise of the Internet or the emergence of social networking, can also result in the creation of new business sectors and redraw competitive dynamics. In knowledge-intensive industries, firms are highly susceptible to "innovation" revision-triggers that are difficult to forecast. Breakthroughs may come from directions least expected (Christensen 1997). As the experience of Silicon Valley has conclusively demonstrated, a nimble start up can overcome the entrenched Goliaths of the industry, and unknown research students, like the Google or the Yahoo founders, may become the next generation of successful entrepreneurs.[2]

Another source of uncertainty is that new innovations often fail to deliver on early promises or take longer to come to fruition. Consider the high expectations surrounding artificial intelligence during the late 1980s, B2B exchanges during the Internet boom years, as well as synthetic fuel and electric vehicles. Technological innovations often force pioneering "first mover" firms to go through "knotholes" before becoming viable. Commercialization is a dynamic and complex process, at least until standards emerge. Examples include PalmPilot, object-oriented software, G3 telecommunications infrastructure, robotic manufacturing, solid-state data-storage, and sputtered media for Winchester disk drives.

As start-ups go public and raise their profiles, they are exposed to additional forces beyond their control, including legal compliance and the need for financial transparency. Changes also occur in the motivational profiles of founding teams and early employees. Founders may be sidelined and a firm may be "professionally" managed as it evolves through its 'adolescence'.

Acquisitions and takeover moves are other types of revision-triggers. Well-publicized examples that clearly changed competitive dynamics in the technology sector include Oracle's acquisition of PeopleSoft, the merger between HP and Compaq, Adobe's acquisition of Macromedia, and Oracle's acquisition of Sun Microsystems. Uncertainties unfold during the acquisition/ merger process, afterwards, during the post-acquisition integration stage, or when the dust settles from an unsuccessful attempt, as was the case with Microsoft's bid to acquire Yahoo. Post-acquisition uncertainties abound, since most of the "knowledge", on which the acquired companies are built, resides in their people. As many large multinationals have found, buying a company without courting the hearts of its key employees, is often a recipe for failure. Disgruntled employees may leave and join, or even form, rival competitors.

An interesting case in point was Xerox during the 1980's. Arguably it had the potential to dominate the disk storage business via acquisitions of Shugart and Century Data, printers via the acquisition of Diablo Systems, and computer communications and interface technologies, through its Palo Alto Research Center (PARC). However, Xerox did not capitalize on this dominant position. As described in

---

[2] Other well-known examples include Jerry Yang and David Filo, the co-founders of Yahoo, Marc Andreessen, the co-founder of Netscape, the founding teams of ROLM and SUN Microsystems, Craig Newmark of Craig's List, and Marc Zuckerberg of Facebook.

Chapter 3, Shugart was disbanded and sold off in the mid-1980s, and PARC technologies later became the foundations of 3Com and Adobe, both founded by former PARC scientists. Eventually, Xerox disengaged from PARC itself.

While a single trigger may be a stimulant for change, adaptation becomes more complex when several revision-triggers coalesce concurrently. Collectively, triggers create a range of uncertainties and transform competitive landscapes on which hot spots can randomly appear and disappear. The conjunction of these triggers often produces pressure points that require "out of the ordinary" or non-standard responses. Super-flexibility can reduce these friction points as a firm maneuvers its dynamic trajectory.

Before describing the various types of maneuvers, induced by revision-triggers, it is essential to specify the object of a maneuver in terms of the "why" and the "when", so that the "how" can make sense. The "when" dimension is about timing, the "why" dimension is about intent. These two dimensions are synthesized into a framework and discussed in the following section.

5.3 Maneuvering: The "Time" Dimension

Business leaders act, according to the reality they face today, and the expectations they may have about tomorrow. These expectations are typically influenced by a firm's historical legacy and its dominant "success recipe". To a limited extent, action can be taken ahead of time; as is the case with R&D initiatives, or a proactive search for suitable acquisitions. In these cases, forecasts, scenarios, predictions, and even hunches, are helpful in figuring out the desired course of action. Oftentimes, action is initiated after the fact, in response to a revision trigger, such as a technical breakthrough, an accident, a customer request, a competitive surprise, or even fashion. The classic "*ex post*" and "*ex ante*" temporal dimensions, used by economists, are helpful distinctions when examining an enterprise's strategic trajectory. However, it is the "ex tempore" dimension, or the "here and now", where super-flexibility is at a premium.

Action is typically initiated at a point of engagement at a specific time. This state of affairs may endure for an instant, a week, a month, a year, or as long as the particular situation, unleashed by a revision trigger, remains in force. In Silicon Valley and other knowledge-intensive ecosystems, an enterprise must maneuver constantly because kaleidoscopic changes, induced by revision-triggers, can rupture short-lived periods of stability. These novel situations provide the stimulus for shifting gears and engaging in maneuvers.

It is difficult to know ahead of time what must be done in the new circumstances. All eventualities cannot be imagined before situations unfold; and real preferences, cannot be anticipated until outcomes have been experienced (March 1981). Indeed, even when predicted, as was the case with the Financial Crisis of 2008, leaders fail to act until we hit the eye of the hurricane. Novelty and spontaneity are not amenable to thoughtful planning.

Actions initiated ahead of time, are typically taken in anticipation of certain events, or in order to change the rules of the game. Firms try to predict the future in different ways. Even new start-ups must project 3-year financial statements and prepare business plans to get funded. Larger enterprises must forecast sales volumes to ensure that manufacturing capacity, inventory and cash are all balanced. Some companies engage in elaborate scenario planning (Schwartz 1991) to develop long-term strategies.

Although forecasting techniques have become much more sophisticated, the problem is that we are continually surprised at how the future unfolds. Things that were previously unthinkable or unimaginable, do occur. These events seem obvious with hindsight, but are shielded from view ahead of time. There are many reasons for these disconnects. Clearly, when moving in unchartered territories, surprises inevitably occur. When expectations are not met, or when events occur that have not been predicted, a firm may need flexibility after the fact. In these cases, attempts are made to correct a mistake or to capitalize on an unexpected opportunity.

Entrepreneurs often rely on intuition or hunches, triggered by their front-line experiences. Economists use expectations of the future as a pivotal dimension of their discipline. Sometimes, things can be planned well ahead of time, before a revision trigger unfolds, as was the case with the introduction of the Euro in 2001.

However, when engaging in high-risk activities, serendipity, luck and freak occurrences also play a role. For example, innovations often go through several "knot-holes" before crystallizing into workable products. Google's search engine started life in "data mining". Yahoo's portal was initially a tracking device for the founders' favorite TV programs. The dilemma is what to do when situations deviate from prior expectations.

While pioneers can inflict revision-triggers and change the rules of the game, many entities are typically forced to adapt. In these cases, they can either act ahead of time, by forecasting and anticipating, or they can respond after the fact. Sometimes it is better to wait and see how situations turn out before engaging in action. Other times it is best to act quickly to capitalize on an unexpected opportunity, or to move out of the way of potentially harmful threats. So the "time" optic is the first dimension of our framework.

5.4 Maneuvering: The "Intent" Dimension

Maneuvering depends on what has to be achieved and why it needs to be done. In sports, competing teams know the rules and there is typically some official, a referee, to ensure compliance with the rules, However, the objective, for example in soccer, is not simply to score goals, but to prevent the other team from scoring goals. Team formations and team tactics are different for offensive and defensive play. However, they must work together in tandem; the real art is to shift gears from offense to the defense at the right time. The sporting analogy may be somewhat simplistic. The rules are clear, the objectives are well defined, and the parameters are stable. Yet there are clear parallels with business.

Similarly, in the military arena, there are several parallels to business that have long been noted. While the complexity and the stakes of warfare are very different, the parallels with business are strong in that a business is an organized grouping of people, capital, technology and knowledge brought together to satisfy user needs, locally and globally. Warfare is about finding and damaging the enemy so that the will to resist is lost. So while the ends differ, the means of achieving them may have some elements in common. A military force must find an advantageous position and successfully engage the enemy. The opponent attempts the same. Sometimes an enemy may be stronger and may force its opponent onto the defensive. Irrespective of the situation, the means of attack and defense are to deploy assets and capabilities to achieve a given objective; in other words by "maneuvering".[3]

It is in playing the game against opponents or competitors that the concept of "intent" enters our framework. Drawing on the sporting and the military analogies, a firm can either go on the offense, for example by attacking a new market segment, or it can go on the defense, by regrouping to withstand an economic downturn. Sometimes an attack may involve a "feint" where the intent is to divert competitors' attention and resources, making the real target easier to attack. Even when all this is done successfully, victory is only achieved when the dislocation produced by the attack is hammered home, just as a crop must be harvested in order to produce profits.

In a similar vein, knowledge enterprises engage in high-risk activities and often fail to realize their intent. This may prompt them to go on the "defensive". A firm may inoculate or immunize itself against risk or potential failure, for example

---

[3] Becoming flexible by means of maneuvers was an essential cornerstone of Napoleon's approach to warfare. This is somewhat reflected in the following anecdote recollected by Gohier commenting on the meeting of Generals Bonaparte and Moreau: Bonaparte told Moreau how anxious he had been to make his acquaintance. "You have just come from Egypt as a conqueror", answered Moreau, "and I am just home from Italy after a great defeat..." he concluded: "It was impossible to prevent our army from being over-whelmed by so many combined forces. Big numbers always beat small ones." "You are right", said Bonaparte, "big numbers always beat small ones." "Still General", said I to Bonaparte, "you have often beaten big armies with smaller ones." "Even in that case", he said," the small numbers were always beaten by big ones." This led him to explain his tactics: "When with inferior forces, I was met by a large army", he said, "having quickly regrouped my own, I fell like lightening on one of the wings, which I routed. I then availed myself of the disorder this manoeuvre never failed to produce within an enemy army, so as to attack it in another part, and again with all my forces. I thus beat the enemy piecemeal; and the ensuing victory was invariably, as you can see, a triumph of the larger over the smaller." The art consisted in securing the numbers, in having the numbers on the selected point of attack; the means of doing this was: an economy of forces. Such mechanics ultimately led to the utilization to the utmost disorder this manoeuvre produces within the enemy army, as well as the moral superiority created by the same manoeuvre within one's own army." That was Napoleon's War (Foch 1921, pp 95-96).

by hedging or by buying insurance. At other times, it may regroup after a failed initiative, and refocus its efforts on achievable goals. When faced with a threat, it may seek cover, attempt to buffer itself, or absorb the shock in some other way.

Unlike sports, however, in business, the balance of play between offense and defense is not binary. Even a "simple" start-up has to fight many battles simultaneously to win. Some of these moves involve attack; others entail defense, but they have to be undertaken at the same time. The degree to which a firm's leadership team is aligned determines how effectively it can shift gears and redeploy its resources. This is dynamic strategy in action.

It is this constant morphing of the center of gravity of the strategic problem, generated by revision-triggers, that highlights the importance of maneuvering and changing gears. Moreover, business ecosystems are like shifting sands, continuously evolving in unexpected ways. What is appropriate one day, may be wrong the next, even in identical circumstances. An army on the move faces unpredictable consequences when engaged in battle. Similarly in the world of high tech businesses, strategic initiatives rarely work out exactly as planned. So the "intent" dimension, and the need to engage in offensive and defensive moves, is the second dimension of our framework.

5.5 Maneuvering to Achieve Super-Flexibility: A Conceptual Framework

In order to develop super-flexible strategies, it makes little sense to focus exclusively on optimal, planned moves "*a priori*". Nor is it sufficient to rely exclusively on "*ex post facto*" actions initiated after the fact. There is a need to engage in offensive and defensive moves, before and after revision-triggers, sometimes simultaneously. Aggregating the "time" and the "intent" dimensions into a conceptual framework helps us identify four categories of maneuvers for achieving super-flexibility.

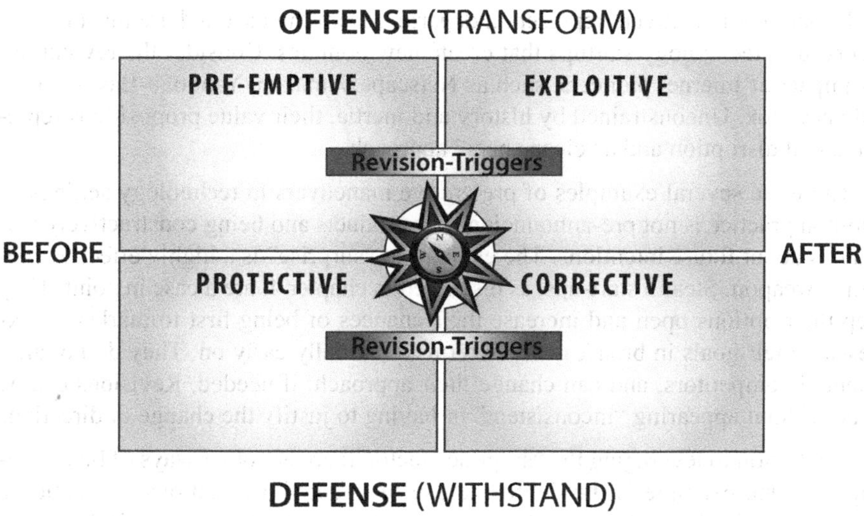

OFFENSE (TRANSFORM)

PRE-EMPTIVE	**EXPLOITIVE**
PROTECTIVE	**CORRECTIVE**

BEFORE ← → AFTER

Revision-Triggers (top and bottom)

DEFENSE (WITHSTAND)

Figure 11. Super-flexible strategies: The maneuvering framework

As depicted in Figure 11, the four types of maneuvers are categorized as "pre-emtive", "protective", "corrective", and "exploitive". For the sake of clarification, each type of maneuver is described individually, although their effectiveness depends on their collective deployment. The challenge is to select and to execute the right combination of maneuvers at a given point in time, and to re-assess their relevance on a continuous basis. The maneuvering framework should be viewed as a diagnostic tool that can be used by business leaders to categorize their strategic initiatives, to identify major gaps, and to assess when to shift gears.

5.5.1 Pre-emptive Maneuvers

Pre-emtive maneuvers are mainly deployed in order to transform the status quo, to innovate, and to seize the initiative. The intention may be to surprise competitors, or to create new rules of engagement. In a technology setting, this form of maneuver typically involves what Heidegger (1977) termed "enframing". The goal is to "bring forth" something new, such as a radical innovation, or a novel distribution channel, altering the rules of the game or the nature of a domain.

Apple's transformation in recent years is a classic example of "pre-emptive" maneuvers. Under Jobs' leadership, the company was re-invented from a "desktop" computer company to a digital consumer electronics entity. It pioneered a new retailing concept with the opening of Apple Stores and the use of "Genius Bars". It introduced the iPod, the iPhone, and iTunes. Through its "disruptive" approach, it created new market segments and developed new rules of engagement.

Pre-emtive maneuvers represent a departure from the past and are most readily observed in technology startups that create new domains. Consider the revolutionary impact of Internet pioneers, such as Netscape, Amazon, Yahoo, e-Bay, Google, and Facebook. Unconstrained by history and inertia, their value propositions represent a real disruption and a "clean sheet" approach.

There are several examples of pre-emtive maneuvers in technology settings. A common practice is not pre-announcing new products and being constructively ambiguous about future intentions. The element of "surprise" is a highly effective pre-emtive weapon. Stealth start-ups, as discussed in chapter 4, are a case in point. They keep their options open and increase their chances of being first to market by expressing their goals in broad, general, terms, especially early on. They do not alert potential competitors, and can change their approach, if needed. Revisions can be made without appearing "inconsistent" or having to justify the change of direction.

In addition to leveraging the "surprise" factor, there are other ways of being pre-emptive. One example is the deliberate use of targeted acquisitions to position a company as a leading-edge provider of new products and services. This is illustrated by Cisco's growth-by-acquisition strategy. It acquired more than 80 companies between 1997-2003, including 23 in 2000. The businesses were, in the main, acquired to provide early access to emerging technologies. They also gave Cisco the opportunity to recruit a number of technology pioneers.[4]

The company used different acquisition formats, including pooling of assets, "spin-ins", subsidiary purchases, asset purchases, and "recruitment" acquisitions. As of March 2003, 1 in 6 Cisco employees were from acquired companies. Most of the deals were closed in 45-60 days, and the IT systems of the acquired firms connected to Cisco's within 2 weeks of purchase.

Cisco's original lead venture capitalist remained on the Board and was a member of its acquisition committee. This enabled Cisco to use its targeted acquisition strategy as a pre-emptive maneuver. It had the opportunity to proactively select and target acquisition candidates that best fitted its product and service portfolio. The acquisition strategy was augmented by a rigorous due diligence process, as well as a well-defined post-acquisition integration strategy. Both pre and post acquisition processes focused on identification and assimilation of key talent, targeted communication to the acquired company employees, and reliance on a dedicated core team of cross-functional experts to guide and monitor the integration process.

The speed of this pre-emptive maneuver, both in closing the deals and, more strategically, in integrating selected parts of acquired firms, contributed to Cisco's

---

[4] For example, Howard Charney became Cisco's EVP of Strategy, after Cisco acquired Grand Junction during the 1990s. Similarly, Judy Estrin became Cisco's Chief Technology Officer in 1995, after Cisco acquired Precept.

leading position in its industry, at a time when its technological leadership was being challenged by other competitors, such as Juniper Networks. By ensuring the continued flow of new technology through its pre-emptive acquisition strategy of series two and series three venture-funded companies, Cisco was able to scale itself, without relying exclusively on internally generated products.

At a more tactical level, pre-emptive maneuvers can also be embedded into products or processes. For example, it is standard practice in the disk drive industry to design a product so that it can be upgraded at a future date to take account of new user needs and advances in technology. In these cases, it is important to anticipate variations that can be later derived from the early models. This approach can leverage the initial design activity over a longer product life cycle, and is especially helpful if the product becomes an industry standard. Moreover, "upgradeability" is also a desired attribute in the acquisition of computer systems, particularly by first-time users (Evans 1982). This theme is further underscored by the "mantra" of agility in IT systems.

Finally, as illustrated in the following example, pre-emptive maneuvers often require the swift execution of a number of actions at the right time. Consider pre-emptive maneuvers of Shugart Corporation in developing the standard setting $5^1/_4$ inch mini-floppy disk drive. In 1976, 8 inch floppy disk drives were the *de jure* industry standard. However, by this time a group of lead users, including manufacturers of word processors and hobby computers, were unhappy with the available options for storage devices.

The product idea was initially conceived during a meeting between a Shugart sales executive and a European customer. Voicing their dissatisfaction with the only available alternative to the 8-inch floppy disk drive used in word processing systems, a cassette tape drive, the customer expressed the need for a smaller removable storage device that could be used for the next generation of desk-top products under development. Shugart's sales executive, having heard similar concerns from other customers, picked up a cocktail napkin and asked if that was about the preferred size of the media. Having received a positive response, he made up a cardboard mock-up and sent it back to the headquarters.

The idea was initially dismissed because the dominant player at the time, IBM, had historically set the industry standard "form factor" for new disk drives. However, when another large customer expressed dissatisfaction with the available alternatives, Shugart spotted a major opportunity. It departed from tradition and acted swiftly to develop a new product. The president developed product specifications on his way back from a customer visit, and assembled the development team the following morning, a Saturday, to work out detailed design criteria and to draw the blueprints. In a pre-emptive move, intended to erect entry barriers, the team set an unusually aggressive manufacturing cost target of $100 for the new product.

This was the first time in the evolution of an OEM (Original Equipment Manufacturer) disk drive that cost had played a critical role in the development process.

Moreover, in a significant departure from standard industry practice, a young engineer tried to meet the aggressive cost targets by using off-the-shelf components. For example, a motor was used from a vending machine and other parts were taken from a cassette drive, with the result that the material cost came to within $5 of the target cost. This move also reduced the development cycle time. The first prototypes were ready in less than six months.

While the product was under development, the company deployed yet another pre-emptive maneuver. A general practice amongst disk drive manufacturers in the OEM business was to communicate new product specifications early in the design cycle. The intention was to ensure compatibility with customers' products. In signing up large OEM orders, Shugart was expected to show its proposed drive (and its new media) to prospective customers. In the process, it would have to divulge valuable intelligence to competitors who would be in a position to copy the new product design. In this case the critical piece of information concerned the size of the diskette. From this information the size or the "form factor" for the new product could be deduced, and a valuable time advantage would be lost.

The problem was resolved by Shugart's decision to send out 5 or 6 different sizes of media to potential customers, all within reasonable proximity to the $5^1/_4$ inch form factor under development. This "constructive ambiguity" gave the firm additional development lead-time. In this case, volume production started within 18 months and enabled Shugart to capture 70% of this market segment. The product became the first non-IBM industry standard OEM peripheral, and some 14 million units were produced worldwide in 1987.

In this case, three complementary, pre-emptive maneuvers were deployed; first, in developing a standard-setting product, initiated as a pre-emptive response to a lead customer's request; second, in using off-the-shelf components to build the product, reducing its manufacturing cost and positioning the company for long-term cost advantage; third, in confusing its competitors about the size of the media diskette and gaining a time advantage with a standard-setting product. Moreover, the speed of action in executing all three maneuvers proved to be critical.

Pre-emptive maneuvers have the potential to be the most "equilibrium shattering" weapon at a firm's disposal, but they can also be highly risky due to the multitude of uncertainties. Keeping intentions ambiguous can result in surprising competitors, but it can also limit market feedback. In addition, pre-emptive maneuvers can inspire knowledge workers to perceive change as a major opportunity. As the co-founder and former CEO of a disk drive firm, observed: *"(In this business) you always have to be pre-emptive and selectively use other maneuvers as needed."*[5]

---

[5] Personal communication with the co-founder of a disk drive company.

5.5.2 Protective Maneuvers

While seeking disruptive advantage through pre-emptive maneuvers, a knowledge enterprise must also guard itself against potentially damaging consequences that it may face when entering new domains. In these circumstances, it is prudent to get some form of insurance, and adopt a hedging strategy; or drawing on a military analogy, to maintain a protected line of retreat.

In a defensive sense, protective maneuvers seek to deflect, absorb, cushion or immunize against the impact of harmful forces. The focus is on defensive moves, deployed ahead of a probable revision-trigger. The old adage of "not having all eggs in one basket" encapsulates the sentiment of this type of maneuver. The objective is to guard against damaging outcomes that may occur when engaging in high-risk actions.

Consider the case of an innovative semi-conductor packaging firm. Its founder, an entrepreneurial scientist, had developed a technology that involved implanting spring loaded test probes to improve the testing of new "Wafer-on-Wafer" integrated circuits. Having raised several rounds of venture funding, its business portfolio was a combination of older "test probes" as well as its path breaking newer products.

As the recession in the technology sector began to bite in 2001, its executive team realized that orders for the new products were lower than expected. Investment bankers had also prepared the ground for an Initial Public Offering in 2002. The recession intensified, especially in the semi-conductor manufacturing sector, historically a leading indicator of change in Silicon Valley. Faced with the reality of limited revenues for an innovative product, the executive team put the new product on hold, and reverted back to the older "cash cow" business.

After a couple of downsizing rounds, the economy did not improve and the move to stem the flow of cash proved justified. The company also started to see growing demand from its customers for its latest technology. At the time, the semiconductor industry was in a cyclical downturn but OEM customers were ordering the latest technology to push the capabilities of their products, including mobile phones and personal computers. Seeing the "skies clearing", it began to ramp up the production of its new product to address growing customer demand. As sales numbers continued to improve, the impact on the bottom line was better than expected, since it had earlier reduced its cost base. This enabled it to remain viable during very challenging times.

Although the situation on Wall Street remained unfavorable, investment bankers had already prepared the way for an IPO. This action reduced the lead-time for promoting the offering to prospective institutional investors. The combined impacts of reduced cost base, positive cash flow, new technology, and a strong order book made it possible to execute the offering during a limited "break in the clouds" on Wall Street in 2003. In addition, key shareholders signed a pledge not to sell the stock for 6 months in order to minimize wide oscillations in share price that typically accompany a public offering.

Common examples of protective maneuvers include reliance on patents and IP (Intellectual property) protection, use of various types of insurance policies, and licensing proprietary designs. Many high tech companies also rely on multiple vendors for critical supplies, and place back-up systems in different locations, in case of earthquakes, natural disasters and other events that may disrupt operations.

Protective maneuvers can also apply to people, policies and organizational infrastructures. For example, a number of larger technology companies in Silicon Valley have adopted innovative approaches to "down-sizing". Many try to reduce cost by lowering headcount, while retaining highly specialized technical talent. Instead of adopting the usual layoff policies, a number of firms offer key employees the option of taking up to a year's leave of absence to do community service or work for non-profit organizations, while retaining health and pension benefits and rights to stock options. In some cases they are paid a percentage of their salary. A review is undertaken after some time, and the target population may be offered full-time employment or allowed to pursue other options. This protective maneuver allows technology firms to downsize without losing key technical talent. It also positions them to ramp up quickly when market conditions improve.

However, as is the case with other types of maneuver, protective moves often require the deployment of several actions. These include anticipating and planning for the worst case, reinforcing vulnerable parts of the business, and keeping critical items, especially financial resources, in reserve. Consider the case of a pioneering technology company in the storage business. During a period of rapid growth, early signals of a market transformation prompted its leaders to embark on a series of protective maneuvers. Sources of potential concern included rumors about the second sourcing practices of a major customer, and a significant build-up of capacity by offshore manufacturers. In a surprise move, the company reduced its domestic employees from 2200 to 900 within a few weeks, and relocated all its manufacturing operations to Asia, where it would benefit from an abundant supply of skilled workers, as well as lower component and labor costs.

A few months later, the storage industry entered a period of severe recession. Less than 10 of the 50 venture-backed start-ups managed to survive, and disk drive operations of several large corporations were discontinued. Despite major industry problems, the company in question was able to avoid a major catastrophe. The protective maneuver had two benefits. First, it built up its customer base among the emerging PC makers, based in Asia. Second, it consolidated its US customer base, largely because of its low cost position. These actions helped the company re-emerge later as a major force in the industry, with a commanding market position.

5.5.3 Corrective Maneuvers

In dynamic, fast-moving ecosystems, potentially damaging events occur for a variety of reasons. These include accidents, mistakes, or competitive challenges. In these situations, defensive actions, in the form of corrective maneuvers, have to be taken *after* the fact. These moves are typically invoked when something goes wrong, when an initiative leads to an undesirable outcome, or when external events generate unfavorable consequences. Corrective maneuvers are about damage control, intended to minimize the negative impact of undesirable situations. Maneuvering, in this corrective sense, refers to the regenerative and recuperative practices needed to recover from traumas, accidents, mistakes and unworkable initiatives.

Several guidelines should be considered when embarking on corrective maneuvers.
- Instead of pointing fingers and assigning blame, as is typically the case when something goes wrong, attention should be focused on acknowledging the problem, and facing the facts as they are, rather than "as we wish them to be".
- Second, it is important to act quickly and apply the brakes early on, using bite-sized measures and focused initiatives, that can restore confidence and credibility.
- Third, time and attention should be focused on generating workable solutions. As is the case in first aid, if a patient is bleeding, a tourniquet must be applied, or, if a bone is broken, a splint can bring immediate stabilization.

Consider, how Steve Jobs turned Apple around after re-assuming its leadership during the late 1990's. At the time, many experts had written the company off and did not view it as viable. Instead of embarking on a new "grand strategy", Jobs concentrated on bite-sized, and rapid, rollout of new products, every 90 days. He focused on what could be tangibly done to fix its problems, areas that were within the company's direct control. They re-packaged and re-branded their products, targeted new users, and opened their own retail stores to provide expert advice in the form of "Genius Bars".

Another example of a corrective maneuver is how Intel fixed a bug in its "Pentium processor" after its initial introduction during the mid-1990s. Although the company initially dismissed the problem as "minor", many early adopters, including Wall Street banks, raised concerns about the new processor. Intel quickly changed its posture, admitted that there was at least a perceived problem, recalled the shipped units so they could be replaced, and apologized for the inconvenience. This rapid corrective maneuver created a favorable image among the user community. They admired the firm for its honesty and integrity, and for demonstrating its commitment to end-users.

Re-integration of Palm and Handspring, two leading providers of hand held computers/organizers, is yet another example of a corrective maneuver. Palm was initially acquired by US Robotics, which itself was later acquired by 3Com, Palm was spun out of 3Com before the company was floated as an independent entity. Meanwhile, the co-founders of the original PalmPilot, had left 3Com/PALM to co-found a new company, called Handspring. They focused the new company on producing a Pilot like device, called the "Visor", and migrated the product into the cell phone business by integrating the "organizer" and the "scheduler" components of the Palm Operating System and software into a larger than normal mobile phone. Faced with approximately a 40% drop in demand for both firms' products, and dwindling share prices, the two firms finally merged in 2003. The cell phone business was later revamped and re-branded and the new entity became a stronger competitor.

Corrective maneuvers were also used by some of the leading venture capital firms during the Valley's "post dot com bubble" downturn. A case in point is the initiative taken by the firm of Mohr, Davidow Ventures (MDV). They first trimmed their $850 million fund back to $650 million in 2002, returning the cash to their limited partners. In early 2003 the fund was paired down, yet again, to $450 million. In addition, the firm closed its offices in Reston (Virginia) and Seattle, and reduced the number of its general partners. The rationale was simple. According to its Managing Partner, the ideal size fund for an early stage investor is between $350-$500 million. Given the reduced levels of investment in the post dot com era, and the number of deals in which a partner could comfortably invest, the firm wanted to reduce expectations of its limited partners and free up its general partners so they could focus on fewer ventures.[6]

A classic example of a corrective maneuver is the case of a disk drive controller company that made a U-turn in its strategy in order to stay in business. When it was founded in 1981, the company had targeted multi-user computer manufacturers, mainly those using the Unix operating system, as its customer base. The founders had pioneered an advanced in-put/output controller technology, termed SCSI or small computer standard interface. However, the target market did not materialize as initially projected because of the rapid diffusion of personal computers.

The industry standard IBM-PC diffused surprisingly fast. However, it used a controller that was a variant of an earlier interface, developed for single-user systems. In order to compete in the PC market, the company faced a clear choice: to emulate the new standard controller product for the PC, or to downsize its powerful controller for the single-user desktop environment. Its executives opted for the second option, and were able to capitalize on short-term opportunities generated by rapid growth in PCs, and PC-compatible systems.

---

[6] Source: The Venture Capital Analyst: Technology Edition, February 2003 Vol. VI (2), Venture One.

The decision to adapt the technology for use in IBM-compatible personal computers was more complex than expected. Since many of its customers were "cloning" IBM's systems, each had developed unique methods to ensure MS-DOS software compatibility. The controller company had to design and develop "semi-custom" controllers to meet these compatibility requirements.

When in 1984 a dramatic shakeout occurred in the personal computer industry, the firm lost over 70% of its customer base in just a few weeks. There was little forewarning of the impending crisis. The problem was made worse because during the initial growth phase, its customers had placed substantial orders, in excess of their requirements, in order to guarantee the timely flow of parts. Needless to say, the impact of the crisis was traumatic and almost terminal. Faced with this difficult situation, another corrective maneuver was deployed.

The company quickly converted its unsaleable customized inventory of finished goods to "liquid" industry standard products, and offered these goods at substantial discounts. This move kept the firm afloat and gave it time to regroup. It was able to follow this strategy, in part, because it had already built up good will and credibility amongst its own vendors, granting them favorable credit terms. The value of this good will was immeasurable during the adjustment period. It sustained the flow of critical components needed to convert the customized inventory into standard products. The point to note is that action taken ahead of time, even in the absence of a specific goal, can create options that can be used at a later stage. The corrective maneuver was effectively executed by rapidly re-working products, and selling them at considerable discounts, a move that surprised its competitors. The founder/CEO even took personal responsibility for sales and used every opportunity, including user group meetings, to sell the "converted" products.

This example has the hallmark of a super-flexible response, in that it needs several actions for effective execution. It also shows that speed of action, and the willingness to back down from the original intent, are sometimes critical for taking corrective action.

5.5.4 Exploitive Maneuvers

Technology firms often find themselves in situations where circumstances or preferences may not unfold as expected. A stroke of luck or being at the right place at the right time, are unpredictable events that have to be capitalized on. Super-flexibility, in this opportunistic sense, is achieved by means of exploitive maneuvers. This type of maneuver is critical, for example, when a new product unexpectedly becomes an industry standard, resulting in rapid expansion of market demand.

Exploitive maneuvers are about focusing resources to rapidly capitalize on emerging opportunities "here and now". They require rapid decision-making and swift concentration and deployment of resources. They are as much a function of executive will as well as availability of liquid resources. Consider how Microsoft made a dramatic shift in its Internet strategy in the aftermath of the success of Netscape and its Navigator browser in 1995. Within a matter of weeks, Microsoft had transformed its Internet focus, from a handful of people to several hundred. Speed of action is critical since exploitive maneuvers are about harvesting opportunities, or avoiding threats, that may suddenly emerge. In military strategy, victory is achieved when a dislocation is consolidated. Many firms fail to achieve this "final victory" because although the right ingredients have been put in place, that final consolidation is ignored.

Consider the controller company discussed earlier. It learned a valuable lesson from its initial experiences. It gradually diversified its customer base to include manufacturers of disk drives, engineering workstations and super-microcomputers. The industry standard eventually migrated upward to the SCSI (small computer standard interface) product that it had pioneered. Although the earlier corrective maneuvers kept the company afloat, they also positioned it for success at a later stage.

By this time, a number of its competitors had integrated forward into the disk drive sector, propelled by the trend toward "embedding" the controller directly onto disk drives. During the course of this industry evolution, the company had devised a computer-aided design system for developing SCSI controllers. These were intended for its own internal use. The objective was to reduce its product development lead-time, and to improve customer service by providing sophisticated test procedures.

As the end-user market became more memory-intensive (due to the diffusion of local area networks, desk top publishing, and computer-aided design) the new standard became dominant. By this time, disk drive manufacturers also started to embed controllers in their products. Their goal was to optimize the higher capacity drives, and to reduce costs. Additionally, embedding a controller directly onto the drive electronics, removed the need for a slot to house a controller printed circuit board inside a desktop device.

This industry trend provided the company with a fleeting opportunity. It packaged the design tools for sale to drive, peripherals and system manufacturers as a complete SCSI computer-aided design system (CAD). The CAD system allowed drive engineers to debug and test a SCSI product. It also enabled a test or a quality engineer to generate complex and repeatable tests and documentation for quality control of SCSI peripherals.

Revenues from the sale of these systems were not significant in themselves. However, this move positioned the company for the long haul by tying its customers to its in-house design and prototyping processes. The move was only possible because of the earlier corrective maneuvers; first, in deciding to downgrade its SCSI controller for the PC environment, second, in diversifying its customer base.

In summary, leadership teams need to engage in exploitive maneuvers by *detecting* and *recognizing* opportunity and threat signals, and by mobilizing executive will and liquid resources. In a similar vein, it is also crucial to exit a "honey pot" before it becomes exhausted, so as not to get stuck with obsolete resources and the remnants of a depleted opportunity. This is a hard lesson learned by many investors during the Internet boom years. Instead of leaving the market before it reached its saturation point, they re-invested their gains in the hope of making even more. The outcome, with hindsight, was easy to predict; it is especially critical to remember this lesson when embarking on exploitive maneuvers.

5.6 Maneuvering and Super-Flexibility

This chapter presented a conceptual framework to help executive teams develop and monitor a dynamic portfolio of strategic initiatives. The objective is to become super-flexible by deploying different types of maneuvers, often in parallel, and to shift gears real-time. Maneuvers are about aligning the intentions, the capabilities and the opportunities facing a knowledge enterprise. The four types of maneuver presented in this chapter provide a framework for developing, aggregating, and monitoring strategic initiatives in dynamic settings.

The capabilities needed to execute each type of maneuver are demonstrably different. Having the liquidity to exploit an unexpected opportunity, for example, by buying a company, is qualitatively different from possessing a resilient disposition to deal with the "hurt" of an accident. Similarly, reliance on insurance, legal protection, buffers or slack, to protect against potentially damaging situations, is different from being agile or versatile when embarking on a pre-emptive maneuver. Clearly, these are related, yet the practicalities of how to act in each situation differ considerably.

Furthermore, in an ever-changing world, the maneuvers framework can be used not only to allocate resources and to prioritize strategic moves, but to assign executive talent to different types of initiatives. Just as soccer teams have different capabilities in defenders versus strikers, businesses also have talent pools that may be better suited to one form of maneuvering, rather than another. It takes a very different person to be a good scanner, quickly recognizing nascent opportunities, compared to a skeptic, who may be ideal in anticipating worst case scenarios and preparing for protective maneuvers. Similarly, a turnaround expert, who is good at instilling a sense of urgency and focusing on corrective maneuvers, is quite different from a creative visionary who thinks about innovative solutions and pre-emptive initiatives.

A related challenge is to balance the needs of today's cash-generating business, while seeding and staffing tomorrow's growth opportunities. Many companies deploy their most seasoned executives for running today's business, while paying lip service to tomorrow. Moreover, corporate venturing initiatives have had a poor track record. With the exception of a few publicized cases, skunkworks, incubators, and internal venture groups have been ineffective in established companies. According to a recent study, major reasons for this failure include: Lack of top management sponsorship and visibility; resentment by the cash-producing parts of the business; and feelings of loneliness, isolation from peer groups, and perceptions of second class citizenship (Campbell et al. 2003).

In order to create a more effective balance between today and tomorrow, attention should be focused on the allocation of roles and staffing profiles for new ventures. If we use the maneuvers framework for talent deployment, it becomes clear that some executives have capabilities that are better suited for today rather than tomorrow. In order to stimulate the development of new initiatives for tomorrow, business leaders can learn from the role played by the established venture community in Silicon Valley. As discussed in chapter 3, venture capitalists have played a pivotal role in hatching and scaling new ventures.

One option may be to select a cadre of seasoned executives to mentor internal venture teams, to act as cross-pollinators, and to provide an objective sounding board for rapid recalibration. In the past, this task had generally been assigned to the up and coming "high potentials" in business development. The underlying logic is that they bring a fresh perspective, and the energy needed to drive new initiatives.

Our observations indicate that venture management needs a blend of seasoned judgment and youthful energy. Nurturing new ventures may be a valuable role for senior executives who are close to retirement, and an avenue for talented knowledge workers who may not fit into current operations. Both groups may be willing to experiment with the unconventional and, as such, are more likely to innovate. Venture executives can address the future, freeing up general managers to focus on today.

In deploying the maneuvering framework, executive teams also have to consider the right combination of actions, and to change gears real-time. We expect tomorrow to be different from today, although it is rare for executive teams to change course midstream, even when they know that they should. This is partly due to the emotional commitment and the investment momentum that may have already been under way. As Bourcet (1888) observed, strategy should be like the branches of a tree, each one leading to the desired outcome.

In today's turbulent world, the center of gravity of strategic problems shift continuously. What might be right one day, may not make sense on another. A dynamic combination of different maneuvers is needed to achieve the appropriate type of flexibility in different contexts. This chapter outlined various forms that these maneuvers might take, although these categories are by no means exhaustive. As illustrated by the examples, the critical point is that *maneuvering for super-flexibility requires combining different capabilities, deploying several actions, and the willingness to change gears and to make swift turns real-time.*

In contrast to approaches that assume a situation has no antecedents, we recognize the influence of prior actions. These constrain the freedom to maneuver, and partly explain why the time dimension is important. While developing the capacity for a super-flexible response is ideally undertaken ahead of time, its actual value is largely realized when maneuvers are executed "in the present", at a point of engagement. As discussed in chapter 2, being super-flexible is as much about being spontaneous, as it is about developing the capability to address contingencies ahead of time. Spontaneity requires revising previous positions, as well as developing new ones "on the spot".

The term "potential surprise" (Shackle 1953) encompasses events that cause future states of the world, as well as stakeholders' values and preferences, to deviate from prior expectations. This problem has been partly addressed by adopting a multi-scenario approach. Clearly, this approach minimizes some of the pitfalls associated with uni-dimensional forecasts. However, since only one future state actually comes into being, it may be expensive to prepare for every imaginable contingency and probably impossible to prepare for the unimaginable. It is, however, precisely because of this paradox that super-flexibility has intuitive value.

In this chapter, we suggest that maneuvering can help business leaders navigate their dynamic trajectory. Like driving a car, maneuvering encompasses different actions, and requires the ability to shift gears real-time. The framework, presented in this chapter, proposes four operational maneuvers as a means of becoming super-flexible.

Super-flexibility is at a premium when the rules of a game are perpetually being redefined, or when the nature of a game itself changes. Experience has shown that it is critical for high technology firms to develop this capability. While the need for super-flexible maneuvers, deployed individually or collectively, is almost self-evident in high technology arenas, its value in other contexts should not be underestimated.

6 Super-Flexible Execution:
Experimenting, Iterating and Recalibrating

How can knowledge workers execute new initiatives when they have limited information, little time, and minimal resources? How can they decide between competing options when there are no clear recipes and blueprints for success? How can they change direction and revise expectations? How can they be systematic and consistent, when uncertainty is an everyday fact of life? We explore these questions to better understand how knowledge workers embark on, and execute pioneering initiatives in dynamic settings.

This chapter is about developing the capability for super-flexible execution. We define super-flexible execution as the capacity to make real-time adjustments as new realities unfold. At an operational level, we present the "recalibration" framework in order to explain how effective teams we have observed engage in action when they face moving targets. Recalibration is about exploring by probing and experimenting, generating fact-based feedback, and making the necessary revisions. Analogous to the scientific model of discovery, we describe the interlinked stages of experimentation, escalation, and integration, as a phased approach to dynamic execution. We conclude the chapter by putting forward a few practical guidelines for implementing the recalibration framework.

6.1 Conceptual Underpinnings

There is an extensive body of research on decision-making and execution. For our purposes, the dominant themes can be clustered into two broad categories: those that emphasize the deliberate, the intentional, and the top-down processes that guide action; and those that highlight the emergent, the spontaneous, and the bottom-up initiatives that coalesce over time.[1]

According to the "deliberate" models, strategies are formulated, on the basis of clear intentions, conscious choices, and careful planning. As depicted in Figure 12, first, objectives are spelled out and preferences clarified. Next, relevant information is collected and analyzed; alternatives are generated and their pros and cons are assessed. Finally, the optimal solution is selected, and the chosen option is implemented. The implicit assumption is that implementation follows planning, and that collecting and analyzing relevant information early on can reduce uncertainties.

---

[1] This chapter draws on several classic streams of research. These include descriptive models of the innovation process (Utterback 1971; Burgelman 1983); features of successful innovations (Rothwell et al. 1974; Maidique and Zirger 1984); factors that impede effective commercialization of innovations (Teece 1987); sources of new innovations (von Hippel, 1986); characteristics of innovative organizations (Kanter 1983, Quinn 1979); organizational arrangements for nurturing innovation (Burgelman and Sayles 1986, Roberts 1980, Romanelli 1987); and profiles of high technology enterprises (Cooper and Bruno, 1977, Maidique and Hayes 1984; Meyer and Roberts 1986). Recent studies of innovation that have influenced our thinking include Christensen (1997) Chesbrough (2003) Christensen & Raynor (2003), Estrin (2009), Kelley (2005).

H. Bahrami, S. Evans, *Super-Flexibility for Knowledge Enterprises*, 2nd ed.,
DOI 10.1007/978-3-642-02447-4_6, © Springer-Verlag Berlin Heidelberg 2010

Figure 12. The deliberate model

The "emergent" viewpoints present the other extreme. Drawing on studies of "radical innovations" and new ventures in established firms, this school of thought suggests that new initiatives typically "emerge" spontaneously through actions of autonomous actors.[2] If the appropriate cultural norms and the right incentive systems are put in place, innovative initiatives will follow. As illustrated in Figure 13, front-line champions, those closest to action, are empowered to act entrepreneurially and are rewarded accordingly.

---

[2] Classic studies on the emergent perspective include: Allison (1971), Lindblom (1959), March and Olsen (1976).

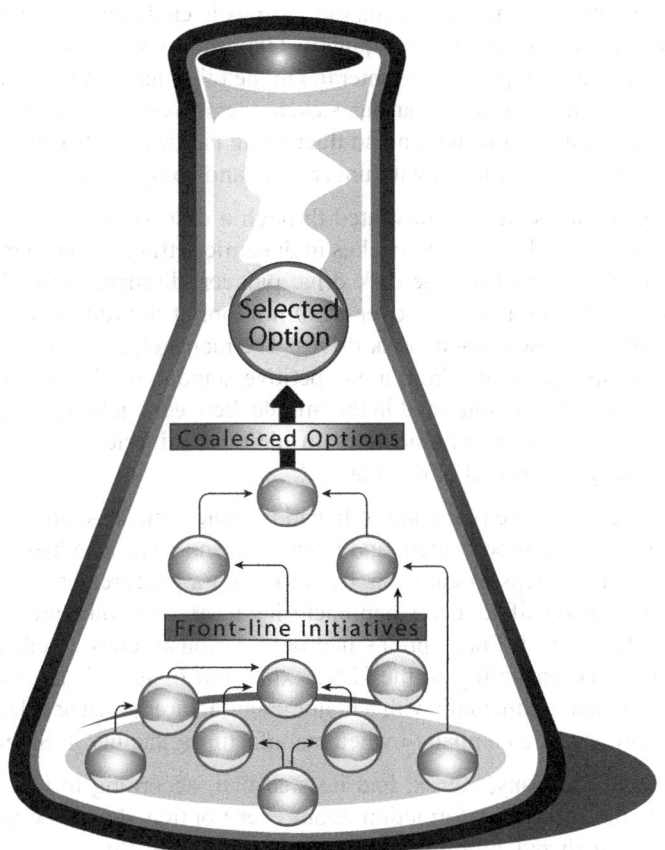

Figure 13. The emergent model

The emergent and the deliberate approaches portray 'pure" modes, at the extreme ends of a spectrum. In reality, our observations suggest that effective execution in dynamic settings is a blend of both. In the emergent mode, there is no intentional effort to create options. Options may be generated through random events, accidents, luck, or individual initiatives. Sole reliance on purely emergent modes can leave an enterprise highly vulnerable. It assumes that effective outcomes depend on luck, serendipity, and forces beyond a firm's control. The purely deliberate mode, on the other hand, does not accommodate spontaneous developments or unique events that may come up unexpectedly. Assumptions embedded in elaborate plans and detailed analyses may become irrelevant by unexpected surprises, such as the departure of a key executive, sudden competitive moves, or the unexpected loss of a critical account.

Executing new initiatives in dynamic settings is challenging. On the one hand, leaders have to be decisive and act quickly. Opportunities are short-lived and competitive advantage is typically ephemeral. On the other hand, it takes time to gather input and to get the buy-in of various stakeholders. Decisions have to be taken in the context of limited information and fluctuating parameters. So how do executive teams move ahead when faced with uncertainty and complexity?

These challenges can be illustrated through a case vignette that demonstrates the limitations of traditional approaches in dynamic settings. Consider the situation facing Shugart Corporation, the disk drive pioneer, discussed in earlier chapters, during the 1980s. With sales of over $250 million, at the time it was the world's largest supplier of low capacity disk drives. The management team was anxious to extend its leading position. From a competitive standpoint, the company was in a difficult position. It was squeezed in the middle, between niche start-ups, as well as large Japanese electronic manufacturers. In addition, unit prices had started to fall in the low capacity floppy end of the market.[3]

This rupturing of the price umbrella had become a major source of pressure on margins. As a result, procurement and manufacturing costs also had to be reduced. Shugart had taken steps to cut costs by setting up a procurement office in Singapore. Attention had shifted to the manufacturing front, so it could provide additional capacity at lower cost. Four options had been seriously considered; creation of a highly automated capability in the U.S.; expansion of its existing manufacturing facility in Mexico; partnership with a major manufacturer (such as a Japanese firm); and establishment of a company-owned manufacturing facility in Singapore.

The parent company, Xerox, had insisted that, according to its own planning procedures, the relevant information about every option should be systematically collected and analyzed, highlighting the costs and the benefits associated with each alternative. This would enable its executives to make an "optimal" decision.

However, the "relevant" information was constantly changing. For example, projected sales price was declining, almost on a weekly basis, due to the rapid penetration of low cost Japanese disk drives in the U.S. market. Component costs (a significant portion of total product cost) were fluctuating. The cost of setting up an offshore facility was increasing because of changing tax laws and rising cost of land and building. Nonetheless, Shugart had to convince its parent, through a detailed strategic and financial plan, that the favored option, the Singapore facility, represented the most optimal solution for lowering manufacturing costs.

The process went on for about 18 months as corporate staff asked for more detailed information and fine-tuned the financial analysis associated with each option. In the meantime, the competitive landscape was being transformed. A

---

[3] For historical details, see "Industry Note: Disk Drives for Small and Microcomputer Systems" (case #S-MM-6N), Stanford University, Graduate School of Business, 1985; and "Planning Manufacturing Capabilities" (case # S-MM-8), Stanford University, Graduate School of Business, 1985).

number of start-ups had already moved to Asia, and Japanese manufacturers were making aggressive inroads into the U.S. market.

No tangible action had yet been taken. The search continued for the "perfect information" on which an "optimal" decision could be based. During the intervening period, Shugart lost a number of its key accounts. This resulted in a significant loss of market share in the low-end floppy disk drive market, where it had traditionally retained a leading position. By 1986, Xerox divested Shugart and the company ceased to exist. Portions of its business were sold to different investors. Although with the benefit of hindsight, it is easy to speculate, many experts believed that if decisive action had been taken early on to lower manufacturing costs, the outcome may have been different.

6.2 The Framework: Recalibration

While there is an abundance of managerial literature on how to make "optimal", "best" or "correct" decisions, there is relatively little attention focused on how to revise a decision if it turns out to be unsatisfactory, or if the assumptions underpinning the original decision change unexpectedly.[4] Many successful innovations or winning business strategies result from many revisions, driven by unfolding circumstances. In technology settings, the challenge is to embark on action and to adjust in evolving circumstances (Brown & Eisenhardt 1998, Burgelman 2002). The imperative is to be decisive, yet surf dynamic waves of uncertainty.

Effective initiatives we have observed over the years share several characteristics: *clear intentions, a distinct point of view, openness to new data, fact-based assessment, and swift revisions.* They can be described as a montage of deliberate intentions, rapid adjustments and emergent learning. While they are not entirely chaotic, elements of luck, timing and spontaneity are clearly important. Nor are they purely deliberate and systematically planned, a priori, although clear preferences and distinct points of view determine their overall direction. Moreover, experiential learning along the way, together with the development of new competencies, highlight their partially emergent character:

"There is a certain way of looking at the world and processing information that is unique to those who are good at dynamic execution. The mistake is to assume that if someone is really smart, they'll figure it out...but you need execution intelligence, not just raw smarts. A great example is Apple's turnaround. The core of what made Apple bounce back was Steve (Jobs') original point of view about user interface and how human beings interact with technology. His point of view on that subject has never changed, ever since Apple designed the first Mac user interface; even at NeXT, he was bringing that point of view to Unix...then as the video/music distribution was changing, he came back to Apple and brought back that original point

---

[4] For a practical perspective on making optimal decisions, see Hammond, Keeney & Raiffa (1999).

of view...you don't need to be a famous entrepreneur to benefit from that lesson.. start with a thesis, gather data, constantly challenge your assumptions, test and experiment, discover things you never thought of before, and re-assess...the worst of all worlds is a leader who wonders from business idea to business idea, and loses a sense of purpose and direction...the truly great entrepreneurs have the ability to have an intense focus and a clear point of view, but are open to testing their assumptions, assimilating new information, and re-thinking the business real-time."[5]

The emphasis is on having a clear point of view, testing, probing, experimenting, learning by doing, seeking new fdata, and continuously re-calibrating.[6] Recalibrations are made as new information is brought to light and as the original technical premises and market assumptions evolve. Following the initial pilots, an idea may be rejected altogether. The deciding factor is practical "relevance" and fact-based assessment, rather than theoretical elegance and informational consistency. As depicted in Figure 14, the recalibration model blends elements of the deliberate and the emergent approaches, with its own unique features.

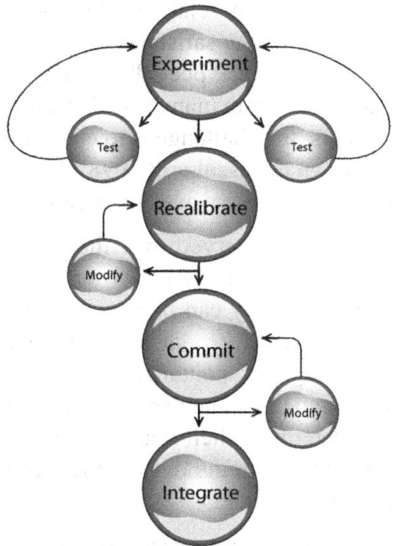

Figure 14. The recalibration model

---

[5] Personal interview with the General Partner of a leading venture firm.

[6] This emphasis on the importance of learning has been noted by other studies. In describing the birth of the video recorder industry, Rosenbloom and Cusumano (1987) discuss how the development of Betamax and VHS by Sony and Japan Victor Corporation were "the tangible results of fifteen years of learning by trying." (p.66). Similarly, Maidique and Zirger (1985) characterize the new product development cycle in high technology firms as a learning process in which innovators learn not only by doing, but also by failing. This in turn results in the development of new alternatives and product concepts.

The process is similar to the scientific method of discovery. Scientists formulate hypotheses and assess their validity by conducting experiments and collecting data. If the evidence does not support the original hypotheses, new hypotheses will be framed, and tested yet again. However, scientists are not in full control of all the salient parameters. A new discovery, or unexpected results, can change the embedded assumptions and even make the work obsolete.

Similarly, in the recalibration framework, the processes of strategy formation and implementation are closely linked together in an iterative process, especially during the early stage of a new initiative. In unpredictable settings, it is impossible to iron out all the uncertainties and "de-risk" strategies through detailed planning and elaborate analyses. Relevant information is not only limited, but also in a state of flux. It may be difficult to establish the technical feasibility of a novel idea, or the viability of executing a new initiative, through "theoretical" planning. By engaging in action, new information can be brought to light, and unforeseen limitations, and new possibilities, identified.

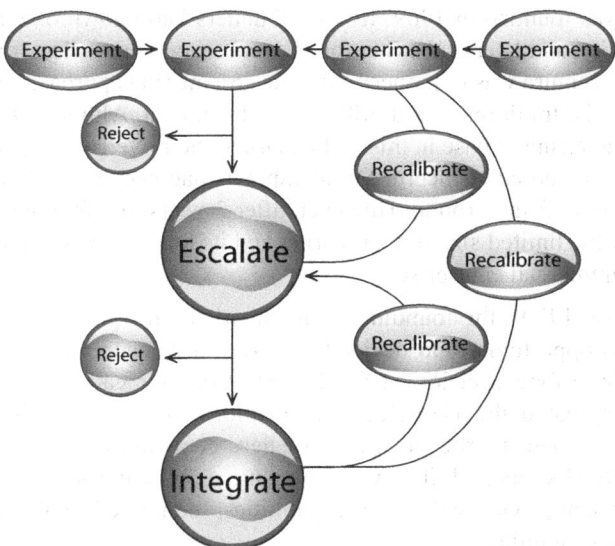

Figure 15. The three phases of the recalibration process

The recalibration process starts with articulating a clear thesis, a bounded hypothesis, or a distinctive point of view around a value proposition. As illustrated in Figure 15, the initial thesis can be rapidly tested through experimentation, piloting and prototyping; the critical factor is to retain the flexibility to modify, iterate and adapt the idea as new developments unfold. The emphasis is on continuous iteration and recalibration through guided experimentation.

6.3 Case History: ROLM Corporation

The recalibration framework is illustrated by drawing on the strategic evolution of ROLM Corporation, a pioneer in the telecommunications industry during the 1970s and 1980s. Later in this chapter, we will describe how a storage company used the recalibration process to enter a new market; in addition, through the perspective of the lead investor, we will examine the iteration and adaptation of the business proposition that eventually became the success formula for Netflix's rise to prominence.

ROLM was a pioneering Silicon Valley company, blazing the trail in unchartered territories. It was the first firm to introduce the concept of off-the-shelf commercial computing to the military market during the early 1970s, an early challenger to AT&T's dominance in the telecommunications equipment field, and a pioneer of "integrated office of the future" during the early 1980s. It was acquired by IBM in 1984 and later become part of Siemens, the global electronics giant.

ROLM was founded in 1969. Its four founders had known one another first at Rice University, and later at the Stanford Engineering School. The founding team's first business venture was to pioneer a unique commercial approach in selling minicomputers to the tradition-bound military establishment. Although the team established a viable business base in this niche market, their overriding goal was to build a sizeable "commercial" concern. Minicomputers had been a timely opportunity to get the business off the ground. However, after 3 years, the founders became concerned about the limited size of that market and its long-term potential for building a sizeable commercial enterprise.

In the early 1970s, the founding team embarked on a pre-emptive search for a new business opportunity and decided to enter the telecommunications business. The 1968 Carterfone decision of the Federal Communications Commission had partially deregulated the US telecommunications industry, opening up the vast telephone equipment market to a host of new companies. The intention was to leverage ROLM's core skills by developing a computer-controlled telephone switching system, with enhanced capabilities, compared with the traditional electromechanical units.

ROLM had to be navigated through the uncertain and stormy seas that characterized the industry. Computing technology was changing the nature of telephones and telecommunications. There was considerable debate about the eventual deregulation of the industry, despite AT&T's concerted efforts to retain its long-standing position as a regulated monopoly. The interconnect distribution channel was just beginning to get off the ground, and competition had intensified with the entry of Japanese and European giants in the field. In short, the industry was in a state of chaos and confusion.

At the time, many expert observers questioned the ability of a young, unknown player, like ROLM, to survive, let alone to prosper in a different arena. Despite the initial, often grave, misgivings of many expert observers, ROLM managed to become a leading telecommunications firm during the next 5 years. By the late 1970s, telecommunications products accounted for almost 70% of its total revenues.

ROLM consolidated its strategic position during the early 1980s by making selected forays into the "office of the future", focusing on integrated voice/data terminals, and computerized voice messaging systems. IBM acquired ROLM in the aftermath of AT&T's divestiture in 1984. At the time of the acquisition, ROLM was called "the ship that is creating the wave of innovation in the field" and a "forerunner in the fast-paced (telecommunications) market."[7] These tributes were clearly reflected in its impressive market performance. After only 10 years in the business, ROLM had managed to capture 15% of the market for office telephone switches, only 9% behind AT&T. Another measure of its remarkable success was the dramatic increase in its stock price. Compared with the 1,920 companies that had gone public since 1975, ROLM's stock had produced the largest long-term relative gain over its initial offering price.

ROLM's pioneering moves were not based on detailed analyses and elaborate plans, but on a few fundamental principles, many informal discussions, and a series of experiments, designed to test the validity of their business propositions. These were initially tested on a small scale. They were later re-calibrated, and either executed on a large scale, with resource commitment and organizational momentum, or discontinued altogether. Recalibration is the hallmark of ROLM's strategic evolution during a 16 year time frame; from military computers, to telecommunications, to energy management, and finally to office systems:

"In building ROLM as a company, we experimented in a number of different areas, people, technology, markets, organization, products and cultural policies... we gave a chance to those whose experience and tangible expertise did not, at least on paper, qualify them to take on certain assignments. For example, our first CFO, took on the assignment to build our direct sales organization during the late 1970s. We were also constantly experimenting with new organizational arrangements. Some worked and some didn't. For example, in 1980 we set up a 3-person top management team to run the company, and before entrepreneurship became popular, we set up a self-contained autonomous division to build and develop our family of digital telephones. But perhaps the biggest experiments involved our strategic diversification, from Mil-Spec computers, to PBXs, to energy management, and finally office systems."[8]

---

[7] San Francisco Chronicle, September 26, 1984; For additional perspectives on the ROLM/IBM merger see the Economist, September 29, 1984 and the Wall street Journal, September 27, 1984.

[8] Personal communication with ROLM's co-founder & CEO.

The approach that ROLM and many successful technology pioneers we have observed can be characterized as a continuous process of engaging, probing, testing, prototyping, and recalibrating. As depicted in Figure 16, the "experimentation" stage clarifies intentions, generates options, assesses feasibility, and tests the stakeholders' initial reaction. The initiative is speeded up and brought into a sharper focus during the crucial "escalation" phase, with greater visibility, concentration of effort, and concerted use of resources. During the final "integration" phase, attempts are made to blend the initiative into the broader strategic and organizational context.

6.3.1 Phase 1: Experimentation

The desire to launch a new initiative may be triggered by several factors. These may include market opportunities, competitive moves, technical breakthroughs, management choices, or random events. ROLM's move into telecommunications, for instance, was initially triggered by the top team's concern over the limited size of the military computer market and its long-term viability for a commercial entity.

"ROLM's objective is to grow to be a large profitable company, in an atmosphere where everyone contributing to that growth, learns, grows and is financially rewarded...The military computer business is currently a good, stable base...however, it has not satisfied our objective of broad customer appeal...our freedom to develop products on our own funds is severely limited...stability and growth are essentially dependent on one...customer...worst of all is our limited flexibility due to business practices that we would undoubtedly sink into...we should (therefore) not sacrifice strategy and principles just for short term growth in the military market..let's realize that that business is good, but limited, and accept it for what it is."[9]

The experimentation phase enables a leadership team to formulate value propositions, test them on a small scale, and generate rapid feedback. Early experimentation has other advantages. It inculcates an organizational mindset willing to embrace new information. It fleshes out viable options, and provides a vehicle for recursive learning. For example, ROLM's technical experiments in office systems during the early 1980s developed its capability base in terminals and information systems, where it had limited prior experience. The over arching objective during this phase is to clarify intentions, develop capability, and create viable options.

Just as scientists use experiments to check the validity of scientific hypotheses, pilots and prototypes can be used to assess the validity of a value proposition. Initiated as deliberate moves, pilots are especially valuable when there are no existing blueprints or proven methods for success. They can be set up in parallel to speed up the learning process. Effective experimentation provides a basis for selecting viable pathways, testing the feasibility of proposed ideas, managing stakeholders' expectations, and re-casting the forged vision.

---

[9] Internal memorandum, ROLM Corporation.

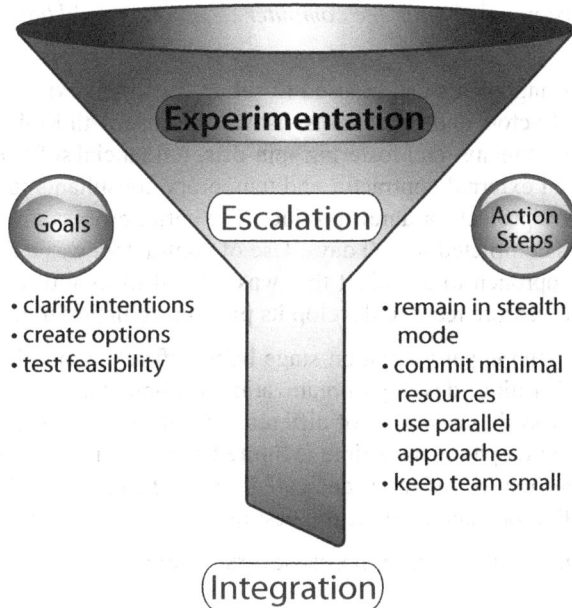
Figure 16. The experimentation phase

For example, technical and marketing experiments were the prelude to ROLM's entry into the telecommunications business during the early 1970s. During this time, there was considerable uncertainty about the eventual deregulation of the industry, the future role of computer technology in telecommunications, and the viability of the emerging interconnect industry as a viable distribution channel. The ROLM team hired a technical consultant, Jim Kasson, to put together a simple prototype. The goal was to find out if it was even feasible to develop a computer-controlled PBX system. The team also recruited a marketing expert, Richard Moley, as the first PBX product manager. Kasson and Moley had both worked for Hewlett Packard and knew each other well.

One of Moley's first initiatives was to interview a number of potential customers about their needs. He also wanted to find out whether they would be willing to buy a PBX system from a young upstart like ROLM. It was these lead user interviews that convinced the team that the opportunity was worth pursuing. It was not just a unique "nice to have"; the idea had traction with lead users. The PBX team could envision the enhanced capabilities that a computer could bring to the plain old telephone:

"Clearly we had the capability, the computer technology, to solve meaningful customer problems, and save them a lot of money ... we could optimize call routings, or handle toll restrictions ... and handling moves and changes would simply

be a matter of re-programming the computer ... no one would have to visit the customer's site."[10]

Different arrangements can be used to set up the initial experiments. These include using contractors and consultants, as was the case with ROLM's PBX, creating internal project teams, and fostering spin-offs. A financial software company, for example, used an external contractor and temporary consultants to staff an aggressive development project for a new product. The entire process, from initial pilot to full launch, was completed in 100 days. Use of contractors was a flexible, fast, and de-politicized approach to a project that was critical to its future success. ROLM used an internal venture team to develop its pioneering line of digital phones.

In summary, the experimentation stage helps refine the initial vision. The process enhances learning, develops organizational momentum, reduces uncertainty, and can help assess the feasibility of different options. However, speed of feedback is crucial during this phase since time is limited and resources are scarce. Effective experimentation requires a small, dedicated, team of thinkers and doers, who can work in a stealth mode and emulate the best qualities of a start-up.

The experimentation phase poses several challenges for entrepreneurs and business leaders:
- It is not feasible to experiment continuously. Leaders need to ensure that time triggers are built into the process, and that there is a definite time line for experimentation.
- They need to keep the ultimate goal in mind, and have a clear idea about "what success looks like". This minimizes problems associated with analysis paralysis and consensus at any cost. Clear end goals and concrete success metrics enable business teams to have a sense of shared reality, yet incorporate different points of view over time.
- Sufficient flexibility should be built in, so the process can adapt over time; this involves setting, and re-setting stakeholder expectations at the outset, and at critical junctures along the way.

6.3.2 Phase 2: Escalation

An experimental attitude and a flexible posture cannot be maintained indefinitely. Once the level of market uncertainty is reduced and the technical feasibility of a new idea is verified, a team must move beyond experimentation and focus on ramping-up promising options. Whereas option generation, action-based exploration, and recursive learning are critical during experimentation, the escalation phase is about focus, speed, momentum and concentration of resources.

---

[10] Personal communication with ROLM's Vice President of Marketing and its first PBX Product Manager.

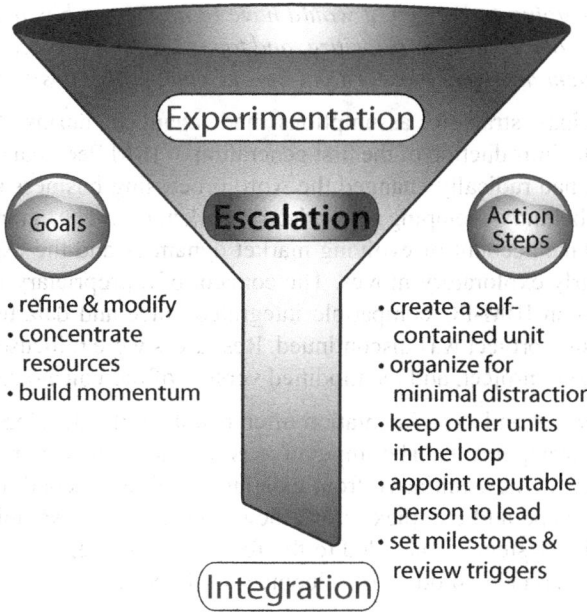

Figure 17. The escalation phase

This stage represents concerted efforts to select and build momentum around the most promising options. It also signals senior management's commitment to a promising initiative. The primary objective is "to put the foot on the gas pedal" and to ramp-up a project that may have a short life cycle.

In the cases we have observed, the decision to escalate, to discontinue, or to revise a project depends on several factors. These include industry dynamics, experiential learning, and organizational expediency. For example, ROLM's initial "grand" strategy in office automation encompassed several products. These included an application processor, a common engine for the telephone switching equipment and the office products, a proprietary, intelligent workstation to integrate voice and data, and various software modules to provide voice messaging, text messaging, and word processing capabilities. These building blocks were to be integrated over time. The total package was expected to provide a comprehensive office automation capability for the end-user.

However, after the initial pilots, it became clear that the strategy was far too complex to execute in its original form. As Bob Maxfield, ROLM's co-founder and the senior executive in charge of the program commented:

"Every time we reviewed the projects, they had slipped another 3 months ... we realized that we weren't getting very far with implementing the grand strategy ... and had underestimated the magnitude of what we had taken on...if (the

strategy) was going to happen, it would have to happen in bits and pieces...so we had to change our approach, prioritize, and focus on those projects that were feasible to implement and were most critical for our competitive positioning."[11]

The original strategic assumptions had changed during the intervening period with the introduction of the first generation of IBM Personal Computers. This development had radically changed the word processing business and undermined the rationale behind developing a proprietary workstation. The "grand strategy" was modified to take account of evolving market dynamics and the experience gained during the early exploratory moves. The concept of a proprietary workstation was modified into an IBM-PC compatible integrated voice and data terminal, and the word processing project was discontinued. Resources were refocused instead on the voice-messaging project, and the modified version of the voice/data terminal.

Escalation beyond experimentation often results in the development of new organizational arrangements. The imperative is to deal with two critical challenges; first, to buffer the new initiative from existing activities; second, to accommodate the growing scope and complexity of a new program. For example, escalation of ROLM's office systems project led to the formation of a separate division with an exclusive focus on new product development initiatives.

Effective project management is also a critical capability during this phase. After all, the initiative is now visible and consumes organizational resources and executive attention. Typically, review triggers are built in to monitor the progress made in implementing pre-defined milestones. These may result in minor revisions or major modifications of the action plan.

New leaders may also emerge during this phase. Since the initiative is no longer a simple pilot, it may need to be guided and 'protected" from internal political realities. A project leader, who may have been effective during the experimentation phase, may not have the skills, the experience, or the network to be an effective bridge-builder and stakeholder manager during escalation. Even in a young start-up, the guru scientist, who may be the visionary behind a technical prototype, may have to give way to an experienced project manager during the escalation phase.

6.3.3 Phase 3: Integration

Once an initiative has been successfully launched, it has to be blended into the mainstream organization. As depicted in Figure 18, the objectives during the "integration" phase are to ensure strategic cohesion across the business portfolio, and to leverage the existing resource infrastructure. A critical task is to devise organizational arrangements that can integrate the new activity into the mainstream organization.

---

[11] Personal communication with ROLM's co-founder and Executive Vice President.

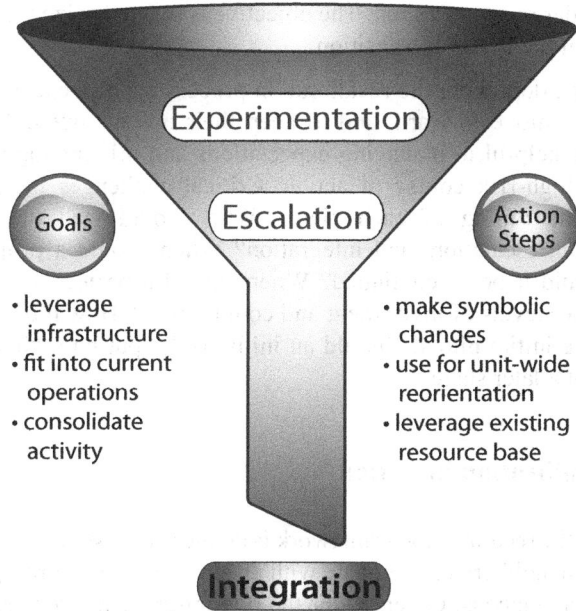

Figure 18. The integration phase

The choice of integration mechanisms depends on two critical factors: first, the expected growth rate for the new business; second, the degree of interdependence between new and existing activities. If, the new business grows rapidly, a separate unit should be set up to focus on its ramp-up; in some cases, the unit may be spun off as a separate business. Well-known examples include Apple's Claris and Sun's Java Divisions. Similarly, if there is limited interdependence between new and existing activities, an autonomous unit may be appropriate. However, if interdependence is high, or if the new business does not grow as rapidly as expected, it can be integrated into the mainstream organization.

For example, ROLM formed an autonomous division to consolidate its PBX business when it had generated enough revenues to warrant the formation of a separate unit. A self-contained unit was appropriate because there was limited interdependence between the minicomputer and the telecommunications businesses. The office systems initiative, on the other hand, was closely linked to the telecommunications business. The two products had to work together and were sold through similar distribution channels to the same customer base. The need for extensive co-ordination prompted a company-wide re-organization and led to the formation of a hybrid structure.

After a new initiative "goes live", symbolic changes are also needed to signal the birth of a "new baby". These may include a change of name, location, logo, leadership, or a broader re-organization. The objective is to emphasize the inflection point and to highlight the need for transition.

In summary, deploying the recalibration process enables executive teams to be decisive and to move forward, and to keep their options open. Additionally, the process can be helpful in managing expectations and minimizing premature commitment to a high-risk course of action. Critical challenges include customized staffing and the timing of each phase. Who should lead the project during experimentation, escalation, and integration? When should a project be initiated and when should it be discontinued? When should a project move on to escalation, with higher levels of investment and commitment? How much time should be allocated to the initial pilots? Should an initiative be put on a "back-burner", and reconsidered at a later stage?

6.4 Recalibration in Action

Implementing the recalibration framework is challenging. Many companies are used to the top-down, deliberate, approach, with an emphasis on planning, data gathering and information analysis. Others favor the bottom-up or the "emergent" approach. The assumption is that innovative ideas emerge, when the environment and the incentives encourage individual champions to initiate new projects.

In technology settings, resources are scarce; time frames are compressed; yet action has to be taken, even when there is limited information. The recalibration framework enables teams to move quickly from idea to action, and to revise expectations based on fact-based feedback. A major trade-off is how to be consistent, yet remain flexible and responsive to new realities.

Consider the use of the recalibration process by a computer storage company in launching a new initiative. The process was kicked off during the annual leadership conference, bringing together its top 100 executives. The objective was to reflect on industry changes and to consider future strategic moves. The explosion of the Internet had opened up new growth options for the company. The leadership conference was focused on how best to leverage emerging market opportunities. Following a series of heated discussions, where contrasting views were presented and debated, the CEO decided to set up two parallel teams. The goal was to explore two different product/service opportunities.

Each team included top performers from different functions. They were given 8 weeks and a small budget to conduct research, listen to experts, interview potential lead users, and brainstorm options. Their findings were later presented to the executive team, laying out different alternatives that could be further explored. The executive team decided to set up two pilot projects to explore the feasibility of the proposed options.

The follow-up experimentation phase lasted for ten weeks. During this time, both teams talked to potential customers and developed technical prototypes. After communicating their findings, it was decided to blend together "the best of both efforts" since neither pilot had generated conclusive results. The recalibrated project later led to the launch of a major new service business for the company and has since become a significant revenue and profit generator.

Another example of recalibration in action is the evolution of Netflix, the pioneer of online, subscription-based, DVD rental service. The story began in 1998 when DVDs were just coming to market. Frustrated by paying $40 in late fees to Blockbuster, the dominant player in the movie rental business, its founder, Reed Hastings, had the insight that there could be a better way to provide the service:

"His thesis was that, unlike the CD, the electronic components that were going to be used in DVD players were also being used in PCs, so the cost curve was going to fall steeply as the components were being commoditized. (The assumption) was that if you could get to the $199 DVD player, consumers would adopt it..but you faced a circular problem..the DVD players were coming out at very high prices, around $700-$800 for the early versions, and there was limited content..Blockbuster wasn't even renting DVDs..why would I buy content if there is no player and why would I buy a player if there is no content. Reed's belief that you had to stimulate this market led him to go to the electronic DVD manufacturers, the content owners, companies like Sony and Toshiba, and presented them with a proposition..we'll aggregate all the content inside one repository called Netflix and we'll create a rental store for the early adopters of DVDs..he was able to put a big red movie ticket called Netflix inside the device and on the reverse side was a free offer..so he aligned the interests of the DVD manufacturers, so they would perpetuate this phenomenon.. but for Netflix, there were several problems. We know (at the time) consumers rented from brick and mortar companies (like Blockbuster); 95% of rentals happened on Thursdays and Fridays but Blockbuster made its margins on late fees, so (Reed's proposition was) if I can rent movies out on DVDs, charge no late fee, and keep the cost down, (then it may work) but consumer behavior is spontaneous..people don't plan ahead and don't want to wait for 2 days to get the DVD in the mail. Then we came up with the subscription idea..you can have so many DVDs at a given point in time and had pretty good uptake. As business became more successful, we had to buy all this content from studios, costing hundreds of millions of dollars. Reed learned that consumers wanted access to an entire catalogue of movies and loved the DVD format; it was about superior quality and no late fees..but how do you scale that? That led to the pioneering notion of revenue sharing..put a little money up front, but studios could share in downstream revenue.. he understood the synergies with content owners and could negotiate those deals..that was the fundamental enabler for scaling the business. Great entrepreneurial leaders always iterate, they look at new data and challenge their own assumptions. At Netflix we were constantly looking at customer satisfaction data, by region, how they checked things out, how reviews were presented..this process of iteration also led to a process of discovery

and yielded new insights....in order to make the subscription business work, you need to develop a preference engine so you can recommend movies based on earlier behavior; second you need a queuing system so you can have video on demand; then the service to customers became seamless..despite these iterations, the cost of customer acquisition was high..when we looked at the data, we noticed that the cost of customer acquisition was a lot lower in the Bay area than in other parts of the country..we were mailing the DVDs from the local post offices and people got their DVDs overnight....word of mouth spread and we got many more customers.. we realized that we needed to set up regional distribution centers..we started one in Idaho, and one in Sacramento, by constantly analyzing the data and iterating the strategy, we moved the business forward..this is an interesting story because it shows how the process of iteration yields new insights and possibilities. Reed's initial thesis "to provide an entire library of movie content to users" has never changed; what changed were the constant refinements on how you deliver that proposition. He was 100% correct about the thesis but 50% right about how to make it happen.[12]

6.5   Guidelines for Implementation

As the ROLM and the Netflix stories indicate, the recalibration framework can be used in several contexts: to start new initiatives; to move beyond an idea towards its execution; and to de-risk pioneering moves in dynamic markets. Our observations point to several guidelines that should be considered when implementing the recalibration process:

Keep the big picture in mind, but implement in small, bite-sized steps.

New initiatives are typically a response to user needs, competitive gaps, pressures for growth, and performance problems. In the absence of a major crisis or an urgent market need, they can languish and get stuck in endless internal debates.

Effective approaches we have observed follow a similar path. There is intense discussion early on, but these conversations move on to focus on pilots and experiments. The emphasis is on generating fact-based feedback by embarking on action. The information can be used to assess the go/no go-decision and to revise the original idea.

Two sets of ground rules are crucial during the early phase: first, it is impor-

---

[12] Personal Interview with an early investor in Netflix, and a member of its Board of Directors; Also see Anita Elberse "Should you invest in the Long Tail?" Harvard Business Review nos 7/8 (July Auhust 2008) pp: 88-96: Anita Elberse and Felix Oberholzer-Gee "Superstars and Underdogs: An Examination of Long Tail Phenomenon in Video Sales. Harvard Business School Working Paper, HBS 07-015, January 30, 2008.

tant to map the tough challenges and the easy tasks, or the "low and the high hanging fruit". This process can create alignment, provide a sense of shared reality, and keep the stakeholders on the same page. However, effective use of the recalibration framework starts with simple tasks that have a quick payoff.[13] Quick wins build confidence, generate credibility, and provide the foundation for taking on tougher challenges.

Develop focused pilots/test a single hypothesis.

New initiatives can turn into political battles. Each faction fights for its own agenda. The pilot is doomed to fail if it is designed to "build consensus", appeal to the lowest common denominator, and minimize criticism from vocal skeptics. In other words, it can get diluted and lose its focus. Although this approach may be politically expedient, it does not generate timely and relevant feedback that can be used to escalate, to curtail or to recalibrate an initiative. As illustrated by the Netflix story, constant iteration is crucial for the success of a new idea.

To avoid this problem, it is important to focus on testing a single value proposition, so the pilot does not get "muddied" by different objectives. When the ROLM team first considered entering the digital PBX business, the main objective was to learn about the risk appetite of telecommunications managers in Fortune 500 companies, their target customers. Would they be willing to give up the relative safety of buying an analog system from AT&T, in favor of using the latest digital technology from an unknown player?

This idea was initially tested by a number of lead user interviews. The PBX product champion talked to 50 telecom managers in Fortune 500 companies. Their response was overwhelming. If the digital PBX could help them account for each department's telephone usage, so they could be billed directly, they would buy the new system, despite the inherent risks. By testing a single critical hypothesis, the ROLM team received first-hand user feedback on a topic that could impact the viability of the entire project.

Keep a low profile early on and express intentions in general terms.

There is a trade-off between being consistent and steadfast on the one hand, and having the built-in flexibility to revise decisions as new realities unfold. This can pose a problem. Leadership teams often limit their ability to recalibrate by raising a venture's profile too early, and by committing to a "specific" course of action prematurely.

---

[13] This is similar to the findings of other studies that have examined profiles of successful change initiatives (see Kotter 1996).

It is easier to recalibrate if leaders keep a low profile early on, and express their intentions in broad, general terms, This enables them to manage stakeholders' expectations, pursue several options within the broader frame of reference, and have the flexibility to recalibrate at a later date. The original idea can even be abandoned, if the expected benefits do not materialize.

This trade-off is reflected in the approach of a new generation of entrepreneurs whose ventures are known as "stealth start-ups". They prefer to "boot-strap" their ventures, maintain a low profile and keep their options open during the crucial early stages. They are more reluctant to raise venture capital during the early phases, and prefer not to disclose their specific intentions to a broader community. Similarly, serial entrepreneurs often stay with their original investors as a way of maintaining "stealth" because they don't have to show their business plan to a broader group of investors.

Stealth start-ups increase their chances of being first to market. They retain the flexibility to recalibrate and change tack, without appearing "inconsistent". Investors are not easily convinced that change is good, when it was the original idea that appealed to them in the first place.

In summary, adopting a stealth posture has two benefits; first, it shades new activities from public view and keeps options open; second, it allows the necessary revisions to be made, without having to justify these to a broader group of stakeholders.

Set up parallel pilots with rapid feedback loops.

Real-time information is critical when operating in dynamic environments. It is no good marching down a path that has become irrelevant or obsolete. Pilots should be set up in order to generate quick feedback, at least before the original assumptions become obsolete. The most successful pilots we have observed tend to have a 30-90 day time frame. If they linger for much longer, the feedback they generate may be interesting, but irrelevant. In the process, the target initiative may lose momentum.

Setting up parallel pilots, to test alternative hypotheses, can speed up the learning cycle. It can also accommodate the views of different stakeholders. The approach can help teams learn from diverse experiences in compressed time frames.

This is how ROLM orchestrated the implementation of its direct sales and service strategy during the late 1970s. At the time there was no "ideal" blueprint. Some favored the acquisition route; others preferred building the sales team from the ground up. The ROLM team adopted a three-pronged approach. They acquired a number of their distributors; they formed joint ventures with a few distributors; and they set up their own direct sales force in major metropolitan areas: *"There was no magic answer ... it had to happen based on given options in each territory ... we tried all three and learned a lot in the process."*[14]

Darwinism is OK — anticipate "worst case" scenarios early and prune out ineffective initiatives.

The dilemma is how to balance emotional and rational drivers when launching a new initiative. On the one hand, fact-based feedback should be used to assess the feasibility of an idea. On the other hand, people have rationalizing tendencies and become emotionally committed to their own ideas, even when there is evidence to the contrary (Staw 1983).

To minimize problems associated with escalation of commitment, it is important to anticipate worse case scenarios ahead of time, to develop a bandwidth of expectations, and to plan contingencies, just in case. What if the technical prototype does not perform according to specification? What if the target market evolves more slowly than expected? What if we lose some of our key technical talent?

These questions should be addressed during the early stages, before stakeholders become committed to a given trajectory. The process enables core teams to consider back-up plans, to discontinue failed initiatives, or to put them on hold.

6.6 Recalibration and Super-Flexibility

The recalibration framework incorporates the importance of rational and emotional drivers in launching new initiatives. It is predicated on the assumption that managing expectations and generating rapid feedback are critical to the ultimate success of a pioneering initiative. If used effectively, the process can help build resilience, enhance agility, and develop versatile capabilities.

Deploying the recalibration approach does not guarantee success. It provides an opportunity to test the feasibility of an idea before escalating financial and psychological commitment. If the experiment turns out to be infeasible, losses can be minimized, without branding it as a failure. An experimental approach can also build resilience by managing stakeholder expectations.

For example, venture capitalists often invest in several start-ups in a "new category". Even with the most sophisticated forecasts, it is difficult to predict which venture will ultimately succeed. By seeding and investing in several start-ups in the same category, they can increase the odds of winning, especially when only one in 30 start-ups, on average, succeed.

---

[14] Personal communication with ROLM's CFO and the senior executive responsible for setting up the sales and service organization.

This approach has other benefits. It can increase the range of experiments and speed up the learning process. It can help develop the experience base of technical professionals. It can encourage variation in product features, and the ability to meet diverse customer needs. It can expand the lead-user base whose feedback is crucial for product iteration. As indicated in chapter 4, some ventures are discontinued, and the most promising elements of others are fused together. This is an illustration of "flexible recycling" at work.

Second, as indicated in the ROLM vignettes, the recalibration approach speeds up the execution process by focusing on several tactical options. This enables a team to take account of diverse situational needs, and speed up the learning cycle. By entering several different areas as a "new category" evolves, or by embracing different standards in a device, start-up teams develop the agility to quickly regroup behind the evolving dominant standard.

Third, generating different options is critical in dynamic settings. An option that may seem ideal one day may be irrelevant when the original assumptions are no longer valid. Exploratory experiments, in the form of action learning, can help develop a range of options, and in the process, enhance the capability base of knowledge workers. They can learn by trying, failing, iterating and recalibrating.

The recalibration approach allows deliberate intentions to be tested against emergent realities. It facilitates dynamic adaptation, especially when embarking on new initiatives in unchartered domains. Actions can be framed in the context of a broad vision. Yet decisions evolve as teams develop new capabilities through experimentation, iteration and prototyping. The approach entails several phases: developing a testable point of view, generating alternatives, experimenting and prototyping, escalating commitment to the most viable option, and integrating the initiatives into the mainstream organization. It is important to iterate and recalibrate during all three phases based as new realities unfold.

It is in this context that super-flexibility is crucial. Recalibration contributes to the development of super-flexible capabilities in several ways:
- It creates versatility by broadening the range of options up front. It also enhances knowledge workers' capabilities by exposing them to a wider range of experiences.
- It instills resilience by removing the stigma of failure and by encouraging recycling and recalibrating. Initiatives are not viewed as being totally right or exactly wrong, but as 'shades of grey" with many different trade-offs.
- It provides liquidity and mobility by recycling failed experiments, re-deploying resources, and channeling knowledge workers towards promising options.

There are clear parallels between the recalibration approach and the process of scientific discovery. Scientists update assumptions and hypotheses by taking account of new discoveries and related breakthroughs (Popper 1972, Feyerabend, 1968). Knowledge workers have to ensure that their intended plan of action is congruent with emerging technological, competitive and market realities. Scientific hypotheses have to be corroborated by experimental data. Forged visions of technology entrepreneurs need to be effectively realized, and corroborated by market feedback:

"...*It is better to loosen things because nobody knows the answer...give people more space to experiment...then after you figure it out, we pull in the reins and march in a particular direction.*" (Andrew Grove, Outlook magazine, 1997).

7 Super-Flexible Organizations: Orgitechting Geo-Distributed Federations

How can a dynamic organization change gears and shift its direction, yet retain a sense of cohesion, purpose and identity? How can it remain robust and resilient, when dealing with crises and downturns, and yet be agile and versatile, to harness new opportunities? How can IT and e-tools enhance organizational connectivity without diluting its social fabric? With geo-distributed global teams, how can a sense of community be achieved?

This chapter is about super-flexible organizational architectures. Like a migrating flock of birds that stay together, yet change their flight path and destination according to the seasons, business leaders face the challenge of creating stable teams and reporting relationships, yet evolving the configuration to adapt to new realities. As the business environment has become more unpredictable, business leaders are searching for organizational recipes that can drive *dynamic* execution.

Our central thesis is that in contrast to the unipolar hierarchies of the industrial age, dynamic organizations are geo-distributed, with several centers of gravity. Analogous to a "federation", each node represents a center of expertise, and makes a unique contribution. Dynamic organizations have 3 core building blocks: the "clustering dimension" or its "anatomy"; the "connective" dimension, depicting its "circulation"; and the "cohesive" dimension, reflecting its "personality". In order to organize for dynamic execution, business leaders have to monitor the three building blocks, make continuous adjustments, and clarify "federal/state" accountabilities and rules of engagement. The term "orgitechting" is used here to describe how technology and organizational design can coalesce to create dynamic enterprises.

In this chapter, we contrast the unipolar organizations of the industrial age, with emerging geo-distributed architectures. We present the "nodal model" as a diagnostic framework. We describe its three core building blocks and conclude by putting forward a few practical tips and suggestions.

7.1 Conceptual Underpinnings

The topic of organizational design has been the focus of considerable research, with wide-ranging practical implications. This is hardly surprising; organizational design is about the *execution* capability of an enterprise. It determines reporting relationships, departmental groupings, accountability patterns, and interaction processes. Fundamentally, it determines the alignment between strategy, structure, culture and talent practices. As the environment has become more volatile and unpredictable, business leaders are searching for novel recipes that can drive *dynamic* execution.

The objective is to strike a balance between generating *focus* on the one hand, and creating *synergies* on the other hand. Simply put, organizational design is about how to segment an entity into roles and positions, and aligning contributions through effective coordination. These dual goals of "segmentation" and "coordination" are termed in the literature as "differentiation" and "integration" (Lawrence & Lorsch 1967).

The dominant design paradigm of the 1960s and the 1970s, known as the "contingency" perspective, suggested that there is no one ideal configuration suitable for different organizations. The appropriate design depends on an organization's age, size, stage of development, societal conditions, growth trajectory and business diversity. A key contribution of this stream of research is the classification of the dominant organizational archetypes that address various situational contingencies. These range from the "simple", entrepreneurial form to the complex multinational corporation (Miller 1987, Mintzberg 1979). However, contingency factors alone do not explain the adoption of different organizational regimes. Notions of strategic "choice" (Child 1972) and "fit" (Miles and Snow 1984) shed light on the diffusion of various forms in different contexts. They explain why some organizational architectures are more popular and widely adopted.

Organizational scholars and practitioners have turned their attention to the transformational impact of new technologies on organizational design principles and practices. Challenges, such as interdependence, speed and velocity, disintermediation, knowledge sharing, paradox and ambiguity, and re-definition of organizational boundaries have taken center stage (Organizational Science 1999). In general, these studies highlight an over arching theme "... *the traditional function of organizational form, namely to buffer the organization from external uncertainties, is no longer the primary task ... as buffering becomes less feasible, we need to offer theories that can help organizations cope with, even embrace, uncertainties.*" (Child & McGrath 2001).

Contemporary approaches focus on emerging organizational architectures that harness change and uncertainty. This stream of work is reflected in notions such as the "horizontal" organization, modular structures, business process re-engineering, and knowledge management. The emphasis is on organizational variables that can be leveraged to live with uncertainty, and to capitalize on the benefits of technology (Galunic & Eisenhardt 2001, Hammer & Champy 1993, Nonaka & Takeuchi 1995, Quinn 1992, Sanchez & Mahoney 1996). Critical areas of research include: How to achieve flexibility as well as efficiency; What is the impact of modularization and standardization; How can charters be changed with speed and efficiency (Child 2001)

Flexible architectures are critical for execution in today's dynamic world. There is minimal time lag between decisions, actions, and outcomes; thinking and doing have to be fused together seamlessly, and developing "agile" entities has become a critical priority. The challenge is how to continuously adapt the organization to address dynamic realities, without causing constant disruption to knowledge workers' productivity and desire for stability; in other words, how can leaders create a sense of cohesion as the business priorities morph and evolve; how to leverage IT tools and

Organizational Challenges of Knowledge Enterprises   125

experiment with novel organizational recipes; how to create "sameness and standardization" across the entire organization, yet enable front-line "states" to exercise initiative and to address local realities.

Walking this tightrope is not an easy task. The remainder of this chapter describes critical organizational building blocks of dynamic entities. The intention is not to present an "ideal" recipe or a magic solution; our goal is to provide a diagnostic toolkit for assessing and monitoring an organization's capacity for *dynamic* execution.

7.2 Organizational Challenges of Knowledge Enterprises

Creating dynamic organizations presents major challenges. Business leaders have to juggle several priorities at the same time. These include the people as well as the business components. Critical people challenges include:

- Grouping experts from different functions into project teams and helping them produce under time pressures and resource constraints.
- Accommodating the diverse styles and expectations of multi-cultural employees with complex inter-personal chemistry.
- Coordinating multiple priorities, cross-functional inputs, different time zones, and distributed teams.
- Enabling teams to continuously update priorities and to make "sudden left turns".

There are also significant challenges on the business side. Consider the following complex balancing acts:

- Creating an organizational system that can sell and service existing products and services, while nurturing the capacity to innovate.
- Remaining disciplined, focused, and frugal, while enabling innovation, experimentation, exploration and learning.
- Connecting distributed teams through e-tools while ensuring the development of a community culture that can nurture emotional connectivity.
- Developing simple processes, templates and metrics, yet ensuring that they can be customized to address unique situations.
- Balancing the need for local responsiveness, in the context of a coordinated global approach.
- Re-organizing to address dynamic priorities, while minimizing potential disruption to knowledge workers' productivity.

The following comment aptly captures some of these dilemmas:
"We want an environment that enhances individual creativity but we do not want chaos ... we want people involved in decisions that affect their work and we want teamwork, yet we want our employees to have a bias toward action ... we want small

groups of dedicated workers but such groups may feel aimless or may be charging in the wrong direction with hidden agendas ... we want people to stretch to reach tough goals, so our real emphasis is on easily-measured short-term growth and profits, but we should also have time to develop our employees for the longer haul, to promote from within, to monitor the atmosphere for creativity."[1]

In view of these complex balancing acts, it is not surprising to find that there is no perfect example, silver bullet or magic solution. Every organization faces different challenges, and has its own unique "DNA". To make matters more complex, business leaders have diverse preferences, experiences and points of view. Instead of searching for the ideal recipe, we have tried to synthesize critical organizational building blocks we have observed over time. By focusing on the critical levers and by using a few illustrative examples, we hope to present a framework that can help our readers diagnose their pain points, and develop practical solutions. This is a complex task and does not lend itself to standard, "one size fits all", generic platitudes.

7.3 Contrasting Static and Dynamic Architectures

Traditional approaches to organizational design were forged during the industrial age, at a time when the business environment was relatively stable and predictable. As Chandler (1962), the pioneering business historian, observed, major re-organizations in Fortune 500 companies took time to unfold and were typically implemented every 5 to 7 years. Standardization, the idea that one approach may fit all, was the norm. This is clearly evident in the way that popular designs, such as the multi-divisional form, have cascaded in different industrial enterprises around the world. In the organizational hierarchies of the industrial age, the premise was mechanistic (Burns & Stalker 1961): first determine what needs to be done, then slot the qualified people into pre-determined roles and positions.

As depicted in Figure 19, the most critical task was segmentation: how to break up the organization into manageable departments, functions, positions, silos, and roles, and create the 'right" reporting structure. Orchestrated through the vertical hierarchy, coordination was viewed as a secondary task. The assumption was that those in senior positions have the time, the authority and the know how to coordinate the activities of those reporting to them. Corporate headquarters was viewed as the enterprise's brain, its central nervous system and control function. In a nutshell, the mechanistic designs were "unipolar" and static, with an HQ-dominated, hierarchical, single center of gravity.

[1] Internal memorandum from the Executive Vice President and co-founder of ROLM on its business philosophy, May 26, 1981.

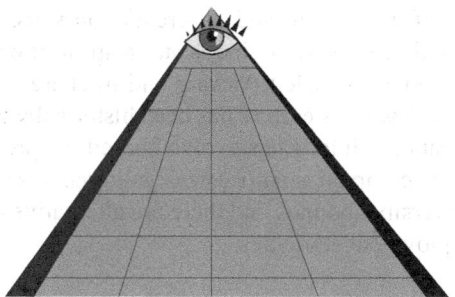 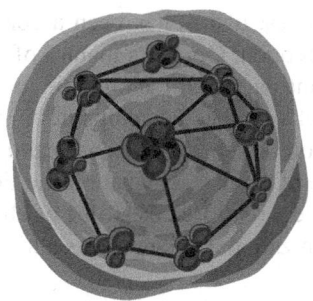

Static Model	Dynamic Model
• Stable & predictable situations	• Unpredictable/dynamic environments
• Segmentation into "silos"	• Cross-functional projects/teams
• Coordination via hierarchy	• Coordination via interaction/processes
• HQ dominated	• Geo-distributed competence centers
• Centralized decision-making	• Federal/state balances
• Ethnocentric approach	• Geocentric approach

Figure 19. Contrasting organizational models

By contrast, dynamic organizations, like living creatures, are "organic". They grow, evolve, morph and adapt. Their adaptive capacity depends on developing many "brains" that can sense and respond to front-line realities; in other words, dynamic organizations are multi-polar, with different centers of gravity. Like an orchestra, each node is a mini-brain, a focused specialist, making a distinctive contribution to the entire entity. The basic building blocks are cross-functional, cross-boundary, cross-geo teams. The teams are fluid and dynamic; their membership changes and evolves; they interact with different stakeholders, peers, superiors, outsourcers, and partners. Roles and assignments continuously evolve; members wear different hats, and perform multiple tasks. Hierarchies exist, but they reflect an individual's accountability, not just their authority and status.

The overarching task is not segmentation but coordination. Leaders have to ensure that fluid, geo-distributed teams are aligned and move in a similar direction. They have to create the "context", and ensure that team members experience "shared reality". Critical coordination tools, as is the case in orchestras, are the conductor and the music; the "music" refers to a team's purpose and intent, its charter, its behavioral norms and its core values. Apple's focus on "computing for the rest of us" has been a cornerstone of its mission and differentiation since its inception. Google's mantra of "never settle for the best" inculcates a spirit of constant innovation and continuous improvement. Hewlett Packard and Intel are both highly-respected companies in Silicon Valley. HP's culture has been historically anchored around "consensus and collaboration", Intel's has evolved based the premise of "constructive confrontation". Some companies emphasize egalitarian norms; others reinforce the value of elitism. Diversity abounds and there are alternative organizational personalities and talent deployment strategies.

7.4 Diagnostic Framework: Building Blocks of Dynamic Organizations

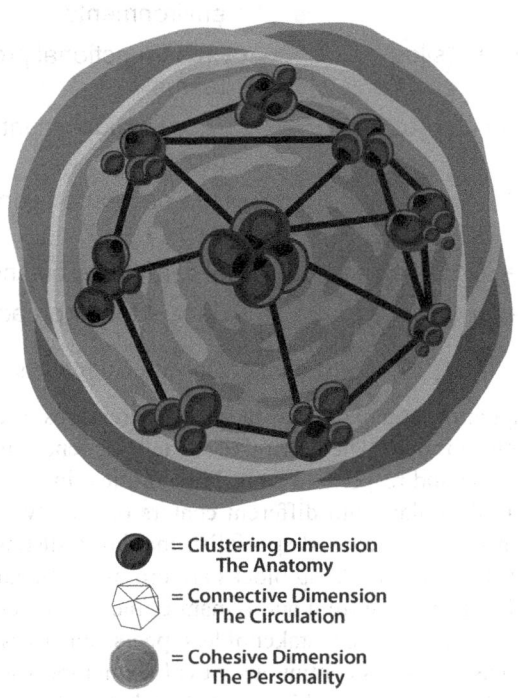

Figure 20. The nodal architecture: A diagnostic framework

As depicted in Figure 20, for diagnostic purposes, we describe dynamic architectures in terms of their 3 core building blocks: the anatomy, or the "clustering" dimension, the "circulation" or the "connective" dimension, and the personality, or the "cohesive" dimension. We use the term "nodal" architecture to aggregate the 3 levers and to provide a diagnostic framework. We argue that "circulation" is the critical coordination tool in emerging dynamic organizations. Yet it has also been the orphan child. This is hardly surprising. Since hierarchies used to perform the critical coordination task in mechanistic designs, the key task of organizational architects was shaping the "anatomy". Today executive teams have to consider all three building blocks, their mix and match, and the required trade-offs.

The clustering dimension describes the anatomy of the enterprise. It addresses the traditional challenge of segmentation: how to partition an entity into manageable work nodes, silos, projects and teams, aggregate the nodes into functions, business units, and regions, and focus the talent pool on targeted assignments. This task requires balancing the needs for speed and agility on the one hand, with stability and cohesion on the other.

The connective dimension is about the enterprise "circulation". The focus is on harnessing synergies, coordinating activities, and creating shared reality. Circulation is largely about interactions, alignment and integration: how to coordinate globally distributed teams by sharing information and know how through business processes, e-tools, key interfaces, personal networks and discussion forums.

The cohesive dimension reflects the "personality" of an enterprise. It is about providing the glue and a unique identity. A blend of the "hard" and the "soft", it is the physical, the intellectual, the financial, the cultural, and the emotional glue that keeps an enterprise together.

7.5 Organizational "Anatomy"

When we ask business leaders to describe their "organization", they typically show us their "org chart". This is hardly surprising. Org charts represent the anatomical foundation, or the skeletal framework, of an entity. They describe reporting relationships, grouping of skills, segmentation into silos, and assignment of responsibility, authority and accountability. They reflect the traditional component of "differentiation" in organizational design.

Dynamic architectures consist of distributed nodes, with different centers of expertise. We use the term "nodal architecture" to depict the notion of "multi-polarity" and distributed capabilities. "Nodes" refer to work units, departments, or project teams with focused deliverables and targeted accountabilities. This is where work is done and talent is deployed.

Several approaches are used to aggregate the nodes. The most common grouping criteria include functions, products, markets, and locations. In multi-product companies, nodes may reflect a company's core products, such as the iPod Division, the "Windows" business unit, or the 'hardware" group. Many R&D nodes are segmented based on time lines; whether they focus on current products or on future priorities; sales teams are typically organized on the basis of locations, the

Americas, Asia-Pacific, Europe, or Middle East. In view of our focus on dynamic architectures, we have found it helpful to categorize the nodes based on two critical dimensions: the frequency of change they experience; and whether they are focused on an on-going assignment or have a temporary focus, in other words the frequency with which they need to be re-organized. This leads us to categorize the nodes into base units and overlay teams.

Base units are the relatively stable component. They are the formal mechanism for grouping talent, and assigning reporting relationships. They refer to functional departments, product divisions, sales offices, manufacturing sites, and research centers. They focus on delivering targeted output and tangible expertise. They are used to compartmentalize work, provide focus, assign accountabilities, and generate a sense of shared identity.

Base units "morph" over time, depending on stage of growth, business imperatives, and preferences of executive teams. As depicted in Figure 21, start-ups organize their base units around the core contributing functions. These include engineering and product development during the early "seed" stage, augmented by other functions, including sales, marketing, and product management, after the first prototype is developed.

More complex functional units are formed as a firm grows and diversifies its product portfolio and market coverage. Sales units, for example, are often segmented into domestic and international sales, or departmentalized on the basis of different customer segments, key accounts, and regional groupings. R&D units are typically segmented into core technologies and application areas, or on the basis of different product units.

Successful firms rapidly outgrow functional base units. The combined pressures of headcount growth and the introduction of new products and services make it necessary to divide the organization into smaller, more focused units. The adopted "divisional" form largely depends on the inter-dependencies between different product families and market segments. These are categorized into "serial", "reciprocal", "pooled', and "multi-dimensional" interdependencies. In view of the close interdependence between technology products, many high tech companies have centralized R&D, supply chain, and operations, and segment the sales function into geographies or industry groups. Support units, including finance, HR, IT and marketing communications, are typically consolidated to minimize duplication; although specialized support-staff are deployed in the divisions as key "liaisons" and interfaces.

As a firm evolves and matures, "groups" and "sectors" are formed based on aggregated categories of product lines, market segments, technologies, or geographies. These groups are the focal points for coordination, while operating units focus on managing day-to-day activities. It should be noted that while these trends represent broad patterns we have observed, the evolution of base units is not necessarily sequential. Some may evolve from functional to group forms; others may revert back to a functional form after a major inflection point, such as a financial crisis, a change of senior management, or a dramatic re-structuring of the business portfolio.

Choosing a segmentation strategy depends on several factors: including growth potential, business interdependencies, critical pain points, leaders' preferences, and industry success recipes. The key point to note is that base units are typically a blend of functional and product clusters, market segments and geographic units. Typically, there is a need to address different trade-offs leading to the formation of multiple reporting lines and complex "matrix" structures. This reporting complexity can inevitably lead to organizational rigidity and inflexibility.

A related challenge is to strike a dynamic balance between stability on the one hand, and flexibility on the other. Business leaders have to be careful about the timing and the frequency of re-organizations: when does it make sense to re-organize the base units; when is it less disruptive to use a project team and avoid a major re-organization.

This balancing act is difficult to achieve. On the one hand, business leaders rely on organizational levers to execute the business strategy. On the other hand, frequent re-organizations can be highly disruptive; they impact knowledge workers' morale and productivity. One option is to view base units as a foundational platform that can provide stability and resilience. Other mechanisms can be used to address the challenge of innovation, and speed. This is where overlay teams can be leveraged. They represent the flexible arm or the rapid deployment capability. They can be used to focus on critical assignments without disrupting the base units.

132 Super-Flexible Organizations: Orgitechting Geo-Distributed Federations

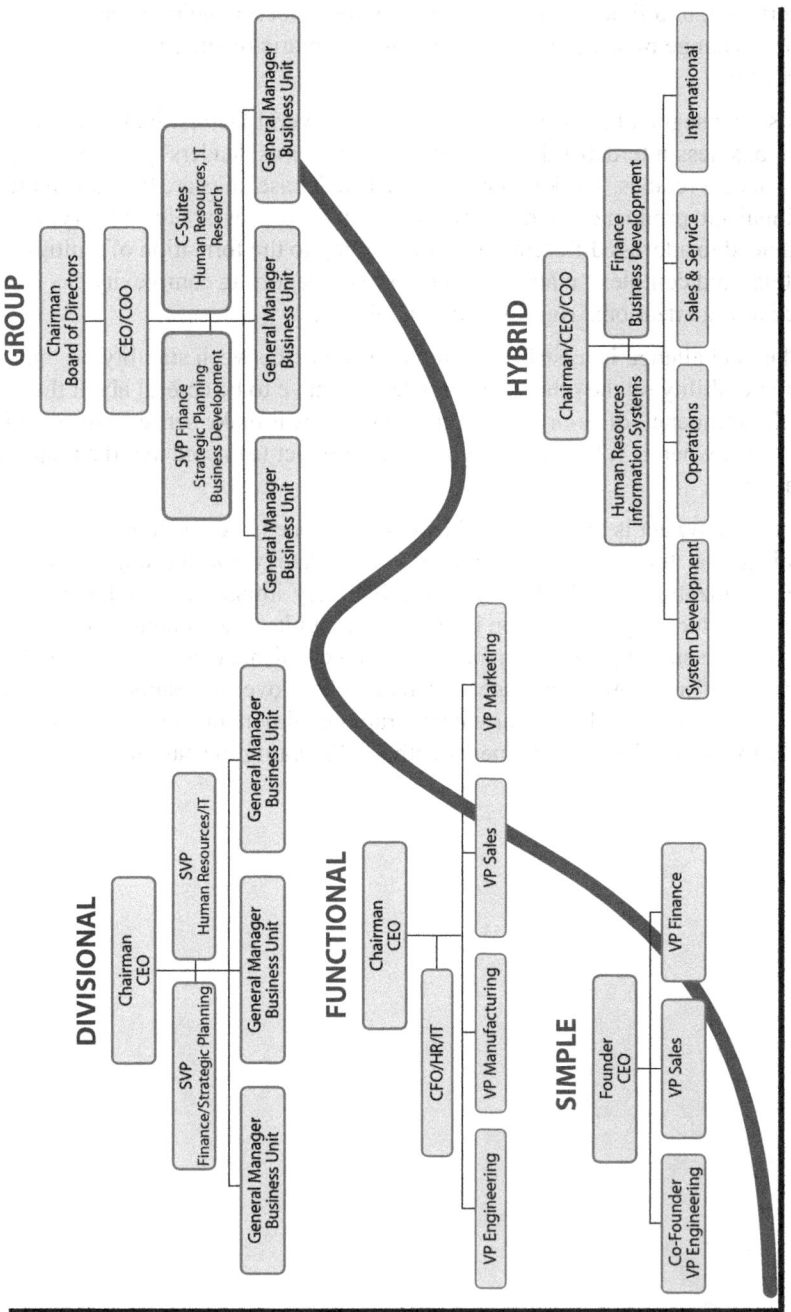

Figure 21. Evolution of the "anatomy" or "base" structure in high tech companies

Overlay teams can be deployed when launching a cross-silo initiatives, such as new product development or entry into a new market. A complementary blend of knowledge-workers can be pooled together at short notice, put to work on new assignments, and disbanded once their task has been accomplished. In some cases, project teams evolve and become the foundation of a new base unit, depending on critical mass and business scope. Consider the reflections of a senior executive of a network storage company:

"We have a functional organization ... it is the most simple from a line of sight perspective ... as our products become more complex and we become geographically dispersed, it starts to fall apart ... so we started what we call virtual business units...they don't own any people ... there'll be a virtual CEO who's responsible for bringing together cross-functional teams ... let's take the example of our CDBU (content delivery business unit) ... it actually has three people and drives fairly significant revenue ... the various functional teams participate as members of both, the functional unit as well as the CDBU."

A complicating factor is that base units and overlay teams are globally distributed, posing additional coordination challenges. This is hardly surprising; high tech companies have to leverage talent pools irrespective of their location. In addition, they have to be "forward deployed" and close to customers, to respond to requests and to customize products and solutions. The resulting organizational model is a complex and intricate matrix, with silos, teams, projects, and departments interacting together in, as one executive put it, a "bowl of spaghetti or at best, a blended fruit salad".

For example, a financial software company set up two units, staffed by technical domain experts and local banking experts, to address the complex needs of its European customers:

"... we wanted our global nodes of competence in close proximity to one another ... so in Europe, we had teams of technical and domain experts in London ... augmented by financial and market experts in various local offices ..., so we could leverage our technical experts on an as-needed basis, and customize solutions for our banking clients out of our local offices in Paris, Milan and Frankfurt ... after all these people knew about the French, the Italian or the German banking conventions."[2]

VeriFone, the pioneer in transaction automation systems, based its global R&D centers in Bangalore and Paris in the 1980s because of the region's expertise in Unix programming and smart card technology. Many disk drive companies set up their procurement and sourcing units in Singapore due to the country's crossroads location and proximity to many sub-system providers.

Given the complex interdependencies that exist in knowledge enterprises, how do you make the anatomy "super-flexible"? How do business leaders balance the need to "withstand" with the imperative to "transform"? The challenge is one of

---

[2] Personal interview with the co-founder and CEO of a financial software company.

timing and frequency: when to use short-term measures, such as project teams, task forces, or virtual business units to focus on new assignments, and when the shift is significant enough to justify a fundamental re-organization of the base structure. Temporary overlays minimize disruption and reduce the de-stabilizing impact of re-organizations. However, project teams need clear charters, focused accountabilities, and clear milestones. Ambiguous charters and accountability "grey zones" often lead to considerable friction, infighting, rigidity and complexity.

7.6 Organizational "Circulation"

Having the right anatomical foundation is necessary but not sufficient. In dynamic settings, there is a critical need for "horizontal" alignment to augment the vertical anatomy. Otherwise, each node may march to its own tune. We suggest horizontal alignment is analogous to enterprise "circulation". Different modes of interaction and information exchange can be used to communicate, coordinate, cross-pollinate and share know how among globally distributed teams. The challenge is summed up in the following comment:

"We like the idea of small, decentralized units with focused accountability...but our products have to play together...our customers buy an integrated system...there is a major element of success that depends on coordination and close cooperation between the units."[3]

Managing reciprocal interdependencies is a major determinant of, and a potential barrier to, organizational flexibility. R&D needs the input of marketing and product management; sales teams need regular input from R&D, service, and operations. Even in start-ups, there are clear interdependencies between engineering and marketing, or operations and sales. While interdependencies can produce synergies, they can also generate "traffic jams" and friction points, especially at "busy" intersections.

As depicted in Figure 22, circulation tools are a blend of the virtual, the organizational, and the personal, spanning e-tools, business processes, cross-silo forums, cross-pollinators and hubs, C suite executives, and personal networks.

---

[3] Personal interview with the co-founder and executive vice president of a telecommunications company.

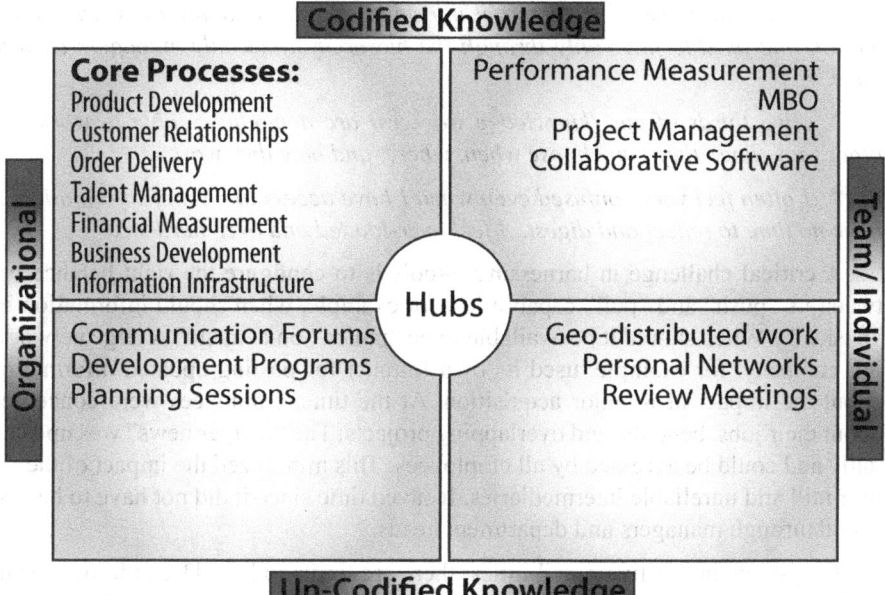

Figure 22. The circulation: Different types of connective tools

e-tools: IT systems have transformed the administrative backbone and the communication infrastructure of business enterprises. In the process, they have also created new organizational challenges. IT's contribution to organizational effectiveness is the codification, aggregation and diffusion of information. e-tools facilitate the deployment of distributed organizations and reliance on virtual teams that operate across time zones, geographies, hierarchies, and enterprise boundaries.

Innovative software, Internet products, and social networking sites have made it possible for nomadic teams to work at any time, from any location. They have made it possible to create inter-connected global entities; like relay teams, tasks can be passed on over different time zones. By means of knowledge management, CRM and other tools, critical information can be distributed, reducing the size of the physical center. Social networking tools have provided real-time broadcast capabilities, and given access to "unfiltered" information. In the process, proliferation of e-tools has also led to information overload and information "toxicity".[4] Information has to be sorted, scanned, absorbed and digested. Consider the following comments on the contribution and the impact of IT from three different perspectives:

---

[4] High technology firms are typically early adopters of new technologies. Many firms are the primary sites for testing their own products, and often serve as beta-test sites for other technology firms.

"...(The real value of IT) is to get information to those doing the work...Information that used to filter only through the hierarchy...that only managers used to have." [5]

"...Two thirds of our (knowledge workers) are nomadic ... able to work any place, any time...they can choose when, where, and how they work." [6]

"...I often feel very confused even when I have access to a lot of information...I have no time to reflect and digest...I feel over-loaded and over-burdened." [7]

A critical challenge in harnessing e-tools is to configure the right balance between its "push" and "pull" capabilities; for example, when should information be "pushed"? When should it be available to be "pulled" on demand? A large networking company, for example, used its own Intranet for posting updated information about the impact of a major acquisition. At the time, employees were concerned about their jobs, benefits, and overlapping projects. The "merger news" was updated daily and could be accessed by all employees. This minimized the impact of the rumor mill and unreliable intermediaries. It saved time since it did not have to be cascaded through managers and department heads.

Despite its innovative possibilities, there are limits to how IT can bridge teams and create effective interactions. For example, the experience of many virtual teams indicates that e-mail is a poor communication tool for building trust, keeping focused accountability, communicating emotionally-charged material, brain-storming, disciplining non-performers, and orienting new employees into the culture. On the other hand, if used effectively, it can be efficient, inexpensive, and help keep "everyone on the same page". The real challenge is to devise customized protocols that en-courage the use of e-tools for communicating "codified" information, while freeing up "face time" for creative dialogue, conflict resolution, and nurturing trust relationships.[8]

Business Processes: IT systems have added a horizontal dimension to the traditional vertical hierarchy. From an organizational standpoint, this impact has been clearly felt in the design, configuration and use of business processes that transcend functional and product silos. They encompass critical activities, including:

- Processes that impact the design, development, production and delivery of products and services, including interaction with vendors and partners. Examples include product development, project management, order entry, product manufacturing, order delivery, and supply chain management.

---

[5] Personal interview with the founder & CEO of a software company.

[6] Personal interview with the IT manager of a networking company.

[7] Personal interview with a project manager in a large technology company.

[8] Examples of codified information include electronic routing of forms, purchasing and ordering supplies, tracking sales proposals and leads, communicating job postings, project status updates, budget templates, and purchase requisition systems.

- Processes that impact the search for, transactions with, and follow-up interactions with customers; examples, include lead generation, lead screening & monitoring, transaction processing, helpdesk, and customer service.
- Processes that impact the measurement and monitoring of financial performance and the allocation of resources, including planning and budgeting, tracking financial results, and consolidating financial information.
- Processes used to manage and compensate knowledge workers during various stages of the employment life cycle. Related sub-processes include talent recruitment (including interview notes and offer letters) talent deployment (such as job postings), training & education (including course catalogues, registration and administration, and content modules), performance and compensation management (such as performance rating, assessing fixed and variable compensation ratios, and external benchmarking) and workforce planning (including "what if" scenarios).
- Processes that impact business development, including search for partnership and acquisition candidates, and integrating new acquisitions. As discussed in chapter 5, companies, such as Cisco, well-known for adopting a growth by acquisition strategy, have popularized the use of acquisition integration processes.

Effective business processes can link vertical silos and keep "everyone on the same page". As depicted in Figure 15, they can break down the silo mentality, facilitate cross-pollination of ideas, and provide operational focus. The challenge is two-fold: first, to ensure that core processes are continuously updated and remain relevant and ever-green; second, to ensure that they are configured around simple templates that can be easily understood, internalized and accessed by multi-cultural and multi-functional stakeholders.

138   Super-Flexible Organizations: Orgitechting Geo-Distributed Federations

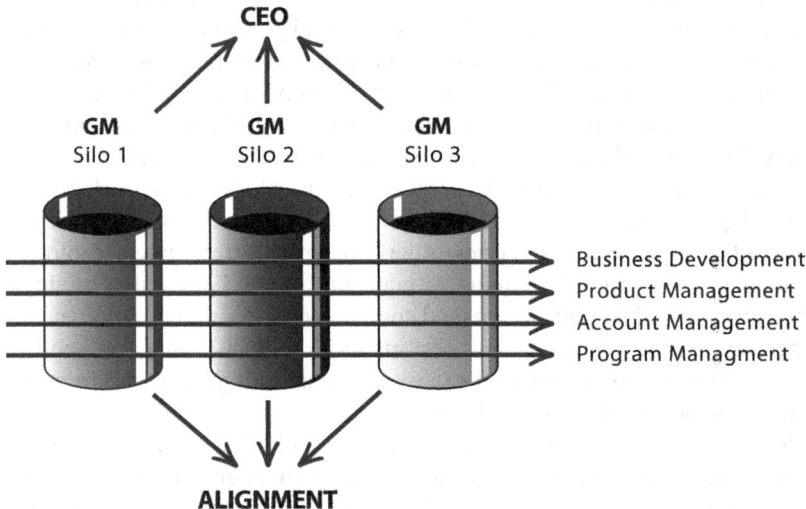

Figure 23. Connecting silos: Horizontal 'circulation'

Cross-Silo Forums: Connectivity is not just about IT-enabled interactions and business processes. Although useful for codifying and cascading know-how, e-tools do not yet capture the spontaneous, the creative, and the emotional dimensions of human interaction. This is where face-to-face forums can be leveraged. By bringing together the leaders, the peers, and the front-liners in appropriate settings, forums can be used to nurture group dialogue, and to provide opportunities for experience sharing and building relationships of trust.

Many technology companies use forums to create shared reality and to break down the silo mentality. They rely on strategy offsites to reflect on the business trajectory. They use operating reviews to synchronize actions plans, and they leverage on-boarding programs to set clear expectations at the outset of the employment relationship.

In recent years, it has become popular to use "leaders as teachers" in order to capture and disseminate tacit know how. A number of established technology companies, such as Intel, have used this approach for over twenty years in their orientation and development programs. GE, under Welch's leadership, further popularized the idea, leveraging it as an enterprise transformation tool. The objective is to spell out "what we do and how we do things around here" and to create opportunities for risk-free dialogue.

Cross-Pollinators: Geo-distributed organizations have many intersection points. Intersection points refer to zones of interdependence where stakeholders' interests converge. This is where cross-pollinators can be positioned and leveraged.

They transcend silos, sit at critical intersections, and can be important sources of alignment and connectivity.

Product management is a clear example of organizational cross-pollination; it is where engineering, marketing, sales, operations, finance and supply chain coalesce to launch a new product or a service. A "connective" challenge is to ensure that critical handoff points can be managed to ensure that traffic can flow smoothly. This is a major pain point for many companies that have complex interdependencies and have developed matrix structures. R&D hands off to marketing; marketing and operations have to be aligned and both need to ensure that they can be synchronized with sales and service. In multi-product, multi-business companies, the challenge is even greater since there are many intersections, entailing different silos and diverse stakeholders.

To further complicate matters, critical interfaces have to be managed with speed and agility. There is no time to assign blame or to abdicate responsibility to others. Words, such as "accountability" and "deliverable" are critical in the organizational vocabulary. The deliverable may have to be produced as a result of extensive coordination with different stakeholders, many of whom may work outside the authority zone of the accountable team. The challenge is to exercise influence without authority, and to synthesize the contributions of others in a way that can lead to effective action.

Product management also highlights the importance of "influence without authority" in cross-pollinator roles. Consider the following comments: *"Product management is about thinking on your feet, staying one step ahead, and being able to project yourself in the minds of colleagues and customers."* Without engineers, nothing would get built; without sales people, nothing is sold; without designers, the product won't look good, but without product managers, everyone will simply fill out the gaps; in the long run, a great product manager can make the difference between winning and losing, but you have to prove it and earn everyone's respect."

Other examples of cross-pollinators are project leaders, account managers, or at a strategic altitude, "C suite executives". For example, a number of software companies have set up the position of "chief solutions officer". The goal is to offer integrated, customized solutions, instead of standard, modular products. These executives are the focal point for strategizing an overall approach, seeking and integrating different functional inputs, and monitoring the progress made towards implementation.

Similarly, at an operational altitude, account managers have to pull together internal resources needed to address complex customer requirements. Product managers sit at the intersection between marketing and engineering. They role is to ensure that different technical and customer requirements are considered in designing and delivering a new product. C-suite executives, account managers, project managers and product managers are examples of 'cross-pollinators" and "hubs". As depicted in Figure 24, they are the focal point for delivering integrated solutions.

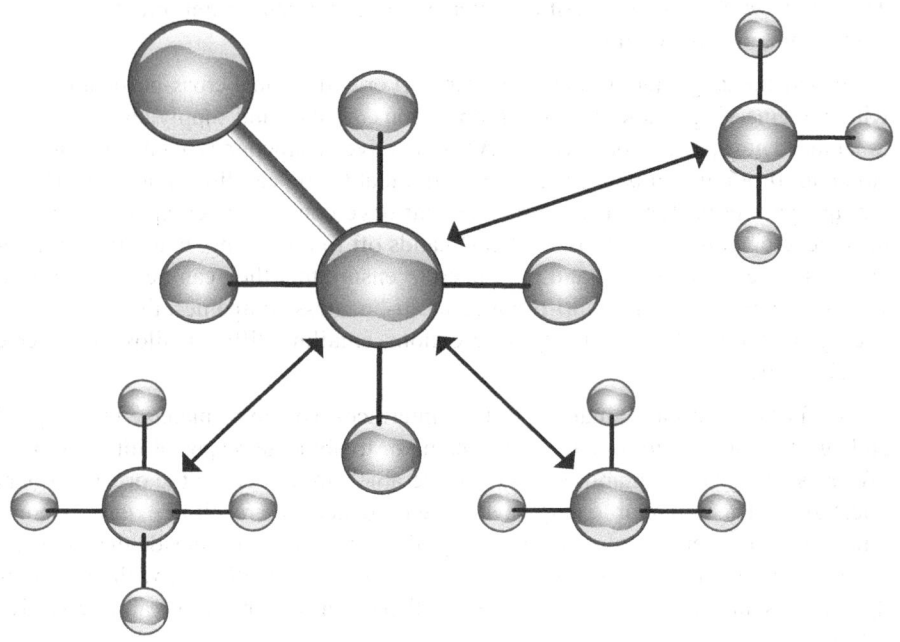

Figure 24. Cross-pollinators and hubs

The challenge is to ensure that those in hub roles have the competence to do the job, and the inter-personal and communication skills that enable them to interact with diverse stakeholders. *"A leader others want to follow, with a gentle style, yet firm when needed".. "those who don't succeed are ego-driven and wave their credentials"*.. The importance of emotional intelligence and strong inter-personal skills is succinctly summed up in the reflections of the CEO of a software company:

"An interesting note is the way that we selected our CIO (Chief information officer) ... who did not grow up through the classic IT organization ... her skill-set was in customer service ... so we chose the diplomatic elements ... to help our various functional organizations come together ... over deep technical experience ... and it has worked very well in our case."

Cross-pollinators can be either enabling catalysts, or major bottlenecks. Sitting at critical intersections, they manage diverse stakeholders and synthesize real-time information. The on-going challenge is to monitor organizational "hot spots" before they turn into traffic jams, and to select credible individuals, with strong influencing skills, to ensure smooth traffic flow.

7.7 Organizational "Personality"

Geo-distributed organizations need some kind of "glue" to bind together the different nodes. The goal is to provide cohesion and a distinctive identity. Otherwise the organization becomes like a bazaar, with each node marching to its own tune. This "cohesive" dimension reflects the "personality" of an enterprise. On the one hand, it is about linking the values and the expectations of knowledge workers to the broader organizational context and business drivers. On the other hand, it is about how external stakeholders view the enterprise and perceive its brand and identity. While financial controls provide the "hard" control glue, core values & talent practices, provide the motivational "soft glue". Cohesive tools are:
- Guiding principles that portray a distinctive organizational personality, and promote a unique talent brand and identity.
- Anchors of stability that can instill resilience during challenging times.
- Leadership pillars that impact daily behaviors; they can be reinforced through effective role-modeling and incentive systems.

Consider the comments of the CEO of a software company on the importance of clear cultural principles:

"...One of our unwritten cultural tenets is that everyone's a sales and support person...and that we should use our own products ... in putting our value tenets together, we wanted to think about "what kind of a company do we want to work for" ...the emphasis is on the company, not the management we even do report cards on how the whole company is living up to its cultural tenets".[9]

Clear values give a distributed global entity a sense of identity and tie together its multi-cultural workforce. This attribute is especially critical since many technology firms generate a significant portion of their sales outside their home base, and have a large population of multi-cultural employees:[10]

"...When you open an office several thousand miles away, it is difficult to export the culture...(so) we make sure that our new employees spend a large part of their time, early on, here at the home base, so they can really experience, feel, and live our culture, and not just read about it."[11]

---

[9] Personal interview with the founder & CEO of a software company.

[10] Successful technology firms develop cultural mindsets that incorporate diverse assumptions and premises. This means balancing core values, reflecting the "home" culture, while accommodating the multi-cultural viewpoints of global customers, employees, and competitors. Several mechanisms are used to blend the two together; These include composition of employees and senior executive teams, short-term sabbaticals to projects outside the "home" base, re-deployment opportunities, real time global communication forums, and global account management systems.

[11] Personal interview with the vice president of worldwide sales of a software company.

The CEO and executive team of a young semiconductor company, for example, use the theme of "intellectual honesty" as a bedrock corporate value. Every employee is expected to be honest in communicating business realities. The message conveyed is that there are no "sacred cows"; you can raise contrarian points of view, as long as you have the factual evidence to support the assertion:

"... we are an intellectually honest company and share facts across the board ... our team is not insecure or arrogant ... so we can talk about facts ... those we like and those that we don't."[12]

The company operates in the US, Germany, Taiwan, Korea, and Japan. The theme of "intellectual honesty" gives its multi-cultural knowledge workers a common communication protocol. It clarifies the corporate "rule of the game" and makes it easier to move between different units. However, it is important to build flexibility in implementing core values. In the US, for example, "intellectual honesty" may mean heated debate and frank exchange of ideas. In Japan, it may be used in one/one conversations instead of in group discussions.

As previous studies have shown, founders play a decisive role in shaping a company's core values during its formative years. Often, they provide the genetic DNA or the cultural imprint of an enterprise (Baron & Hannan 2002, Chatman & Cha 2003). Cultural norms can be decisive in shaping talent practices. For example, Google's core value of "encouraging creativity" is reinforced by its corporate policy that allows engineers to spend up to 20% of their time on a project of their choice; their notion of "data drives decisions" means that almost every decision, including hiring decisions, are based on some form of quantitative analysis (in the case of new hires, GPA scores are used to partly assess the candidates).

While core values and behavioral norms can be a powerful engagement, socialization and control tool, they can also make an organization rigid and inflexible. To minimize rigidity, cultural norms should be reviewed at critical inflection points. The pulse has to be taken to ensure that the organizational personality is in synch with emerging business realities. It is not useful to emphasize the importance of consensus-based decision-making, for example, if business realities demand decisive action and rapid execution.

Our observations point to four categories of talent practices that reflect an organization's personality:

Screening & recruiting for "fit": The productivity of knowledge workers depends on the appropriate fit between personal values, expectations, and competencies and the organization's context, values, and business focus. A knowledge worker who values consensus, for example, may not fit into a confrontational environment. Someone who is interested in work/life balance, may not be the right fit for a hard-

---

[12] Personal interview with the founder and CEO of a semiconductor company.

driving start-up. An expert specialist, who may be uncomfortable taking on assignments outside his or her core expertise, may not fit into an environment where employees are expected to wear different hats and switch between assignments at short notice. Values "fit" can be best assessed during the initial recruiting phase, when expectations on both sides have yet to be set. Popular approaches include employee referral programs, extensive interviews over extended time-frames, internships, consulting assignments, and targeted recruiting.

Performance management and compensation systems: A related challenge is to ensure that desired values can be reinforced through compensation and performance management systems. If "intellectual honesty" is the desired norm, it has to be reinforced through the feedback process. Those who communicate "bad news" should be recognized and rewarded. If customer service is the norm, it has to be reflected in the reward system and promotion criteria. We have seen some variation in the way that Silicon Valley companies use performance management and compensation systems. Some assume that effective screening during the early recruiting cycle, or referrals from "reliable sources who know us", or alignment through compensation, provide sufficient reinforcement. Others have rigorous performance management systems, with forced rankings built into the cycle.

The selected approach depends on the size of the organization, the attitude of its leaders, and its stage of development. Start-ups, for example, tend to rely on informal screening and the ownership structure to promote alignment. Established companies rely on formal compensation and performance management tools. Whatever the context, the challenge is to ensure that there is a clear "line of sight" between an individual's performance and behavior, and the organization's desired values and cultural norms.

Visible signals: In fast-moving domains, people pay attention to signals they can quickly scan and readily observe. Visible signals can be a powerful tool to reinforce desired behaviors. Many companies use symbols and signals, intentionally and unintentionally, to convey their personality and to communicate their core values. For example, HP and Intel have historically underscored their egalitarian norms by using open-plan offices and same-size cubicles. In many companies, employees, regardless of rank and position, have similar travel privileges.

Visible signals apply to other daily routines. The founder of a network server company wanted to promote the critical importance of responsive customer service. He used the executive teams' business cards as a visible signal to convey the message. Every executive officer had his/her home phone number printed on their business cards. The rationale was to give customers an opportunity to contact them at any time. The CEO even set up a red phone as the "hotline" in his office, so he could be contacted directly. The employee surveys indicated that the "golden rule" of customer responsiveness, symbolized by the "red phone", was not just a platitude. The fact that the CEO and the top team were willing to "walk the talk" reinforced the desired value in a visible way.

Workplace design: Symbolic norms can also be conveyed through workplace design. Facilities' layout can convey egalitarian sentiments or reinforce hierarchical norms. They can highlight the importance of group interaction or individual contribution. They can signal transparency versus secrecy. If aligned with behavioral norms, and business success factors, workplace design can create a sense of community, and facilitate the development of trust. Attention has also focused on how physical and virtual spaces should be aligned to bring about "convergent" architecture (Huang 2001).

During an encounter between senior executives from a European multi-national and a young knowledge worker from Silicon Valley, the conversation turned to whether cultural norms had a real impact on daily behaviors and perceptions. The knowledge worker was asked whether the stated culture of "fairness and egalitarianism", promoted by her company, was reinforced by the leaders' daily actions. The response was immediate: *"when you come and visit our campus (you'll notice that).... the CEO's cubicle is exactly the same size as mine and he doesn't have any windows either"*. Consider the campus layout of a global company in Menlo Park, California. Like many others in Silicon Valley, it was designed to facilitate group collaboration and informal interaction. A key design feature is a central thoroughfare, analogous to "downtown" or "main street", with office complexes built around it. This is viewed as a central artery for the entire campus community. Knowledge workers from different departments "bump" into each other as a matter of course. The staircases are wider than normal to allow for team conversations. White boards are placed along the corridors so people can be spontaneous and share their creative thoughts. Common spaces take center-stage, while individual cubicles are less attractive.

In summary, the cohesive dimension is critical in organizational design. It can instill bedrock values, provide "sameness", and give emotional cohesion in a distributed organization. It can disseminate an entity's core DNA. It can be used to screen and select new talent; it can project a distinctive talent brand for recruiting and retaining knowledge workers. The key challenge is to "figure out what has to be the same so that everything else can be different." In other words, it is important to clarify and communicate the non-negotiable behavioral norms that every organizational citizen is expected to live by, and to reinforce these through the appropriate talent practices and symbolic norms.

7.8. Illustrative Case Study

This section describes a case vignette to illustrate the three organizational design levers of anatomy, circulation and personality. While the company in question is highly successful, the vignette should be viewed as "food for thought", rather than as "best practice". It shows the three building blocks of at work. In this example, the "circulation" is at the heart of the company's approach to organizational design.

ABC is a large public company in the network storage business. Founded in 1991, it has 7000 employees, several development centers, and operates in more than 60 countries. It was spun off from another Silicon Valley company that was a pioneer in the file-server business.

The anatomy: It has a classic functional structure and makes extensive use of temporary teams, projects, and task forces to focus on new opportunities. Various approaches are used to address coordination bottlenecks. These include reliance on virtual business units (that don't own many people, but address new opportunities, and typically drive significant revenue), monthly cross-functional meetings of every team, cross-functional product reviews, and annual thematic meeting of its top 100 executives. Its leaders characterize their organization as "networked silos" and use the term in their internal communication and orientation programs.

The circulation: In addition to conventional meetings, the company relies on several virtual meetings, including a quarterly "all hands" meetings with the entire employee base around the world. The objective is to keep "everyone on the same page" and update them on important trends that impact the business. This demonstrates how e-tools can be used to link up distributed units and provide flexibility in real-time communication.

The program entails live quarterly broadcasts by the senior executive team, discussing new priorities and major achievements in order to "inform, align, and focus". Using its own technology and "content delivery network", the goal is to "strengthen communication and build bridges." The broadcast connects the corporate HQ, four remote development sites, and 33 sales and customer service offices around the world. Live broadcasts are also recorded for those who are unable to join in. They are segmented into bite-sized segments, each lasting less than 2 minutes, Remote locations have their own meetings, before and after the live broadcast, and discuss the implications for their function and geography.

ABC's VP of Product Development & East Coast Operations reflected on the value of live broadcasts: *"we have acquired a number of companies here and you want these new employees to be successful, to feel connected, and to be fully integrated ... I wasn't always effective when I tried to explain our culture to them. But after watching a few streamed "all hands" meetings, they started to get it. Our culture became real and understandable to them."*

The point of this case is that ABC leveraged the potential of new technology to create a novel form of connectivity; one that creates a neighborhood feel in a distributed entity; one that can convey a key message, while recognizing the significance of inclusion; one that can be used offensively, to launch new products, and defensively, to emphasize the need for expense cuts:

In response to the general economic downturn, the company called on its employees to exercise restraint in discretionary spending *"... we launched the* campaign by sending an e-mail, with links to a VOD (video on demand-modular segments of a live broadcast linked to specific topics and themes) by our CEO, which enabled us to come together quickly as a company. It was as though someone had turned off a faucet. Discretionary spending simply stopped." The money saved contributed significantly to the company's financial health. "To reinforce the message, we followed up with monthly VODs from other executives. As companies grow, they tend to lose agility, but this kind of communication can restore it."

The personality: Like many start-ups, the founding team had codified their core values early on, depicting its desired "personality" and the kind of entity we wanted to build. "... *Our culture can be summed up as flexible and light on its feet. Our original tagline was "fast, simple, and reliable". We keep repeating these words all the time and judge everything we do based on them ... these are more than just aspirations written on a piece of paper ... we actually use them to structure the organization and to measure our performance ... so, for example, fast is measured in terms of how quickly we close our books, get the product out, and get the stock options out to our employees.*"

7.9 Implementation Guidelines

What does it take to create a dynamic, geo-distributed architecture? What may be a few practical starting points? How can leadership teams keep the big picture in mind, but implement in bite-sized steps? Our observations highlight the importance of several critical actions. These include:
- Modifying the role of corporate headquarters
- Developing clear and actionable "federal" mandates
- Placing effective cross-pollinators and hubs at major intersections
- Improving organizational 'circulation" and the connective component

Visiting executives to Silicon Valley ask us a common question: Who or what is the center of power in Silicon Valley? Who was in charge of creating the "grand-plan" that led to the rise of the "Valley"? They expect the answer to be the venture capital community. After all, they provide the risk capital, and have the power to make or break a new venture. However, as indicated in chapter 3, this is clearly not the case. While the venture community is an important component of the ecosystem in "hatching" and scaling new ventures, it needs the contribution of others; the universities and research laboratories, the support infrastructure of specialists, and above all, the passion, creativity and dedication of entrepreneurial knowledge workers.

The implication for established enterprises is clear. To create a super-flexible organization, they need to distribute the enterprise's brainpower by modifying the role of corporate headquarters. Corporate units should be re-organized along modular lines, with differentiated portfolios of tasks and accountabilities. This transformation process is already underway in many global companies. It has been driven by the need to cut costs, reduce overhead expenses, provide flexibility, and create financial transparency. The pace of change is further accelerated as many administrative functions, historically undertaken by corporate staff, have been automated and embedded in IT systems.

Business entities clearly need corporate functions to provide control, consistency and uniformity. However, in today's dynamic environment, corporate staff should behave, not as omnipotent rulers, but as accountable colleagues, with clear roles and success metrics. *Critical success factors include clarity around value-added deliverables, roles and accountabilities, interaction rules, "taxation" policies, and performance metrics.* The experiences of established firms in Silicon Valley indicate that corporate staff have to undertake several tasks, often in parallel. As depicted in Figure 21, these include:

- The compliance, or the "enforcer" role, focusing on activities that are mandated by law and that ensure effective governance; examples include investor relations and corporate audit.
- The business driver, or the "director" role, emphasizing activities that are linked to the execution of selected business initiatives. Examples vary, depending on the company in question. If "growth-by-acquisition", is the preferred strategy, as was the case at Cisco for more than two decades, the business development team may wear the "director" hat; if talent deployment is of critical concern, as was the case at GE under Jack Welch, it may include performance assessment, executive compensation, and succession planning. In many energy and engineering companies, the director role involves the health and safety function.
- The "service provider" role, emphasizing activities that can be leveraged across the entire organization. The objective is to minimize duplication, reduce overhead costs, and provide centers of competence for delivering critical services. Examples include business services, talent recruitment, facilities management, and IT services.
- The "cross-pollinator" role, focusing on two related tasks; first, that of a catalyst for sharing best practices, leveraging common interests and synthesizing complementary capabilities. Examples include workforce mobility and talent deployment; second, creating the "glue" to tie together the enterprise community, and to develop a distinctive 'brand" identity. Examples include corporate communication, brand management and leadership development.

However, these categories are broad indicators, and should not be viewed as rigid segmentation criteria. They should be used as food for thought and as a framework for discussion. As is the case with 'phenotype plasticity" in evolutionary biology and discussed in chapter 2, every company is unique. It has its own DNA, executive pre-dispositions, industry practices, cultural norms, and administrative legacy. To make matters more complicated, every corporate function may fulfill a number of these roles concurrently. For example, HR fulfills an enforcement role (ensuring compliance with hiring and firing practices in accordance with different legal frameworks), a "director role (reflected in executive compensation and performance assessment), a cross-pollinator role (in orchestrating leadership development), and a service provider role (in recruiting talent).

The point to note is that corporate functions should help orchestrate the strategic vision, develop the organizational infrastructure, and create the cultural glue that can leverage synergies, and ensure unity of mission and purpose. However, these tasks should be undertaken *together with the line units, not dictated to them.* As corporate teams consider their future direction, they should think about their roles and accountabilities, but more importantly, they should consider behavioral norms and interaction ground rules. *It is not just what they do, but how they interact with other units, that is the critical success factor.*

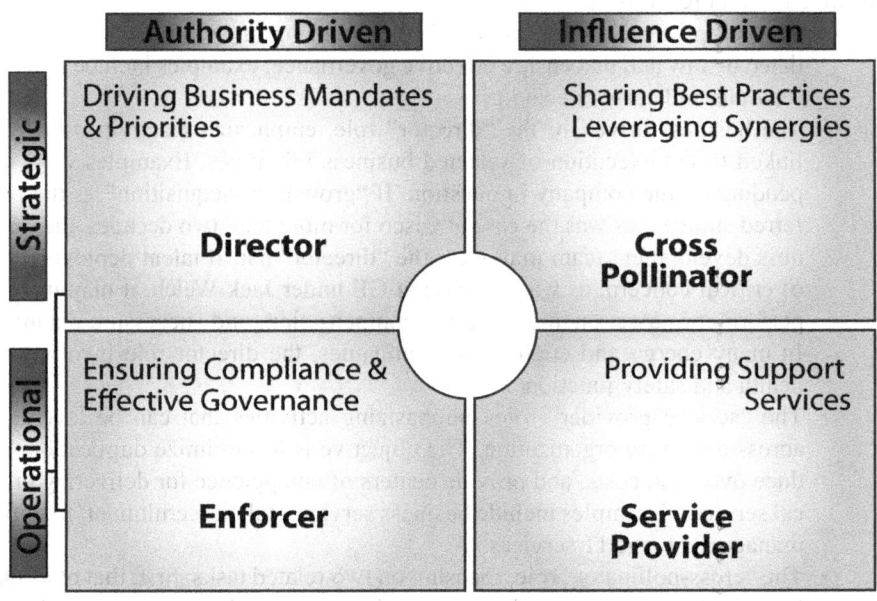

Figure 25. Differentiated task portfolio for corporate/ HQ functions

Apart from developing a differentiated task portfolio, it is also important to staff corporate units by blending together complementary capabilities. Experienced line operators can inject a front-line, business perspective, while functional experts can provide specialist know how. A global engineering company, for example, appoints experienced line managers to head up its corporate HR function for up to three years. Functional HR specialists augment the business perspective by providing expert input on staffing, compensation, succession planning, relocation, and leadership development. While line executives move on to other assignments, functional specialists stay with the function and provide a sense of continuity.

A related challenge is to ensure that discussion forums are periodically set up to address contentious issues between lines managers and corporate staff. Critical topics include "federal rules", "corporate processes" and "tax policies". Sources of corporate funding and allocation of overhead expenses continue to generate tension in many companies. These topics occupy a great deal of executive time and mindshare. The tension can be partly addressed by setting up discussion forums, and by providing factual transparency around concrete deliverables and resource utilization.

A second critical step in implementing geo-distributed architectures is to think in terms of "trade-offs" rather than "either/or" binary choices. For example, traditional structures have been viewed as either centralized, with tight central control, or decentralized, leaving line managers a great deal of autonomy. Designing a geo-distributed architecture is less about centralization/decentralization and more about clarifying "federal/state" balances. Federal mandates are "non-negotiable" groundrules that apply to every citizen. "what has to be the same across all the units, so that everything else can be locally customized." They may address core values and behavioral norms, such as ethics and integrity. They may focus on financial targets, or on strategic imperatives, such as GE's mandate that "every business has to be a #1 or a #2 player in its market". They may apply to corporate processes, such as product development, project management, business development, or customer relationship management. They may include talent practices, including succession planning and leadership development, or the use of a common brand, and a standard look and feel.

A case in point is the positioning of IT groups. In several technology companies we have observed, "corporate or group IT" provides the standard IT infrastructure and communication services. This is funded through corporate "G&A". However, business units can take the lead in identifying their own "customized application needs". They may use the "corporate IT function" as an "internal vendor", or go outside for sourcing the required services. In other words, each "state" can fund its own customized applications. The critical task is to clarify federal "mandates" so that other initiatives can be locally customized.

Third, while IT tools provide connectivity in the context of "codified" knowledge, individual initiative is needed to cross-pollinate tacit know-how. This is where "hubs" and "super hubs" can be leveraged. They can be viewed as bridges and connectors. They refer to knowledge workers who sit at critical intersections, often between silos. If deployed effectively, hubs can minimize filtering, synthesize input, and provide real-time connectivity. This capability allows danger and opportunity signals to be rapidly transmitted across the organization. The challenge is to identify critical organizational "hotspots" or intersections and to assign credible individuals to staff hub roles.

Finally, in view of our traditional emphasis on the vertical hierarchy, emphasis has to shift to the horizontal dimension. The typical breakdowns we observe have little to do with elegant structures; they have a lot to do with communication, keeping everyone on the same page, and creating shared reality. This is where organizational "circulation" comes into play. Leaders have to identify "circulatory" bottlenecks that impede flexible action. The solution may entail modifying a core business process (such as how to set and reset business priorities, how to develop a dynamic process for resource allocation, and how to install a portfolio alignment process), and creating opportunities for creative dialogue and risk-free cross-pollination.

7.10. Geo-Distributed Organizations and Super-Flexibility

In this chapter, we suggested that dynamic organizations are geo-distributed and multi-polar. They resemble "federal" systems with several centers of gravity. Federal mandates, in the form of mission and values, behavioral norms, talent practices, business processes, and brand identity, can provide "sameness", and give cohesion. "States" can exercise discretion in configuring context-specific policies and practices.[13]

Geo-distributed architectures can be super-flexible in several ways. Their modular, multi-polar, nature is amenable to adaptation and evolution. Nodes can be added, spun off, dissolved, or enlarged. They can be dissected, segmented, and re-positioned. They can be kept small to provide accountability and speed. They can be enlarged to minimize duplication. They may be semi-permanent to execute routine activities. They can be temporary, focusing on projects that have a limited life cycle. They can be used as templates for integrating acquisitions. The critical challenge is to minimize coordination needs and complex interdependencies, and enable teams and projects to interact and provide opportunities for cross-pollination.

Developing the core building blocks is the first step towards creating a super-flexible organization. It is a necessary but not a sufficient condition. While many firms try to develop the foundation, they do not behave in a super-flexible manner. This may be due to overemphasis on one building block (such as technology or anatomy) at the expense of others; relying on "old rules" while playing a new game, passive leadership, cosmetic gestures, or lack of accountability. Those that strive to be super-flexible reinforce its importance through concrete initiatives, and are vigilant at taking the pulse and recalibrating at critical junctures.

The real differentiator is how to deploy and leverage these building blocks; how to influence knowledge workers' attitude and disposition, and how to tune in to reality in a timely manner. It is no good having the organizational anatomy, without the desire or the mindset to deploy it. Similarly, having the right mindset cannot go far in the absence of core capabilities and skills.

---

[13] There are parallels between the nodal architecture and the notion of a "heterarchy" observed in Swedish multinationals. See Hedlund (1986).

The challenge is exacerbated in today's complex, matrix organizational jungle. Business leaders have to walk a tightrope between several tensions: balancing federal mandates and state needs, creating stable anchors and providing the capacity to "make sudden left turns", developing the right anatomical infrastructure, but ensuring that there is effective circulation. There are no perfect solutions or formulas to consider. The art of super-flexible organizational design is not about being either totally chaotic or tightly synchronized. Effective utilization of IT and remote work protocols does not reduce the importance of behavioral norms, personal networks, emotional connectivity and face-to-face interaction. The focus must be on generating short-term results while not losing sight of the long-term direction. Front line workers should be listened to and regularly surveyed, but there also needs to be clear mandates and directional guidelines from the top.

Geo-distributed organizations do not fit into the "either/or" mechanistic premises of our industrial age thinking. Leaders have to accommodate knowledge workers' need for inspirational guidance on the one hand, and self-management on the other. Teams should be focused with clear accountabilities and minimal coordination needs, yet they should interact with each other to create synergies and to provide the capacity for innovative thinking.

We need versatile capabilities to address, on the one hand, technological sophistication, complex innovation, short-lived opportunities, and competitive intensity, and on the other hand, effective ways to assemble, engage, guide and motivate expectant knowledge workers. We need to think more in terms of "shades of gray", establishing "trade-offs", and continuous "fine-tuning" of the organizational architecture, and less in terms of ideal configurations and perfect solutions. This is not a simple task and does not lend itself to "cure all" or "one size fits all" solutions.

This chapter has focused on organizational building blocks that enable an enterprise to withstand turbulence and to transform in the face of uncertainty; Many leaders try to create this balance by walking a tightrope between opposing tensions. Their organizational systems are not totally chaotic, but they are not in total control. A frugal cost-conscious mentality pervades their style; yet they try to learn, to experiment and to innovate. Management teams are not mavericks, yet many embody entrepreneurial zeal and anti-bureaucratic sentiments.

Business leaders have different points of view in addressing these challenges. The three dimensions of anatomy, circulation, and personality, should be viewed as components of a diagnostic toolkit. They provide a common vocabulary and a checklist of options that can be used as food for thought during the design process.

Creating super-flexible organizations poses a major challenge because our experiences, vocabularies, and expectations have evolved to address the challenges of the industrial era, and its inherent focus on standardization, binary thinking, and uni-dimensional recipes. While the current turbulence in the business environment offers exciting opportunities for experimentation, innovation, and diversity in organizational designs, we have to be willing to lift our blindfolds, and to move away from standard, "one size fits all" magic solutions.

8 Super-Flexible Leadership: Aligning Knowledge Workers Through Peer-Peer Practices

How do business leaders keep knowledge workers emotionally engaged and intellectually focused? How do they set clear mandates, yet create room for entrepreneurial initiatives? How do they guide geo-distributed teams and provide a sense of community?

Silicon Valley is an entrepreneurial ecosystem built on knowledge-based assets. A critical challenge is how to recruit, engage, motivate, develop, guide, and retain knowledge workers. This task presents a dilemma: On the one hand, knowledge workers do not want to be micro-managed; on the other hand, they have to be guided, coached, directed, and ultimately "aligned".

This chapter focuses on super-flexible leadership: how to engage, lead, and collaborate in dynamic settings. We suggest that a critical leadership challenge is to align and realign knowledge workers as new realities unfold; to keep them on the 'same page" and create "shared reality"; to set clear guidelines and clarify the non-negotiables; to seek input yet make decisions on a timely basis.

Effective leaders we have observed *align* their teams by using "*peer-peer*" practices. Peer-peer leadership is about switching gears, navigating at different altitudes, and changing hats, depending on the context. It means specifying clear boundaries and allowing room for creative dialog; setting up diverse teams with different points of view, but with a shared mission and sense of purpose; recognizing the importance of emotional drivers and ensuring that intellectual and financial motivators are also considered. Effective leaders walk a fine line between apparent extremes without becoming schizophrenic; in a nutshell, they can "place iron hands into velvet gloves".

8.1 Who Are Knowledge Workers?

Peter Drucker first coined the term "knowledge worker" during the 1950s to describe a new category of employees who use their "knowhow" to create value. We use the term to refer to employees with unique, often intangible, intellectual capital or expertise. They are professionals who cannot be easily replaced, and whose contribution is critical to an enterprise's success. Their knowhow has to be captured, codified, transformed, and packaged into marketable products and services. A related challenge is to coordinate the contributions of geo-distributed, multicultural teams. Engaging and motivating these core contributors is a critical priority since it has a direct impact on the performance of a knowledge-based entity.

Knowledge workers take on various guises. We have found it helpful to segment them based on the *type* of know-how they possess and how their expertise can be deployed. As depicted in Figure 26, some may be engaged in creative processes, such as R&D, product design and business development. Others may be engaged in the application of knowledge, with a primary focus on real-time execution; examples include sales teams and customer service professionals. Others may sit at the intersection between the two, including product managers and marketing professionals.

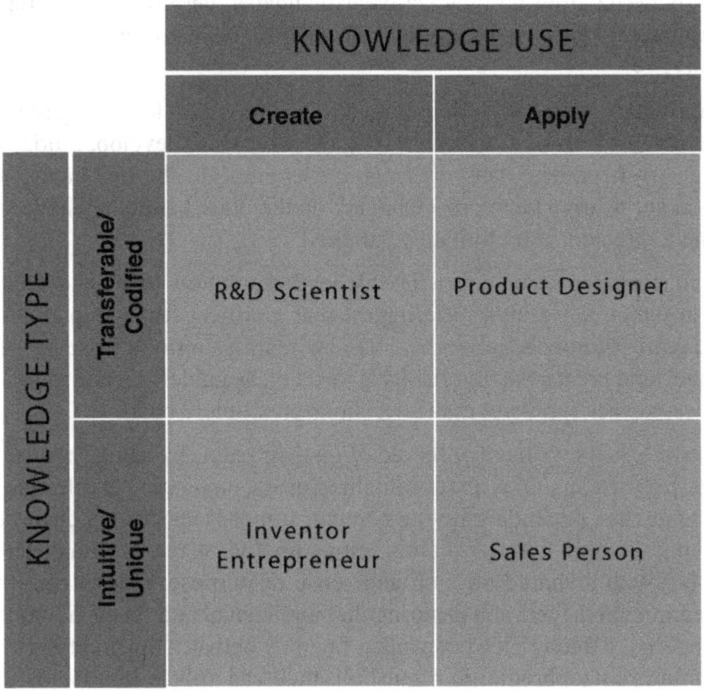

		KNOWLEDGE USE	
		Create	Apply
KNOWLEDGE TYPE	Transferable/ Codified	R&D Scientist	Product Designer
	Intuitive/ Unique	Inventor Entrepreneur	Sales Person

Figure 26. Categories of knowledge workers

The challenge is to enable knowledge workers from different backgrounds and diverse disciplines to pool together their collective talents in realizing common goals. These practices are typically a blend of the 'hard" and the "soft"; for example, how to deliver results under tight deadlines with limited resources; and how to generate emotional commitment and intellectual engagement.

8.2   What Makes Knowledge Workers Tick?

Knowledge workers have diverse and complex motivational patterns. They expect to have "good chemistry" with their peer group, want intellectually challenging assignments, and desire recognition and feedback. Work is intense, and thanks to e-tools, they are always accessible and reachable. It is difficult to disentangle "careers" from "life styles". Professional and personal lives are typically intertwined. As a senior executive in an established high tech company reflects:

"...Our people want honesty and openness, expect challenging work, support for learning, respect and recognition, and control over how work gets done ... they basically want to make a difference."

Our observations point to three categories of motivators that are important to knowledge workers. These include:
- **"Fair" compensation,** in terms of how total compensation compares with similar jobs in the company and in the industry.
- **Intellectual engagement,** including opportunities to grow, learn, stretch and remain employable.
- **"Emotional" connectivity,** reflecting the relationship between the knowledge worker, the boss, and the peer group, as well as the fit be-tween personal and organizational values.

Clearly, the mix varies depending on the individual, the context and the role. Some knowledge workers emphasize financial rewards; others value intellectual or emotional drivers. Some want to achieve; others want to belong; some want to be recognized; others want to make a difference. Although it is important to recognize the importance of all three drivers, our observations indicate that emotional engagement is especially critical. Work is intense and all consuming. Many projects are pioneering, address narrow market windows, and entail collaborative teamwork. Commitment depends on how a knowledge worker is touched in the heart. Emotional engagement can build trust and give teams the capacity to do that little bit extra when resources are in short supply, or provide the resilience to face difficult times.

Creating emotional bonds presents several challenges. Many knowledge workers have to function in distributed, multi-cultural contexts. There is limited face time and minimal opportunities to build trust. They experience information "overload" and conflicting priorities. They are always on, accessible and reachable; Burnout and lack of work/life balance are everyday realities.

These challenges are not easy to address. Leaders have to accommodate diverse styles, motivational traits, and lifestyle expectations. They have to retain mobile knowledge workers with different motivations and expectations. They need to exercise "influence" without formal authority. They have to deal with big egos and "prima donna" attitudes. A critical imperative is to turn arrogance into commitment, and to provide "guidance" without "supervision"; as the CEO of a financial software company observed:

"...Our knowledge workers are typically individual contributors who have healthy egos ... want to build their skill sets, have to make a difference in our industry, and are motivated by a spirit of discovery."

Everyone has to be a doer in some capacity. Initiative, versatility, and the capacity for self-management are critical for success. There is little time for micro management, handholding, detailed supervision, and checking the "rule book". The modern knowledge worker is analogous to a "digital artisan", having to create tangible value out of intangible know-how, under tight deadlines, competitive pressures, limited resources, and incomplete information, in dynamic contexts.

8.3 Peer-Peer Leadership

The challenge is to develop a leadership style that can align knowledge workers in a dynamic world, and keep them on the "same page" as priorities evolve. Effective approaches we have observed are a mixture of soft influence and hard authority, analogous to "placing an iron hand into a velvet glove". On the one hand, leaders have to be decisive, set clear direction, and make the tough calls. They have to confront non-performers, and resolve conflict on a daily basis. On the other hand, they have to exercise influence without authority, be a team player, listen carefully, and empathize with different points of view. Effective leadership in a knowledge-based entity is about integrating both dimensions and switching gears be-tween the two, without coming across as inconsistent or as schizophrenic. This is easier said than done, especially in view of different motivational patterns, and the dynamic nature of knowledge-based businesses.

At an operational level, we use the term "peer-peer" to describe daily practices of effective leaders we have observed. As depicted in Figure 27, differences between "parent-child" and "peer-peer" leadership are deceptively simple. In a peer-peer regime:

- The "boss" is the fulcrum of accountability, not just authority. Authority has to be earned through tangible expertise and concrete contributions. It is not a "given" due to rank, seniority, position, and title.
- The relationship between superior and subordinate is multi-faceted, not binary. The boss may be the source of authority in one context, and the follower and the doer in another. The challenge is to recognize when to take off one hat and put on another.
- One size does not fit all. Every knowledge worker is unique, in terms of achieving style, cultural background, motivational driver, and personality profiles. Some need detailed guidance; others are self-directed. Some need constant recognition and feedback; others are self-motivated. Some take the initiative and make things happen; others expect to be told what to do. Leaders have to customize their approach and address the unique expectations of different knowledge workers.

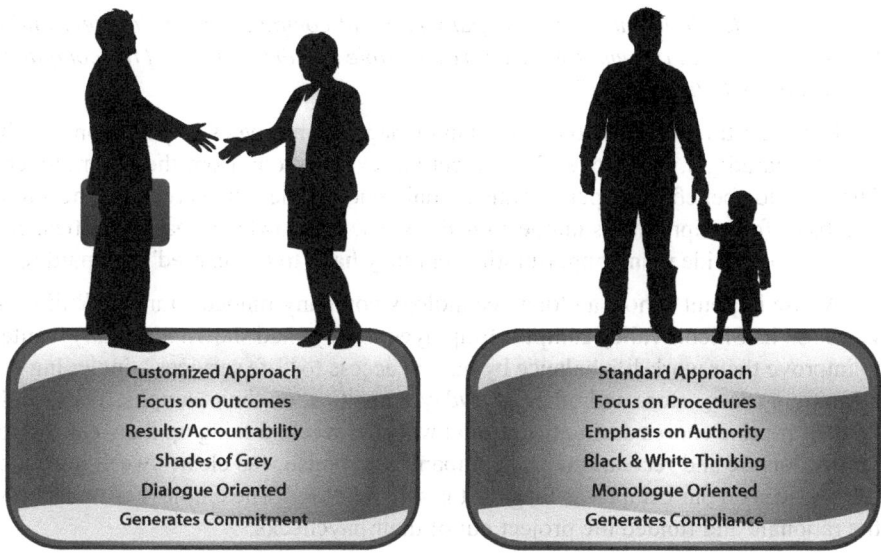

Figure 27. Comparing "parent-child" and "peer-peer" leadership practices

- The focus is on the "what" and the "why" rather than the "how". Leaders' most critical task is to explain the higher-order purpose, to clarify the desired outcomes, and to discuss the execution ground rules. There is no time to micro-manage and provide detailed supervision in rapidly changing environments.
- Relationships are predicated on having conversations and creating opportunities for dialogue. The intention is to arrive at options and decisions to which knowledge workers can commit, and to take the pulse at critical junctions.

Peer-peer practices impact daily activities. They influence hiring and firing, conflict resolution, communication styles, and attitudes towards authority, loyalty, and career development. Bosses are challenged and questioned. Conflict resolution is about brainstorming, rapid problem solving, factual assessment and getting to the core of an issue. Promotion practices are based on reputations and merit, rather than on seniority or patronage.

Communicating context, grounded in "brutal honesty", rather than "sugarcoated" reality is critical in building trust; authority is another word for accountability, being responsible for critical outcomes, rather than having the formal power to tell others what to do. Loyalty is analogous to an intense friendship, which may or may not last, rather than the traditional obligations of a binding marriage. Employees are in the driving seat of their own careers; employers provide the tools and the opportunities. As a senior executive observed:

"Career development in our company is about competency development and is learner-oriented ... our employees are responsible to learn ... it is not the company's responsibility to train them."

Peer-peer thinking is also reflected in managing employees' expectations. In the parental paradigm, "employees" have certain expectations from their "employer". They include benefits and perks, educational opportunities and career advancement. The basis for reciprocity is unquestioned loyalty. In knowledge-based entities, employers do provide many opportunities, but they have to be "earned" and paid for.

A case in point is how a global technology company funded a range of "life services" on its Silicon Valley campus. Employee surveys had shown that many wanted to improve their work-life balance by having access to "life services", including dry cleaning, grocery store and other everyday amenities, on their campus. They could do their routine chores during the normal working week, freeing up the weekend for family, leisure and recreation. The company's response was clear: "we'll introduce life services on our campus as long as it is self-funding." The employees understood the rationale and funded the project out of their paychecks.

Peer-peer thinking puts the emphasis on meritocracy and egalitarian norms. For example, employees of many companies in Silicon Valley, regardless of rank and position, fly coach and have similar offices or cubicles. Power is based on one's reputation and value-added contributions.

The "peer" mentality is also reflected in employees' access to, and control of, personal information. Due to the diffusion of e-tools, knowledge workers have access to their confidential personal records and can update these on a regular basis. The underlying thought process is that "I am responsible for the information". As an HR leader observed:

"In traditional companies, we tend to build our systems for the 1% (of employees) who might abuse the opportunity...not the 99% who do it right."

8.4 Front-Line Practices

Knowledge workers resemble nomadic tribes. They move between projects, teams and companies, as they look for new challenges and opportunities. Consider the following vignette:

"Meeta is in her late 30s. An Indian by birth, she completed her engineering degree in India and came to Silicon Valley during the early 1990s. She studied at Stanford University as a Masters student in Computer Science. After graduating, she worked in product management for a large software company and left after 2.5 years to join a start-up, founded by a former Stanford colleague. She left the start-up a year later when they failed to get the financing needed to expand the business. She joined the product management team of a mid-sized software company, and enrolled in Berkeley's Executive MBA program. She was laid off a year later, when the technology industry faced a major downturn. Through her Berkeley and Stanford network, she came across an opportunity in a venture-backed start-up, focusing on security software. She joined the company as their first marketing professional, left 18 months later, and together with another colleague, started her own company."

During her 17 years in Silicon Valley, Meeta has worked for four different companies, attended two major universities, started her own company, but has lived in the same ecosystem. Employers recognize that career mobility and inter-company movement is a critical feature of a knowledge-based ecosystem. Leadership strategies and talent practices have to take account of the dynamic nature of the employment life cycle.

Peer-peer leadership in such a dynamic setting is not a lofty ideal, but about behavioral norms and daily practices. Some address "emotional" drivers; for example, the need to feel "connected", or to be "recognized". Others are focused on accomplishing tasks, and delivering results under tight deadlines. We have synthesized effective practices we have observed into four inter-related themes:

- **Ensuring knowledge worker "fit":** Although there are common motivational patterns, every knowledge worker is unique. The environment, incentives, and practices that motivate one knowledge worker may be different to those influencing another. This is why there should be a fit between personal goals, values, and expectations, and an entity's desired purpose and behavioral norms.
- **Providing structured freedom:** Knowledge workers want to be guided, not managed. Effective guidance implies that limits have to be set. Clear non-negotiables, rather than detailed rules and procedures, can strike a balance between guided direction on the one hand, and individual empowerment on the other. Collaborative goal setting and regular feedback are critical enablers in this context.
- **Creating shared reality:** Knowledge workers have to understand how the work "context" has changed, and how their individual contribution may fit into the bigger picture. The business "story" has to be told and re-told as new realities unfold. As the founder of a software company observed: "my real job is to try and keep everyone, inside and outside, on the same page".
- **Orchestrating distributed teamwork:** No single knowledge worker has all the expertise needed for the completion of an urgent and complex assignment. Since work is done in distributed teams, knowledge workers have to be selected, "fused" and guided for virtual collaboration.

8.4.1. Ensuring Knowledge Worker Fit

In recent years there has been extensive discussion about "talent" or employment brand. Many companies have tried to differentiate themselves on the basis of the talent pool they attract, and the culture they create. This is in stark contrast to the traditional ideas of standardization and the notion that "one size fits all". Historically, business entities recruited talent on the basis of "person-job" fit. The goal was to ensure that there is a fit between the needs of the job and the experience and the qualifications of the individual. Historically, this approach made sense. People were recruited to fill pre-determined roles in hierarchical settings. They worked in relatively stable entities for their entire careers and were viewed as inter-changeable.

The challenge in a knowledge-driven enterprise is different. The organization is in a constant state of flux; priorities change continuously; roles are forged around capabilities and reputations. In these settings, it is important to ensure that there is a fit between a knowledge worker's values, motivations, and expectations, and the organization's norms, values, and context.[1] Effective "fit" is likely to create a win-win situation and minimize unwanted turnover. As the founder of a high tech company commented:

"When I recruit, I try to understand the person's motivation and attitude first... if they don't have a particular skill, they can learn on the job ... if they have the wrong motivation and attitude, no amount of skill and experience can help fill the gap."

Various approaches are used to ensure person-organization fit. These include employee referral programs, peer screening, internships, probations, and consulting assignments. A number of firms rely on behavioral inter-viewing, and look for critical competencies and personality traits. Others test the fit in a real-time work context; the candidate may work on an assignment as a contractor or as a consultant, giving both sides tangible opportunities to test the values "fit".

Consider the case of a global company whose culture is based on "constructive confrontation". Employees use conflict as a problem-solving tool. The recruiter on a university campus wanted to simulate the realities of working in a "confrontational" environment. During the first interview, he didn't engage in "small talk". Instead, he put a stopwatch on a table, and asked the candidates to draw a chip design in a given time frame. The students who were being interviewed, had different reactions to this "no-nonsense" experience. Some thought it was an honest and direct way to assess their technical competence. Others felt humiliated and patronized. Clearly, a simple interview helped both parties assess how they would fit into a confrontational culture.

Behavioral fit can also be reinforced through performance assessment, regular feedback, and personal coaching. The objective is to evaluate performance based on tangible contributions and observable behavior. This is easier said than done. There

---
[1] Chatman and Cha 2003, O'Reilly & Chatman 1996.

are challenges involved in making "objective" assessments of knowledge-based deliverables. Many high tech companies have set up "total performance management systems". The goal is to define and operationalize behaviors that exemplify bedrock values, with coaching and feedback built into the cycle. In many cases, equal weight is given to the behaviors, not only to the business results.

Consider the experience of a semiconductor equipment company. Its performance management process clarifies desired behaviors, based on eight "core values". These include "achievement", "honesty and integrity", "innovation and continuous improvement", "mutual trust and respect", "open communication", "ownership and accountability", "teamwork", and "think: customer, company, individual".

For example, "ownership and accountability" is described as: "takes responsibility for one's own actions or the actions of one's group, whether successful or unsuccessful. Takes initiative for problem solving, both within and outside the scope of their responsibility, and stays with the issue until it is successfully resolved. Delivers on commitments." Teamwork is described as "Proactively identifies cross-organizational issues where partnering leads to resolution. Works with others cooperatively to achieve a common goal. Focuses on company priorities. Represents his/her interests and yet is fair to other groups. Actions taken are in support of the common good. Ensures all team members are clear on their objectives, roles and responsibilities." A comprehensive feedback process is used to gauge actual behavior in undertaking daily tasks.

8.4.2. Providing Structured Freedom

Even volunteers need rules of conduct and a framework within which to operate. Otherwise, the organization becomes like a dysfunctional orchestra, with each specialist "playing its own tune". This presents a leadership dilemma. On the one hand, knowledge workers want to be led, guided, and engaged. On the other hand, they demand the freedom to act independently and to use their discretion. A major challenge facing team leaders is to clarify the non-negotiables or the 'golden rules", so that "the what and the why" as well as the "do's and don'ts" can be clearly understood, Clear rules of conduct provide "structured freedom". Front-liners can use their discretion in the context of clear boundaries. Our observations point to three categories of non-negotiables that make a difference.
- Contextual non-negotiables spell out the broader purpose and clarify how the assignment fits into the bigger picture: "we want to be in the remote storage business and this project is a key element of making that happen ... we are focusing on the end-users of storage products rather than distributors...your team's focus will be on core product design ... we'll sub-contract the peripheral design elements."

- Behavioral non-negotiables spell out the critical behaviors that are essential for the project's success and that take account of the enterprise's core values. At a micro level, they clarify the basic do's and don'ts of implementation. "A key element of our core values is collaboration and teamwork...on a practical level, this means that you have to identify the most critical stakeholders, keep them in the loop, and get their input on a regular basis."
- Project non-negotiables specify desired results and critical success metrics. They clarify the deliverables, the time frame, the resources, and the accountabilities. "... we are looking for a working prototype by the end of the year ...a budget of $500,000 has been allocated for this project..,we want to set up two parallel teams ... each team is directly accountable for developing a prototype...the executive team needs weekly updates on critical milestones... the team reports to Jane on engineering design and to Joe on budgeting."

Clear guidelines are especially important for geo-distributed virtual, teams. Without the forced discipline and the context cues of physical co-location, geo-distributed teams and nomadic workers need a framework within which to operate. True empowerment goes hand in hand with clear direction.

A case in point is the approach used by a software company. Their core values emphasize self-initiative and a sense of urgency in making things happen. These are reinforced through guidelines that enable teams to challenge existing processes. Process improvement teams can be formed by groups of at least five employees to challenge a process or an operating policy, if they follow a pre-determined methodology for generating constructive solutions.

In practice, the approach works as follows: the company provides a voluntary training and certification program on process improvement. Employees can enroll in the program and spend their own time to complete it. If five certified employees agree that the process should be improved, they can get together, form a team, follow the methodology, and propose changes to management. The system allows front-line employees to challenge working practices, although there are no guarantees that their recommendations would be implemented.

In summary, setting clear guidelines provides opportunities for delegation. As one executive observed:

"... we like to treat our people as adults ... instead of micro managing, we expect them to internalize a few key guidelines, like our mission and values, and to act within the scope of those guidelines."

8.4.3. Creating Shared Reality

Knowledge-based companies operate in dynamic settings. An objective that makes sense today may become irrelevant tomorrow. This makes it necessary to communicate and re-communicate the context in which work is embedded. It is the challenge of creating shared reality—ensuring that leaders can regularly take the pulse, to recalibrate, and to re-tell the business story; in the words of a high tech CEO "... *we let our people know what the vision is or how it is changing, but then let them decide what they are going to do (to make it happen)*".

A critical catalyst in creating shared reality is effective interaction be-tween the leaders and the front-liners. Direct "line of sight" makes it possible to identify opportunities early, implement decisions quickly, and forge a spirit of community. The analogy with guerrilla warfare is useful in this context:

"...the principles of guerrilla warfare are useful for managers who find themselves in a constantly changing environment...in the heat of the battle, a guerrilla commander needs accurate information and the ability to communicate quickly with the troops...successful guerrilla forces are led by commanders who also are in the thick of the battle...willing to get in the trenches."[2]

Several approaches are used to create shared reality, including informal interactions, open-plan offices, on-boarding sessions, and development programs. E-tools and social networking provide novel opportunities for communication across hierarchical levels, functional silos, and organizational boundaries. High tech companies are early adopters of new technologies. Many firms are the primary sites for testing their own products, and serve as beta-test sites for other technology products. Popular tools include collaborative software, video bytes, "state of the project" podcasts, team Wikis, pulse surveys and customer dialogues. Cited benefits included senior executives' ability to stay in touch with front-line realities, rapid transmission of information across time zones, and information transparency and immediacy.

There are limits to how IT can capture intangible know-how. As knowledge workers are constantly bombarded with virtual information, they need to interpret, aggregate and synthesize. As indicated in chapter 7, they need hubs and aggregators to update, filter and interpret information; these include websites, individuals, teams, departments or a blend of all. Hubs are analogous to neural connectors. They fuse, connect, integrate, synthesize, and synergize. They put people in touch with one another, become critical points of contact, help cross-pollinate expertise and bring in different points of view.

At a departmental level, we have observed four categories of hubs at work. Core hubs refer to critical line activities, including research & development, sales, customer service, supply chain management, and product management. Control hubs are the finance, accounting, and treasury functions. Infrastructure or foundation hubs, such as IT, HR, facilities, education and learning, shape the work context and provide the skeletal back-bone of the organization. Finally, strategic hubs link today's business to tomorrow's opportunities. Examples include strategic investment, venture teams, business development, and alliance management.

---

[2] Gibbons 1987

Hubs perform multiple tasks in parallel. Consider a software company whose product divisions are organized around functional groups. Hub roles are assigned to group executives who concurrently perform a number of roles.

Managing vertical linkages: With operational responsibility for the divisions under their control, they spearhead the coordination and implementation of divisional strategies, and are the focal point for resolving inter-divisional tensions.

Coordinating horizontal inter-dependencies: Group executives re-solve inter-group concerns and are accountable for decisions that cross group boundaries. For example the executive in charge of system development is responsible for addressing product development issues with his counterparts in sales, operations, international, and finance groups.

Fusing strategic and operational roles: Group executives, as members of the top management team, are collectively responsible for charting the strategic direction.

Hubs can also act as blockers and inhibitors of communication and dialogue. Critical success factors include their perceived reputation, expertise, credibility, and interaction skills. They need the versatility to deal with multiple agendas, the flexibility to "speak the languages" of different stakeholders, and the inter-personal skills to relate to knowledge workers from different cultures and functional backgrounds.

8.4.4. Orchestrating Distributed Teamwork

As discussed in chapter 7, teams are the organizational backbone, and the anatomical building block, of knowledge-based entities. Knowledge work is complex, requiring the contribution of different specialists. No one has all the expertise needed to complete an urgent and complex assignment. Some teams work on on-going assignments, such as account management or customer service. Others work on projects with a deadline and a limited life cycle, as is the case with new product or business development. As a result, knowledge workers have to be selected, "fused" and blended together for dynamic teamwork.

Many teams are geo-distributed. They operate inter-dependently and are separated by time, distance and culture. Team members may come from different educational, cultural, linguistic, functional and generational backgrounds. Geo-distributed teams represent the most challenging type of collaborative work: facing high levels of task complexity, coupled with high levels of uncertainty.

Geo-distributed teamwork is about balancing variety, spontaneity, and complementaries on the one hand, with uniformity, predictability, and consistency on the other. This is why is it critical to balance the subjective dimensions of teamwork, such as trust and chemistry, with "objective" dimensions, such as setting clear ground rules for conflict resolution. Effective teams we have observed share the following characteristics.

- **Team complementarity and chemistry**
They blend different skills and points of view, but have a unified mission and sense of purpose. Much like sports teams, they strive for common goals and shared outcomes. At the same time, they represent different functions, complementary capabilities, and cross-cultural perspectives. They assemble eternal optimists and devil's advocates, thinkers and doers, pragmatists and idealists, talkers and listeners, and "cowboys and suits". Effective team leaders try to build relationships of trust by engaging in intense discussion at the beginning of an assignment. Face-to-face interactions early on give team members the opportunity to check their chemistry, get to know one another, present different points of view, and in the process, build relationships of trust. Virtual interactions are more effective when team members have had the opportunity to meet face-to-face (Hinds & Kiesler 2002).
- **Critical ground rules**
Effective teams develop clear ground rules for addressing critical challenges. These include protocols for resolving conflict, building consensus, and collaborating remotely. Clear ground-rules enable teams to de-personalize problems and resolve conflict on a factual basis (Griffith et al. 2003). In addition, they minimize coordination bottlenecks in resolving one-off problems.

  Since virtual work entails extensive coordination, effective teams rely on structured team interactions. For example, they segment their meetings into information sharing, decision-making, and brainstorming categories and develop customized ground-rules for each type of interaction. Brainstorming meetings may incorporate input from diverse sources, including customers, peers, vendors or partners. Informational meetings may be based on standard templates that provide consistency and uniformity. Decision-making contexts are more complex. They need advanced preparation and one/one conversations. It is easier to conduct informational meetings remotely, whereas brainstorming meetings are more effective when they are "face-to-face".
- **Clear charters and accountabilities**
Effective leaders assign clear roles and accountabilities to their team members, in the context of well-defined team charters. Role clarity does not have to be limited to a member's technical or functional contributions. They may also incorporate different stakeholder perspectives. For example, team members may be asked to think from the vantage point of a "devil's advocate", a potential customer, a future competitor, or a front-liner.

  Inculcating cognitive diversity can have two benefits. It gives team members an opportunity to make unique contributions to the team effort, over and above their functional expertise. It can also be a real-time "development" opportunity and a stretch assignment. For example, an engineer, who has to think about product features from the vantage point of a customer,

may become more versatile as a result of having to put herself in someone else's shoes.
- **Common understanding of the low/high hanging fruit**
Effective leaders recognize the broad range of challenges involved in undertaking team assignments. They try to boost team members' confidence and enhance the team's credibility by producing tangible deliverables early on. A practical approach is to map out the "high and the low hanging fruit", or the easy and the difficult tasks, at the beginning of an assignment. Effective teams initially focus on the easy tasks that have a quick payoff. Tangible deliverables can generate credibility and build confidence during the crucial early stages of a team assignment.

8.5   Aligning and Super-Flexibility

Knowledge enterprises are a montage of versatile capabilities, informal networks, and professional relationships, rather than a series of pre-determined roles and positions in mechanistic hierarchies. Their productivity depends on knowledge workers' capabilities, commitments, motivations, and relationships. They cannot be programmed around pre-determined roles and positions. It is crucial for team leaders to align their members around a shared purpose and to re-align them as new realities unfold.

The *aligning* orientation of knowledge enterprises and the supervisory tilt of industrial entities differ in three areas: leading knowledge workers in a peer-peer, rather than a parent-child, paradigm; exercising control by providing "context", setting clear expectations, clarifying non-negotiables, and developing critical ground-rules; and recognizing the importance of *emotional*, as well as financial and intellectual, drivers in motivating knowledge workers.

The ebbs and flows of today's work environments are such that knowledge workers have to be continuously seconded to different assignments, often, with little notice and minimal planning. Staffing for this level of variability implies that it is more important to match the motivation and the values of an individual to the norms and over arching purpose of an organization.

Peer-peer leadership has re-defined traditional expectations of the employer-employee relationship. Loyalty is analogous to an intense friendship, rather than a long-lasting marriage. The employer provides training resources, an organizational network, and career opportunities. However, it is up to individuals to manage their own careers:

A knowledge worker's effectiveness in getting things done is based on competence and credibility, perceived reputation, and network of relationships. In this context, titles, seniority, and spans of control are not necessarily significant determinants of success. Effective knowledge workers have the flexibility and the confidence to re-purpose their capabilities when new needs arise; as the co-founder of a medical diagnostics company observed: *"I want to recruit people who are absolute experts in a given area but who can also apply their talents to other areas; "A" class players in their field, but also "B" & "C" class players in other fields."*

9 Becoming Super-Flexible: The Enterprise in Motion

What can we learn about dynamic adaptation from Silicon Valley's entrepreneurial ecosystem? How should we rejuvenate our industrial age practices to address the challenge of perpetual innovation and continuous transformation? How can the ideas presented in this book help us lead in a dynamic world? This final chapter is focused on these critical questions.

During the past two decades, we have hosted many delegations of senior executives, board members, and government officials from different parts of the world. Their goal was to get a glimpse into disruptive technologies and innovative products, to learn about entrepreneurship and new venture formation, and to find out about new leadership practices and organizational experiments. We concluded each visit by debriefing our visitors on their key impressions. This chapter is partly a synthesis of their takeaways. Our views have also been shaped by teaching this material to our graduate students at Berkeley and Carnegie Mellon, and to knowledge workers in different parts of the world, where our frameworks and ideas have been interpreted through the lens of other cultures and business experiences.

During these conversations a major discussion topic is how historical legacy and active inertia influence leaders' perspectives, and in the process, shape their decisions and actions. So our starting point is to compare foundational assumptions that differentiate industrial-age thinking from new approaches that address dynamic realities. How do you lead when your world is no longer anchored in *"terra firma"* but is a raft floating on a whitewater river? How do you organize and coordinate when you can choose from a plethora of collaborative software tools and social networks? How do you nurture disruptive innovation when the old game was about extending the life cycle of blockbuster products? These core assumptions underpin leadership practices, organizational architectures, business strategies, and ultimately, our approach towards enterprise adaptation. We hope to highlight the traps we can fall into and to isolate a few critical levers that can be used to reinvent established enterprises for today's dynamic world.

9.1 New Game/ Old Rules

Traditional entities have been architected for a primary purpose: to provide stability, continuity and predictability, with an emphasis on withstanding turbulence. Their over arching goal was to produce standard products and durable services that can withstand the test of time; consider Henry Ford's famous maxim "give it to them in any color as long as it's black". Stability, predictability and standardization were the over arching goals.

Silicon Valley enterprises are dynamic; they thrive on novelty and innovation. Products and services have a short half-life. They are architected more as *mobile* entities that can surf successive waves, and adapt to new realities as they unfold. This process entails changing direction, passengers and destinations as conditions evolve and priorities morph. The critical challenge is to think in new ways, to revisit our core assumptions, and to re-orient our mental models.

Today, enterprises should be viewed as "mobile", capable of surfing successive waves of innovation, and harnessing the ups and downs of market transformation and business uncertainty. It is no longer feasible for business leaders to think of themselves as architects and builders. Instead, we have to think more like drivers, navigators, and pioneers who may change vehicles, direction, passengers and destination as conditions change and preferences evolve. By re-conceptualizing the enterprise as a *"mobile"*, rather than as a *"static"* entity, we are in a better position to shift our mindsets, re-configure our organizational DNA, speed up the adaptation process, and unleash the capacity for enterprise renewal.

The need to view the enterprise as a dynamic construct has been noted by several scholars in recent years. Concepts, such as dynamic "capabilities" (Conner & Prahalad 1996, Henderson 1994, Teece et al. 1997), dynamic "communities" (Galunic & Eisenhardt 2001), and dynamic "boundaries" (Afuah 2001) have gained theoretical momentum. From an organizational standpoint, dynamic constructs extend the original notion of "organic" structures (Burns and Stalker 1961), a term used to depict organizational forms that can operate in changing environments.

Naturally, core assumptions and mental models do not change overnight. There are many barriers to overcome. People are creatures of habit and don't find it easy to change. We are constrained by institutionalized norms, administrative heritage and active inertia. Our tendency is to rely on tried and tested recipes within familiar comfort zones. We are reluctant to take risks and experiment with new approaches in the absence of major crises or dramatic market failures. This is understandable. There is a lot to lose, and little to gain, at least in the short term.

The starting point is to build awareness and improve our understanding. Today we are somewhat schizophrenic; we are playing a new game but relying on old rules. In order to make an effective transition, we have to re-examine the foundational assumptions that differentiate the old from the new. These include:
- Tight integration versus loose coupling
- Focus on "consistency" versus emphasis on "relevance"
- Unipolar versus multipolar organizational architectures
- Viewing the enterprise as a 'meritocracy" rather than as an "aristocracy"

Tight integration versus loose coupling: Traditional entities have been vertically integrated and operate like giant "super-tankers" with complex interdependencies. They are slow to move and find it challenging to make decisions; changes made to one part are likely to impact others. They change direction, configuration and crew only when they face a major crisis. The typical strategic response is to rely on "big bang" solutions, such as re-organizations, acquisitions, or the appointment of new CEOs.

Silicon Valley enterprises are modular. They are configured like an armada of boats, of different shapes and sizes, moving at varying speeds but towards the same destination. They are made up of cross-functional, cross-geography, cross-boundary and cross-silo teams that interact, cross-pollinate, and strive to innovate. They have to continuously adapt to changing ecosystem conditions. When the weather changes or the currents shift, their modular nature facilitates rapid adaptation. As described in chapters 5 and 6, maneuvering, recalibrating, and experimenting are features of everyday life.

In addition, as discussed in chapters 3 and 4, Silicon Valley entities have open borders and thrive on collaborative partnerships. They concentrate on core activities and outsource support services. They are members of a diverse ecosystem that include "originators", "hatcheries", "lubricants" and "generators". They provide variable, just-in-time, complementary expertise, so an entity can get traction by focusing on its unique competencies.

Consistency versus relevance: Traditional entities place a high value on "consistency". This is hardly surprising since maintaining the "status quo" is critically important. The focus is on doing "what you said you'd do" and so deviation from the "norm" is discouraged. Things happen because they have "already been announced" or because "they are on the calendar", not because they still make sense. This is in sharp contrast to common practices in Silicon Valley, where entrepreneurial teams thrive on "empirical pragmatism". Although an idea may have made sense yesterday, it has to be adjusted in line with today's realities.

Personal exposure to front-line realities makes it easier to recalibrate and to develop corrective actions based on real-time feedback. Knowledge workers can make decisions based on the world "as it is" today, rather than the "way we wish it to be" or the "way it was yesterday". Traditional businesses find it difficult to recalibrate, partly because "courtiers" cushion their leaders from front-line realities. Positioned between the leaders and the front-liners, they act as filters and transmitters, often shielding leaders from "unfavorable" news. By the time reality unfolds, it may be too late to make the necessary recalibrations or to embark on corrective actions. As discussed in chapter 7, leaders have to ensure that they can take the organization's pulse real-time through fluid "circulation", and confront reality as "it is", rather than the way we "wish it to be"

Unipolar versus multi-polar organizational architectures: Traditional approaches to organizational design emphasize "unipolarity", with emphasis on a single center of power, residing at the top. Historically, we have used terms, such as "headquarters/subsidiary" and "centralization/decentralization", to depict the distribution of authority along the vertical hierarchy. By contrast, Silicon Valley enterprises are multi-polar. They have different centers of gravity and diverse clusters of expertise. The focus is not on centralization or decentralization, but as discussed in chapter 7, on "federal/state" balancing acts.

"Federal" rules apply to every "citizen"; They may reflect core values, as is the case with Google's "eat your own dog food" and "hire by committee", or Adobe's aspiration to be "genuine, sincere, trustworthy and reliable"; They may specify core processes, such as business development, customer relationship management, product development, or talent deployment; They may address financial targets, resource allocation, and brand identity.

Federal rules have to be counter-balanced by discretions granted to "states". Every "state" needs the flexibility to address its unique front-line realities. The objective is to balance "uniformity" on the one hand, and "diversity" on the other. The challenge is to figure out what has to be the same across the entire enterprise so that everything else can be flexibly customized. The list of federal rules, however, must be kept to a minimum; otherwise complexity creeps in and impedes adaptive behavior.

Meritocracy versus aristocracy: Traditional corporations have historically viewed the leader as the all-knowing, omnipotent ruler. In knowledge-intensive settings, no one individual has all the expertise needed to undertake complex tasks in real-time contexts. A leader has to rely on the collective wisdom, the specialized expertise, and the complementary capabilities of other team members. His or her most significant contribution is to be the symbolic focal point, the "fair-minded judge", the creator of the "context", and the synthesizer of team decisions. Differences between the two leadership models is depicted in the context of "parent-child" versus "peer-peer" practices described in Chapter 8.

In addition, knowledge workers are rewarded based on how they con-tribute in concrete, measurable ways, not by whether they have "paid their dues and been loyal subjects". Personal reputation, based on tangible contributions, is the ultimate source of credibility. As indicated in chapter 8, "brutal honesty" and "fact-based" performance assessments are the norm, not the exception. In short, Silicon Valley entities strive to operate more like "meritocracies', rather than 'aristocracies".

In summary, industrial-age entities cannot be reinvented overnight. There are no magic formulas or standard solutions. By examining the foundational assumptions that differentiate the old from the new, we hope to help our readers diagnose business practices that impede adaptation. This assessment can be a prelude to organizational "spring cleaning"; they can think about "what to keep", "what to discard", and "what to acquire", in terms of new capabilities, new configurations, and new behaviors. This task cannot be undertaken as a "one shot deal". It is a process of periodic reflection and continuous improvement. We hope that the foundational assumptions described in this chapter can be a trigger for discussion and provide food for thought.

9.2. Concluding Thoughts

As described in chapter 2, dynamic adaptation is about becoming super-flexible, developing and deploying a broad range of capabilities, from agility, versatility and adaptability, to robustness, resilience and hedging. Some of these capabilities, such as resilience and robustness, provide the capacity to withstand turbulence. Others, such as versatility and agility, are about transitioning and adapting to new realities. As depicted in Table 8, these capabilities impact different aspects of an enterprise. It is no good having a super-flexible strategy without the supporting organizational architecture. A flexible structure has to be brought to life through dynamic leadership practices. This is why our five action principles for becoming super-flexible focus on the "total" enterprise, not just its individual components. They address strategic management as well as organizational design. They focus on leadership practices as well as execution processes. We present an integrated perspective by describing the multi-dimensional capabilities that facilitate adaptation.

CONCEPTS	IMPLICATIONS FOR KNOWLEDGE ENTERPRISES
Adaptability	Willingness to do things differently. Is related to enterprise strategy and values, especially the attitude and role modeling behavior of leaders.
Agility	Detecting danger and opportunity signals and taking appropriate action in a timely manner; impacts scanning capabilities, decision-making processes, conflict resolution, and cross-silo coordination.
Elasticity	Allowing units to expand or contract as business conditions change; impacts enterprise architecture, especially in forming and dissolving collaborative partnerships.
Liquidity	Moving people and assets around with minimum friction or penalty costs; impacts talent deployment and resource allocation.
Malleability	Shifting resources across silos, depending on critical priorities; impacts deployment of talent and financial resources.
Mobility	Re-deploying talent, assets and capabilities around the enterprise and the ecosystem; impacts talent and asset deployment.
Modularity	Setting up scalable, plug and play, work units with compatible interconnects; impacts organizational architecture and business processes.

CONCEPTS	IMPLICATIONS FOR KNOWLEDGE ENTERPRISES
Robustness	Creating a solid core to fall back on; impacts core values, encoded competencies, brand position, and financial reserves.
Resilience	Re-growing damaged parts and re-establishing credibility; impacts core values, business reputation, and leaders' behavior and attitude.
Versatility	Recruiting and developing people with the ability to do different assignments; customizing products and services for different market segments; evolving a single product into a family of different products; impacts recruiting policies, product development, and diversification options.

Table 8. Different attributes of super-flexibility and their impact

In conclusion, becoming super-flexible by developing the capacity for dynamic adaptation revolves around five basic principles:

- Super-flexibility is a continuous *balancing act; it is about shifting gears between withstanding turbulence and transforming to adapt to new realities.* In this sense, continuity and change have to coexist. A key challenge is to figure out what has to stay the same, so that everything else can adapt and morph. In practical terms, leaders have to engage in spring-cleaning on a regular basis: they have to think about what to keep, what to add and what to discard. As discussed in chapters 4 and 6, systematic "spring cleaning", recycling failed initiatives, "recalibrating", and "selectively pulling the plug" are critical in this context.
- Super-flexibility is about moving forward by shedding old skin. However, this situation can present a dilemma; we tend to give up our old habits when we experience *friction and go through difficult 'knot-holes'*. It is important to view *friction as a constructive force in dynamic adaptation.* The challenge is to harness friction and generate positive movement. As discussed in chapters 7 and 8, one way to turn friction into a constructive catalyst is to identify organizational hotspots, and to proactively place hubs and cross-pollinators at critical intersections.
- Super-flexibility is about *creating several centers of gravity and "not putting all eggs in one basket"*. It reflects a shift in thinking from "one best way" to "let a thousand flowers bloom". This theme is reflected in two principles: maneuvering and orgitechting. Maneuvering emphasizes the deployment of preemptive, opportunistic, protective and corrective initiatives. The objective is to develop a flexible business portfolio, spanning offensive and defensive

components. Orgitechting highlights the inherent flexibility associated with a multi-polar, geo-distributed, organizational architecture.
- Super-flexibility, as is the case in evolutionary biology and discussed in chapter 2, is not only about "*genotype plasticity*", at the level of the "species", but also about "*phenotype plasticity*", how basic principles of adaptation can be applied at the level of the individual organism. There is no universal formula that can be applied to every organization. Although conceptual principles may be relevant at the macro altitude of the "species", solutions have to be customized and adapted to address different situations and contextual realities.
- Super-flexibility is made easier by *keeping things simple*; it is difficult enough to change without the added impediment of complexity. Duke of Wellington partly attributed his victory against Napoleon to the fact that he "used rope" while Napoleon relied on a "*splendid piece of harness, it looks very well... until it gets broken and then you are done for. I made my campaigns of ropes. If anything went wrong, I tied a knot and went on.*" (Longford 1969, p.442).

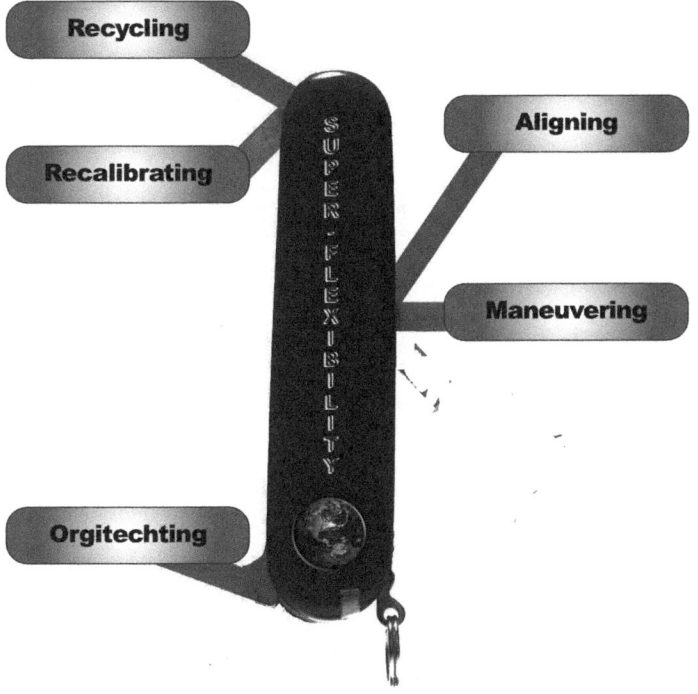

Figure 28. Super-Flexibility in action: A toolkit for dynamic adaptation

The principles and frameworks presented in this book can help simplify life for knowledge workers. Our goal is to give our readers the toolkit they need to diagnose problems on the fly, and to develop adaptive solutions on the spot. Spontaneity, agility, and the capacity for rapid problem solving will be critical leadership capabilities in the future. We hope the ideas presented in this book can help our readers develop the capacity for dynamic adaptation as they face diverse challenges and opportunities in the dynamic world of the 21st century.

10 References and Additional Readings

Aaker, D.A. & Mascarenhas, B. (1984). "The Need for Strategic Flexibility." Journal of Business Strategy, 5(2), 74-82

Abraham, W.C. & Bear, M. F. (1996). "Metaplasticity: the plasticity of synaptic plasticity." Trends in Neuroscience, 19(4), 126-130

Abraham, W.C. (2008). "Metaplasticity: tuning synapses and networks for plasticity." Nature Reviews of Neuroscience, 9(5), 387

Acharya, V.V. & Bisin, A. (2009). "Managerial hedging, equity ownership, and firm value." RAND Journal of Economics, 40(1), 47-77

Ackoff, R.L. (1977). "Towards Flexible Organizations: A Multidimensional Approach." Omega, 5(6), 649-662

Adamides, E.E. & Pomonis, N. (2009). "Modular Organizations and Strategic Flexibility: The Mediating Role of Knowledge Management Strategy." Chapter VI, 118-131 In E. Aou-Zeid (Ed.): Knowledge Management and Business Strategies. Idea Group Inc.

Adamides, E., Stamboulis, Y., & Pomonis, N. (2005). "Modularity and Strategic Flexibility: A Cognitive and Dynamic Perspective." Boston MA: The 23rd International Conference of the System Dynamics Society

Adler, P.S. (1988). "Managing Flexible Automation." California Management Review, 30(3), 34-56,

Adler, P.S., Goldoftas, B. & Levine, D.I. (1999). "Flexibility Versus Efficiency? A Case Study of Model Changeovers in the Toyota Production System." Organization Science, 10(1), 43-68

Agrawal, A.A. (2007). "Macroevolution of plant defense strategies." Trends in Ecology and Evolution, 22(2), 103-109

Agrawal, A.A. (2001). "Phenotype Plasticity in the Interactions and Evolution of Species." Science's Compass Review, 294, 321-328

Agrawal, A.A. & Fishbein, M. (2008). "Phylogenetic escalation and decline of plant defense strategies." Proceedings of the National Academy of Science, 105(29), 10057-10060

Albrecht, J.W. & Hart, A.G. (1983). "A Putty-Clay Model of Demand Uncertainty and Investment." Scandinavian Journal of Economics, 85(3), 393-402

Allen, L. & Pantzalis, C. (1996). "Valuation of Operating Flexibility of Multinational Corporations." Journal of International Business Studies, 27(4), 633-653

Allen, P.M., Datta, P.P. & Christopher, M. (2006). "Improving the Resilience and Performance of Organizations using Multi-Agent Modelling of Complex Production-Distribution Systems." Risk Management, 8(4), 294-309

Allison, G.T. (1971): Essence of Decision: Explaining the Cuban Missile Crisis. Boston, MA: Little Brown & Co.

Amador, M., Werning, I. & Angeletos, G.M. (2006). "Commitment vs. Flexibility." Econometrica, 74(2), 365-396

Ancel, L.W. & Fontana, W. (2000). "Plasticity, Evolvability, and Modularity in RNA." Journal of Experimental Zoology (Mol Dev Evol) 288, 242-283

Anderies, J.M., Janssen, M.A. & Ostrom, E. (2003). "Design Principles for Robustness of Institutions in Social-Ecological Systems." Paper prepared for the Workshop in Political Theory and Policy Analysis. Indiana University Working Paper #W03-10

Ansoff, H.I. (1965): Corporate Strategy. Harmondsworth: Penguin Books

Ansoff, H.I. (1975). "Managing Strategic Surprise by Response to Weak Signals." California Management Review, 8(2), 21-33

Arrow, K.J. (1995). "A Note on Freedom and Flexibility." in Choice, Welfare, and Development: A Festschrift in Honor of Amartya Sen." K. Basu, P. Pattanaik, and K. Suzumara, (Eds.): Oxford: Clarendon Press

Arteta, B.M. & Giachetti, R.E. (2004). "A measure of agility as the complexity of the enterprise system." Robotics and Computer-Integrated Manufacturing, 20(6), 495-503

Assens, C. (2000). "Stability and plasticity in self-organized networks." European Journal of Economic and Social Systems, 14(4), 311-332

Augier, M. & Teece, D.J. (2009). "Dynamic Capabilities and the Role of Managers in Business Strategy and Economic Performance." Organizational Science, 20(2), 410-42

Backman, J. (1940). "Flexibility of Cheese Prices." Journal of Political Economy, 48(4), 579-582

Backman, J. (1940). "The Causes of Price Inflexibility." The Quarterly Journal of Economics, 54(3), 474-489

Backman, J. (1948). "Price Inflexibility—War and Postwar." The Journal of Political Economy, 56(5), 428-437

Bahrami, H. & Evans, S. (1988). "Stratocracy in High Technology Firms." California Management Review, 30(1), 51-66, Winter 1987, reprinted in G. Carroll & D. Vogel (Eds.) (1988): Organizational Approaches to Strategy. Cambridge, MA: Ballinger

Bahrami, H. & Evans, S. (1989a). "Strategy Making in High Technology Firms: The Empiricist Mode." California Management Review, 31(2), 107-128

Bahrami H. & Evans, S. (1989b). "Emerging Organizational Regimes in High Technology Firms: The Bi-modal Form." Human Resource Management, 28(1), 25-50

Bahrami, H. (1992). "The Emerging Flexible Organization: Perspectives from Silicon Valley." California Management Review, 34(4), 33-52

Bahrami, H. & Evans, S. (1995). "Flexible Recycling & High-Technology Entrepreneurship." California Management Review, 37(3), 33-52

Bahrami, H. & Evans, S. (1997). "Human Resource Leadership in Knowledge-based Entities: Shaping the Context of Work." Human Resource Management Journal, 36(1), 23-28

Bahrami, H. & Evans, S. (2000). "Flexible Recycling and High Technology Entrepreneurship." In M. Kenney (Ed.): Understanding Silicon Valley: The Anatomy of an Entrepreneurial Region. Stanford CA: Stanford University Press

Bahrami, H. & Evans, S. (2003) "Architecting Flexible Enterprises: Organizational Design in the Post-Internet Era." in H. Osterle and R. Winter (Eds.): Business Engineering. Berlin, Heidelberg: Springer

Bahrami, H. & Evans, S. (2006). "Managing High-Tech Knowledge Workers: Lessons from Silicon Valley." Peking University, PKU Business Review, 20(3), 68-72

Baldwin, C.Y., & Clark, K.B. (1997). "Managing in an Age of Modularity." Harvard Business Review, 75(5), 84-93

Baldwin, C.Y., & Clark, K.B. (2000): Design Rules: The Power of Modularity. Vol. 1. Cambridge MA: MIT Press

Baldwin, C.Y. (2001). "The Value and Costs of Modularity." Power Point Slides, Harvard Business School, July 21, 2001 http://www.rieti.go.jp/jp/events/e01071301/pdf/baldwin.pdf, (accessed on 12/19/09)

Baldwin, C.Y. & Woodard, C.J. (2007). "Competition in Modular Clusters." Harvard Business School Working Papers Series # 08-043

Bargigli, L. (2005). "The Limits of Modularity in Innovation and Production." Centre for Research on Innovation and Internationalization, Università Commerciale "Luigi Bocconi", Milano, Italy, CESPRI Working Paper WP #176

Baron, J. & Hannan, M. (2002). "Organizational Blueprints for Success in High-Tech Start-Ups." California Management Review, 44(3), 8-36

Bartram, S.M. (2006). "The Use of Options in Corporate Risk Management." Managerial Finance, 32(2), 160-181

Bartram, S.M. (2008). "What Lies Beneath: Foreign Exchange, Rate Exposure, Hedging and Cash Flows." Journal of Banking and Finance, 32(8), 1508-1521

Bartram, S.M. & Atetz, K. (2009). "Corporate Hedging and Shareholder Value." Munich Re, MPRA, working paper # 14015

Bartlett, C. & Ghoshal, S. (1988). "Organizing for Worldwide Effectiveness." California Management Review, 31(1), 54-75

Barnes, S.J. (2003). "Enterprise mobility: Concept and examples." International Journal of Mobile Communications, 1(4), 341-359

Basole, R.C. (2007). "Strategic Planning for Enterprise Mobility: A Readiness-Centric Approach." AMCIS 2007 Proceedings, Paper # 491

Basole, R.C. (2009). "Visualization of inter-firm relations in a converging mobile ecosystem." Journal of Information Technology, 24(2), 144-159

Baumgärtner, S. & Strunz, S. (2009). "Economic insurance value of ecosystem resilience." University of Lüneberg, Working Paper Series in Economics #132

Bayne, B.L. (2004). "Phenotype Flexibility and Physiological Tradeoffs in the Feeding and Growth of Marine Bivalve Mollusks." Integrative and Comparable Biology, 44(6), 425-432

Belderbos, R. & Zou, J. (2007). "On the growth of foreign affiliates: multinational plant networks, joint ventures and flexibility." Journal of International Business Studies, 38(7), 1095-1112

Bernanke, B.S. (1983). "Irreversibility, Uncertainty, and Cyclical Investment."

The Quarterly Journal of Economics, 98(1), 85-106

Bertsimas, D. & Sim, M. (2004). "The Price of Robustness." Operations Research, 52(1), 35-53

Benjaafar, S., Morin, T.L. & Talavge J.J. (1995). "The strategic value of flexibility in sequential decision making." The European Journal of Operational Research, 82(3), 439-457

Biller, B. & Xiang, C. (2008). "Flexible Capacity Investment Strategies for Global Firms." Tepper School of Business, Carnegie Mellon University, WP-2008-E39

Birkinshaw, J. & Gibson, C.B. (2004). "Building ambidexterity into an organization." MIT Sloan Management Review, 45(4) 47-55

Bish. E.K., Muriel, A., & Biler, S. (2005). "Managing Flexible Capacity in a Make-to-Order Environment." Management Science, 51(2), 167-180

Blais, B. & Mariotti, T. (2005). "Strategic Liquidity Supply and Security Design." Review of Economic Studies, 72(3), 615-649

Bonder, S. (1976). "Versatility: An Objective for Military Planning." Keynote address presented at the 37th Military Operations Research Symposium, Fort Bliss, Texas

Bonder, S. (1979). "Changing the Future of Operations Research." Operations Research, 27(2), 209-224

Boroloi, S.K., Cooper, W.W. & Matsuo H. (1999). "Flexibility, Adaptability, and Efficiency in Manufacturing Systems." Production and Operations Management, 8(2), 133-150

Bourcét, J.P. (1776): Principles de la Guerre de Montagne. Paris

Bourgeois, L.J., & Eisenhardt, K.M. (1987). "The Anatomy of the Living Dead in the Computer Industry." California Management Review, 30(1), 143-159

Bourgeois, L.J. (1981). "On the measurement of organizational slack." Academy of Management Review, 6(1), 29-39

Brand F.S. and Jax, K. (2007). "Focusing on the Meaning(s) of Resilience: Resilience as a Descriptive Concept and a Boundary Object." Ecology and Society, 12(1), 23

Breschi, S., & Lissoni, F. (2006). "Mobility of inventors and the geography of knowledge spillovers. New evidence on US data," Centre for Research on Innovation and Internationalisation, Università Commerciale "Luigi Bocconi", Milano, Italy, CESPRI Working Papers #184

Briscoe, F. (2007). "From Iron Cage to Iron Shield? How Bureaucracy Enables Temporal Flexibility for Professional Service Workers." Organization Science, 18(2), 1526-5455

Briscoe, F. (2006). "Temporal Flexibility and Careers: The Role of Large Scale Organizations for Physicians." Industrial and Labor Relations Review, 60(1), 67-83

Brock, W.A. & Carpenter, S.R. (2009). "Interacting Regime Shifts in Ecosystems: Implication for Early Warnings." The Beijer Institute foe Ecological Economics, Discussion Paper # 217

Brown, S. & Eisenhardt, K. (1998): Competing on the Edge. Cambridge, MA: Harvard Business School Press

Breschi, S. & Lissoni, F. (2006). "Mobility of inventors and the geography of knowledge spillovers. New evidence from US data." Università Commerciale "Luigi Bocconi", Milano, Italy, CESPRI Working Paper WP #184

Brusoni, S. & Roberto, F. (2005). "Modularity as an Entry Strategy: The invasion of new niches in the LAN equipment industry." CESPRI Working Papers Centre for Research on Innovation and Internationalization, Università Commerciale "Luigi Bocconi", Milano, Italy, CESPRI Working Paper WP 171, Milano, Italy

Brusoni, S., Marengo, L., Prencipe A., & Valente, M. (2007). "The Value and Costs of Modularity: A Cognitive Perspective." SPRU Electronic Working Paper Series 123, University of Sussex, SPRU - Science and Technology Policy Research, Published in European Management Review, 4(2), 121–132

Buganza, T. & Verganti, R. (2006). " Life-Cycle Flexibility: How to Measure and Improve the Innovative Capability in Turbulent Times." Journal of Product Innovation Management, 23(5), 393-407

Burgelman, R.A. (1983). "A Process Model of Internal Corporate Venturing in the Diversified Major Firm." Administrative Science Quarterly, 28(2), 223-244

Burgelman, R.A. (2002): Strategy is Destiny. New York NY: The Free Press

Burgelman, R.A. (2002). "Strategy as a Vector and the Inertia of Co-evolutionary Lock-in." Administrative Science Quarterly, 47(2), 325-357

Burgelman, R.A. & Sayles, L.R. (1986): Inside Corporate Innovation. New York NY: The Free Press

Burns, T. & Stalker, G.M. (1961): The Management of Innovation. London: Tavistock

Buzacott, J.A. (1982). "The Fundamental Principles of Flexibility in Manufacturing Systems." Brighton: U.K.: Proceedings of the First International Conference on Flexible Manufacturing Systems

Buzacott, J.A. & Mandelbaum, M. (2008). "Flexibility in manufacturing and services: achievements, insights and challenges." Flexible Services and Manufacturing Journal, 20(1-2), 13-58

Byrd, T.A. & Turner, D.E. (2000). "Measuring the Flexibility of Information Technology Infrastructure: Exploratory Analysis of a Construct." Journal of Management Information Systems, 17(1), 167-208

Caldentey, R., & Haugh, M.B. (2009). "Supply Contracts with Financial Hedging." Operations Research, 57(1), 47-65

Carley, D.H. & Cryer, T.L. (1964). "Flexibility of Operation in Dairy Manufacturing Plants: Changes 1944-1961." U.S.D.A. Agricultural Economic Report #61

Carpenter, S., Walker, B., Anderies, J.M., & Abel, N. (2001). "From Metaphor to Measurement: Resilience of What to What?" Ecosystems 4: 765-781

Carpenter, S.R., Folke, C., Scheffer, M., & Westley, F. R. (2009)."Resilience: accounting for the non-computable." Ecology and Society, 14(1): Apt 13. Retrieved from http://www.ecologyandsociety.org/articles/2819.html

Carver, C.S. (1998). "Resilience and Thriving: Issues, Models, and Linkages." Journal of Social Issues, 54(2), 245-266

Chapin III, F.S., Hoel, M., Carpenter, S. R., Lubchenco, J., Walker, B., Callaghan, T.V., Folke, C., Levin, S. A., Mäler, K-G., Nilsson, C., Barrett, S., Berkes, F., Crépin, A-S., Danell, S., Rosswall, T., Starrett, D., Xepapadeas, A. & Zimov, S.A. (2006). "Building Resilience and Adaptation to Manage Arctic Change." AMBIO, Journal of the Human Environment, 35(4), 198-202

Chandler, A.D. (1962): Strategy and Structure. Cambridge MA: MIT Press

Chandra, C. & Grabis, J. (2009). "Role of flexibility in supply chain and modeling - Introduction to the special issue." Omega, 37(4), 743-745

Chatman, J.A. & Cha, S.E. (2003). "Leading by Leveraging Culture." California Management Review, 45(4), 20-34

Cheema, A. & Soman, D. (2006). "Malleable Mental Accounting: The Effect of Flexibility on the Justification of Attractive Spending and Consumption Decisions." Journal of Consumer Psychology, 16(1) 33-44

Chen, W. & Kemper, L. (1999). "Robust Design for Achieving Flexibility in Multidisciplinary Design." AIAA Journal, 37(8), 982-989

Chesborough, H.W. (2003): Open Innovation. Cambridge MA: Harvard Business School Press

Child, J. (1972). "Organization Structure, Environment and Performance: The Role of Strategic Choice." Sociology, 6(1) 1-22

Child, J. & McGrath, R.G. (2001) "Organizations Unfettered: Organizational Form in an Information-intensive Economy". Academy of Management Journal, (Special Research Forum on New & Evolving Organizational Forms), 44(6) 1135-1148

Child, J. & Smith, C. (1987) "The Context and Process of Organizational Transformation: Cadbury Limited in its Sector." Journal of Management Studies, 24(6), 565-593

Chisholm, R.A. & Filotas, E. (2007). "Ecosystem Resilience and the Paradox of Enrichment" The Santa Fe Institute

Chisholm, R.A. & Filotas, E. (2009). "Critical Slowing Down as an Indicator of Transitions in Two-species Models" Journal of Theoretical Biology, 257(1), 142-149

Christensen, C.M. (1997): The Innovator's Dilemma. Cambridge MA: Harvard Business School Press

Christensen, C.M. & Raynor, M.E. (2003): The Innovator's Solution. Cambridge MA: Harvard Business School Press

Clemons, E.K. & Santamaria, J.A. (2002). "Maneuver Warfare." Harvard Business Review, 80(4), 56-65

Coffield, F.J. (1999) "Breaking the Consensus, Lifelong Learning as Social Control." European Conference on Lifelong Learning

Collingridge, D. (1981): The Social Control of Technology, London: Palgrave MacMillan

Collingridge, D. (1983). "Hedging and Flexing: Two Ways of Choosing under Ignorance." Technological Forecasting & Social Change, 23(2), 161-172

Collins, N.R. (1956). "Gains in Profits from Flexible as Compared with Inflexible Use of Resources with Reference to the Specialized Grain Producing Firm." Unpublished Ph.D. Dissertation, Harvard University

Comfort, L.K., Sungu,Y., Johnson, D. & Dunn, M. (2001). "Complex Systems in Crisis: Anticipation and Resilience in Dynamic Environments." Journal of Contingencies and Crisis Management, 5(3), 144-158

Cooper, A.C. & Bruno, A. (1977). "Success Among High Technology Firms." Business Horizons, 20(2), 16-22

Copeland, T.E. & Keenan, P.T. (1998). "How much is flexibility worth?" The McKinsey Quarterly, (2), 38-49

Cowden, J.M. & Trelogan, H.C. (1948). "Flexibility of Operation in Dairy Manufacturing Plants." U.S.D.A. Circular #799

Cyert, R.M. & March, J.G. (1963): A Behavioral Theory of the Firm. Englewood Cliffs N.J: Prentice Hall

Daoudal, G. & Debanne, D. (2003). "Long-Term Plasticity of Intrinsic Excitability: Learning Rules and Mechanisms." Learning and Memory, 10(6), 456-465

Davis, J.P., Eisenhardt, K.M., & Bingham, C.B. (2009). "Optimal Structure, Market Dynamism, and the Strategy of Simple Rules." Administrative Science Quarterly, 54(3), 413-452

Day, R.H. (1969). "Flexible Utility and Myopic Expectation in Economics." Oxford Economic Papers, New Series, 21(3), 299-311

De Groote, X. (1994). "The Flexibility of Production Processes: A General Framework." Management Science, 40(7), 933-945

De Leeuw, A.C.J. & Volberda, H.W. (1996). "On the Concept of Flexibility: A Dual Control Perspective." Omega

De Meyer, A., Nakane, J., Miller, J.G., & Ferdows, K. (1989). "Flexibility: The Next Competitive Battle. The Manufacturing Futures Survey." Strategic Management Journal, 10(2), 135-144

Desell, T, El Maghraoui, K, & Varela, C.A. (2007). "Malleable applications for scalable high performance computing." Cluster Computing, 10(3), 323-337

DeSteno D. & Salovey P. (1997). "Structural Dynamism in the Concept of Self: A Flexible Model for a Malleable Concept." Review of General Psychology, 1(4), 389-409

De Toni, A. & Tonchia, S. (1998). "Manufacturing Flexibility: a literature review." International Journal of Production Research, 36(6), 1587-1617

DeWitt, T.J. (1998). "Costs and limits of phenotypic plasticity: Tests with predator-induced morphology and life history in a freshwater snail". Journal of Evolutionary Biology, 11(4), 465-480

DeWitt, T. J. & Scheiner, S.M. (Eds.) (2004): Phenotypic Plasticity Functional and Conceptual Approaches. Oxford University Press

Devine, J. (1985). "The Versatility of Human Locomotion." American Anthropologist, New Series, 87(3), 550-570

Ding, Q., Dong, L. & Kouvelis, P. (2007). "On the Integration of Production and Financial Hedging Decisions in Global Markets." Operations Research, 55(3), 470-489

Draaisma, J.J.F. & Mol, A. (1977). "Is Steam Cracker Flexibility Economical?" Hydrocarbon Processing, 56(4), 149-155

Doz, Y. & Kosonen, M. (2008): Fast Strategy: How Strategic Agility will help you stay ahead of the Game. Wharton School Publishing

Duncan, R.B. (1976). "The ambidextrous organization: Designing dual structures for innovation." In L.R. Kilmann, L.R. Pondy & D. Slevin (Eds.) The Management of Organization Vol. 1, 167-188. North Holland NY, Elsevier

Dyer, L. & Ericksen, J. (2006). "Dynamic Organizations: Achieving Marketplace Agility through Workforce Scalability." Cornell University ILR School, CAHRS Working Paper #06-12

Dyer, L. & Ericksen, J. (2008). "Complexity Based Agile Enterprises: Putting Self-Organizing Emergence to Work." Cornell University ILR School, CAHRS Working Paper #08-01

Dybå, T., & Dingsøyr, T. (2008). "Empirical studies of agile software development: A systematic review." Information and Software Technology, 50(9-10), 833-859

Earle, E.M. (1943): Makers of Modern Strategy. Princeton NJ: Princeton University Press

Eccles, H.E. (1959): Logistics and the National Defense. London: Stackpole Company

Ekstrom, M.A. & Bjornsson, H.C. (2003). "Evaluating IT investments in Construction: Accounting for strategic flexibility." Center for Integrated Facility Engineering, Stanford University, CFE Technical Report#136,

Elberse, A. & Oberholzer-Gee, F. (2006). "Superstars and Underdogs: An Examination of the Long Tail Phenomenon in Video Sales." Harvard Business School, Working Paper Series #07-015

Elberse, A. (2008) "Should you invest in the long tail." Harvard Business Review 86 (7/8), 319-343

Eppink, D.J. (1978a). "Managing the Unforeseen: A Study of Flexibility." Unpublished Ph.D. Dissertation, Vrije Unviersiteit, Amsterdam

Eppink, D.J. (1978b). "Planning for Strategic Flexibility." Long Range Planning, 11(4), 9-15

Ethiraj, S.K., Levinthal, D. and Roy, R.R. (2008). "The Dual Role of Modularity: Innovation and Imitation." Management Science, 54(5), 939-955

Evans, J.S. (1982a). "Flexibility in Policy Formation." Unpublished Ph.D. Thesis, Technology Policy Unit, Aston University

Evans, J.S. (1982b): Strategic Flexibility in Business. Menlo Park CA: S.R.I. International, Business Intelligence Program, Research Report #678

Evans, J.S. (1991). "Strategic Flexibility for High Technology Maneuvers." Journal of Management Studies, 28(1), 69-89

Feldman, M.S. & Pentland, P.J. (2003). "Reconceptualizing organizational routines as a source of flexibility and change." Administrative Science Quarterly, 48(1), 94-118

Feyerabend, P.K. (1968). "How to be a Good Empiricist- a Plea for Tolerance in Matters Epistemological." in P.H. Nidditch, (Ed.): The Philosophy of Science, Oxford University Press

Fiegenbaum, A. and Karnani, A. (1991). "Output Flexibility- A Competitive Advantage for Small Firms." Strategic Management Journal, 12(2), 1001-114

Fiegenbaum, A., Thomas, H., & Tang, M-J. (2001). "Linking Hypercompetition and Strategic Group Theories: Strategic Maneuvering in the US Insurance Industry." Managerial Decision Economics, 22(4-5), 265–279

Fiering, M.B. (1982) "A Screening Model to Quantify Resilience." Water Resources Research, 18(1), 27-32

Foch, F. (1921): The Principles of War. (Third Impression translated by H. Belloc), London: Chapman & Hall

Fong, C. & McCabe, K. (1999). "Are decisions under risk malleable?" Proceedings of the National Academy of Science, 96, 10927-10932

Fraser, R.W. (1985) "Demand Fluctuations, Inventory and Flexibility." Australian Economic Papers, 23(42), 105-111

Freeman, R.C., A. Horsley, V.T.P. Jervis, A.B. Robertson, & Townsend, J. (1974). "SAPPHO updated- Project SAPPHO." Research Policy 3(3), 258-291

French, B.C., Sammet, L.L. & Bressler, R.G. (1956). "Economic Efficiency in Plant Operations with Special Reference to the Marketing of California Pears." Hilgardia, 24(19), 543-721

Friedman, Y. & Reklaitis, G.V. (1975). "Flexible Solutions to Linear programs Under Uncertainty: Inequality Constraints." AIChE Journal, 21(1), 77-83

Fuller, J.F.C. (1946): Armament and History. London: Eyre & Spottiswoode

Fuss, M. A. (1977). "The Demand for Energy in Canadian Manufacturing." Journal of Econometrics, 5(1), 89-116

Fuss, M. A. (1977). "The Structure of Technology over Time: A Model for Testing the "Putty-Clay Hypothesis." Econometrica, 45(8), 1797-1821

Gamba, A. & Fusari, N. (2009). "Valuing Modularity as a Real Option." Management Science, 5(11), 1877-1896

Galunic, D.C. & Eisenhardt, KM. (2001). "Architectural Innovation and Modular Corporate Forms." The Academy of Management Journal, 44(6), 1229-1249

Gavetti, G. & Rivkin, J.W. (2007). "Rationality and Plasticity over Time: Toward a Grounded Theory of the Origin of Strategies." Organization Science, 18(3), 420-439

Gebauer, J. & Schober, F. (2006). "Information System Flexibility and the Cost Efficiency of Business Processes." Journal of the AIS, 7(3), 122-147

Gebauer, J. & Lee, F. (2007)." Enterprise System Flexibility and Implementation Strategies: Aligning Theory with Evidence from a Case Study." Information Systems Management, 25(1), 71-82

Gebauer, J. & Lee, F. (2008). "Enterprise System Flexibility and Implementation Strategies: Aligning Theory with Evidence from a Case Study." Information Systems Security, 25(1), 71-82

Gerwin, D. (1982). "Do's and Don'ts of Computerized Manufacturing." Harvard Business Review March-April, 60(2), 107-116

Gerwin, D. (1993). "Manufacturing Flexibility: A Strategic Perspective." Management Science, 39(4), 395-410

Ghosal, S. & Bartlett, C.A. (1997): The Individualized Corporation. New York NY: Harper Collins

von Ghyczy, T., Bassford, C. & von Oetinger, B. (2003): Clausewitz on Strategy. New York: Wiley

Giachetti, R.E., Martinez, L.D. Sáenz, O.S. & Chen, C-S. (2003). "Analysis of the structural measures of flexibility and agility using a measurement theoretical framework." International Journal of Production Economics, 86(1), 47-62

Gibson, C.B. & Birkinshaw, J. (2004). "The Antecedents, Consequences, and Mediating Role of Organizational Ambidexterity." Academy of Management Journal, 47(2), 209-226

Gibbons, F.M. (1987). "The Secrets of Guerrilla Management." Inc. Magazine, February: 124-125

Gist, M.E. & Mitchell, T.R. (1992). "Self-Efficacy: A Theoretical Analysis of its Determinants and Malleability." Academy of Management Review, 17(2), 183-211

Glatzel, C., Helmke, S. & Wine, J. (2009) "Building a flexible supply chain for uncertain times." McKinsey Quarterly March

Goldman, S.M. (1974). "Flexibility and the Demand for Money." Journal of Economic Theory, 9(2), 203-222

Goldman, S.M. (1978). "Portfolio Choice and Flexibility." Journal of Monetary Economics, 4(2), 263-279

Gong, Z. & Hu, S. (2008) "An economic evaluation of product mix flexibility." Omega, 36(5), 852-864

Gregorius, H.R. & Kleinschmit, J.R.G. (1999). "The Environmental Dichotomy of Adaptation and the Role of Genetic Diversity." Silvae Genetica, 48(3/4), 193-199

Grewal, R. & Tansuhaj, P. (2001). "Building Organizational Capabilities for Managing Economic Crisis: The Role of Market Orientation and Strategic Flexibility." Journal of Marketing, 65(2), 67-80

Grove, A. (1996): Only the Paranoid Survive. New York: Doubleday

Grümm, H. R. (1976). "Definitions of Resilience." International Institute for Applied Systems Analysis, Vienna: Research Report #76-6

Grümm, H.R. and Breitenecker, M. (1981). Economic Evolutions and Their Resilience: A Model. International Institute for Applied Systems Analysis, Vienna: Research Report 81-5

Guerico, V.J. (1981). "Feedstock Flexibility." Chemical Engineering, 82(2), 63-65

Gunderson, L. (1999). "Resilience, Flexibility and Adaptive Management - Antidotes for Spurious Certitude?" Conservation Ecology 3(1), 7

Gunderson L.H. & Holling, C.S. (2001): Panarchy: Understanding Transformations in Human and Natural Systems. Washgington DC: Is-land Press

Gupta, Y.P. & Goyal S. (1989). "Flexibility of manufacturing systems: Concepts and measurements." European Journal of Operational Research, 43(2), 119-135

Hagen, E. H. and Hammerstein, P. (2005). "Evolutionary Biology and the Strategic View of Ontogeny: Genetic Strategies provide Robustness and Flexibility in the Life Course." Research in Human Development, 21(1&2), 87-101

Hahlway, W. (1966). C. von Clausewitz: Schriften. Aufsätze, Studien Briefe, Götingen

Hamblin, D.J. (2002). "Re-thinking the Management of Flexibility - a Study of the Aerospace Industry." Journal of the Operational Research Society, 53(3), 272-282

Hambrecht, W.R. (1984). "Venture Capital and The Growth of Silicon Valley." California Management Review, 26(2), 74-82

Hamel, G. (2000). "Waking Up IBM." Harvard Business Review, 78(4), 137-148

Hamel, G. & Valikangas, L. (2003). "The Quest for Resilience." Harvard Business Review, 81(9), 52-63

Hammer, M. & Champy, J. (1993): Re-engineering the Corporation: A Manifesto for Business Revolution. New York: Harper Business

Hammond, J.S., Keeney, R.L., & Raiffa, H. (1999): Smart Choices: A practical guide to making better decisions. Cambridge MA: Harvard Business School Press

Hanel, R., Thurner, S., & Tsallis, C. (2008)."On the robustness of q-expectation values and Rényi entropy." Santa Fe Institute Working Paper #08-12-059

Harker, J.M., Brede, D.W., Pattison, R.E., Santana, G.R. & Taft, L.G. (1981). "A Quarter Century of Disk Drive Innovation." IBM Journal of Research and Development, 25(5), 677-690

Harrigan, K.R. (1980). "The Effect of Exit Barriers on Strategic Flexibility." Strategic Management Journal, 1(2), 165-176

Harrigan, K.R. (1985): Strategic Flexibility: A Management Guide for Changing Times, Lexington MA: D.C. Heath and Company

Hart, A.G. (1937a). "Anticipations, Business Planning and the Cycle." Quarterly Journal of Economics, 51(2), 272-293

Hart, A.G. (1937b). "Failure and Fulfillment of Expectations in Business Fluctuations." Review of Economics and Statistics, 19(2), 69-78

Hart A.G. (1940): Anticipations, Uncertainty and Dynamic Planning. University of Chicago Press

Hatum, A. & Pettigrew, A. (2006). "Determinants of Organizational Flexibility: A Study in an Emerging Economy." British Journal of Management, 17(2), 115-137

Hashimoto, T., Stedinger, J.R., & Loucks, D.P. (1982a). "Reliability, Resiliency and Vulnerability Criteria for Water Resource System Performance Evaluation." Water Resources Research, 18 (1), 14-20

Hashimoto, T., Stedinger, J.R. & Loucks, D.P. (1982). "Robustness of Water Resources System." Water Resources Research, 18 (1), 21-26

Heckhausen, J. & Singer, T. (2001). "Plasticity in Human Behavior across the Lifespan." in N.J. Smelser and P.B. Balter (Eds.) International Encyclopedia of the Social and Behavioral Sciences, pp. 11497-11501, Elsevier Science Ltd. New York

Hedlund, G. (1986). "The Hypermodern MNC: a Heterarchy" Human Resource Management, 25(1), 9-35

Heidegger, M. (1977): The Question Concerning Technology. Translated by W. Lovitt, London: Harper & Row

Heimann, S.R. & Lusk, E.J. (1976). "Decision Flexibility: An Alternative Evaluation Criterion." The Accounting Review, 51(1), 51-64

Helbing, D., Deutsch, A., Diez, S., Peters, K, Kalaidzidis, Y., Kathrin Padberg, K., Lämmer, S., Johansson, A., Breier, G., Schulze, F. & Zerial, M. (2009). "BioLogistics and the Struggle for Efficiency: Concepts and Perspectives." Santa Fe Institute Working Paper # 09-10-041

Henderson, R. M. "The Evolution of Integrative Capability: Innovation in Cardiovascular Drug Discovery." Industrial and Corporate Change, 3(3), 607-630

Henry, C. (1974). "Investment Decisions Under Uncertainty: The Irreversibility Effect." The American Economic Review, 64(6), 1006-1012

Highsmith, J. (2001). "Agile Software Development: The Business of Innovation." IEEE Computer, 34(9), 120-127

Highsmith, J. (2002): Agile Software Development Ecosystems. Addison Wesley

Hill S.L., Burrows M.T., Hughes R.N. (2003). "The efficiency of adaptive search tactics for different prey distribution patterns: a simulation model based on the behaviour of juvenile plaice." Journal of Fish Biology, 63(1), 117-130

Hinds, P.J. & Kiesler, S. (2002): Distributed Work. Cambridge MA: M.I.T. Press von Hippel, E. (1986). "Lead Users: A Source of Novel Product Concepts." Management Science, 32(7), 791-805

von Hippel, E.A. (1976). "Users as Innovators." Technology Review, 5, 212-239

Hittle, J.D. (1947): Jomini's Art of War. Harrisburg, PA: The Telegraph Press

Hoetker, G. (2006). "Do modular products lead to modular organizations?" Strategic Management Journal, 27(6), 501-518

Hoetker, G. (2007). "Modularity and the Impact of Buyer-Supplier Relationships on the Survival of Suppliers." Management Science, 53(2), 178-191

Holling, C.S. (1973). "Resilience and Stability of Ecological Systems." Annual Review of Ecology and Systematics, 4, 301-321

Holling C.S., Folk, C., Gunderson, L. & Mäler, K.G. (2000): " Resilience of Ecosystems, Economic Institutions and Institutions." Final Report John D. & Catherine T. MacArthur Foundation

Holopainen H. (2002). "Corporate Governance Structures: How Investment Incentives Interact with Strategic Flexibility." EBHA Annual Conference, Helsinki

Hong. H. & Rady, S. (2002). "Strategic Trading and Learning about Liquidity." Journal of Financial Markets, 5(4), 419-450

Howard-Grenville, J.A. (2005). "The Persistence of Flexible Organizational Routines: The Role of Agency and Organizational Context." Organization Science, 16(6), 618-636

Huang, J. (2001). "Future Space: A Blueprint for Future Architecture." Harvard Business Review, 79(4), 149-157

Huchzermeier, A. & Cohen, M.A. (1996). "Valuing Operational Flexibility under Exchange Rate Risk." Operations Research, (Special Issue on New Directions in Operations Management), 44(1), 100-113

Hughes R.N. (2005). "Lessons in modularity: the evolutionary ecology of colonial invertebrates." Scientia Marina, 69 (Suppl.1), 169-179

Hutchinson, G.K. & Wynne, B.E. (1973). "A Flexible Manufacturing System." Industrial Engineering, 5(10), 10-17

Iravani, S.M.R., Buzacott, J.A. & Posner, M.J.M. (2003). "Operations and Shipment Scheduling of Batch on a Flexible Machine." Operations Research, 51(4), 585-601

Jansen, J.J.P., Temelaar, M.P., van den Bosch, F.A.J. & Volberda, H. W. (2009). "Structural Differentiation and Ambidexterity: The Mediating Role of Integration Mechanisms." Organization Science, 20(4), 797-811

Janssen, M.A. & Anderies, J.M. (2007). "Robustness Trade-offs in Social-Ecological Systems." International Journal of the Commons, 1(1), 43-65

Janssen, M.A. & Ostrom, E. (2006). "Resilience, vulnerability, and adaptation: A cross-cutting theme of the International Human Dimensions Programme on Global Environmental Change." Global Environmental Change, 16(3), 237-239

Jedlika, P. (2002). "Synaptic plasticity, metaplasticity and bcm theory." Bratislavke Lekartke Listy, 103(4-5), 137-143

Jen, E. (2004): Robust Design: Biological, Ecological and Engineering Case Studies. Oxford University Press

Johnson, G. (1988). "Rethinking Incrementalism." Strategic Management Journal, 9(1), 75-91

Jones, R.A. & Ostroy, J.M. (1976). "Liquidity as Flexibility." Department of Economics, U.C.L.A.: Discussion Paper # 73

Jones, R.A. & Ostroy, J.M. (1984). "Flexibility and Uncertainty." Review of Economic Studies, 51(164), 13-32

Kanter, R.M. (1983): The Change Masters. New York, Simon & Schuster

Karuppan, C.M. & Karuppan, M. (2008). "Resilience of super users' mental models of enterprise-wide systems." European Journal of Information Systems, 17(1), 29-46

Katila, R., Rosenberger J.D. & Eisenardt, K.M. (2008). "Swimming with the Sharks; Technology Ventures, Defense Mechanisms and Corporate Relationships." Administrative Science Quarterly, 53(2), 295-332

Keeney, R.L. (1983). "Issues in Evaluating Standards." Interfaces, 13(2), 12-22

Kelley, T. (2005): The Ten Faces of Innovation. New York: Doubleday

Kennedy, J.S., Forsyth, P.A., & Vetzal, K.R. (2009). "Dynamic Hedging under Jump Diffusion with Transaction Costs." Operations Research, 57(5), 541-559

Kenney, M. (Ed.) (2000): Understanding Silicon Valley. Stanford University Press

Kenney, M. & Florida, R. (2000). "Venture Capital in Silicon Valley: Fueling New Firm Formation" in M. Kenney, (Ed.) "Understanding Silicon Valley." Stanford University Press

Kerchner, O.G. (1966). "Economic Comparisons of Flexible and Specialized Plants in the Minnesota Dairy Manufacturing Industry." Unpublished Ph.D. Dissertation, University of Minnesota

Khan, A.K. & Pillania, R.K. (2008). "Strategic sourcing for supply chain agility and firms' performance." Management Decision, 46(10), 1508-1530

Kickert, W.J.M. (1985). "The magic word flexibility." International Studies of Management and Organization, 14(4), 6–31

Kindleberger, C.P. (1937). "Flexibility in Demand in International Trade Theory." Quarterly Journal of Economics 51(2), 352-361

Kinzig, A. P., Ryan, P., Etienne, M., Allison, H., Elmqvist,T. & Walker, B. H. (2006). "Resilience and Regime Shifts: Assessing Cascading Effects." Ecology and Society, 11(1), 20

Kitano, H. (2004). "Biological Robustness." Nature Reviews Genetics 5(11), 826-835

Klaus, J.D. (2005). "Strategic Mobility Innovation: Options and Oversight Issues." CADRE/PC Report 2005-15

Klein, B.H. & Meckling, W. (1958)."Application of O.R. to Development Decisions." Operations Research, 6(3), 352-363

Klemm, K. & Stadler, P. (2008). "A Note on Fundamental, Non-fundamental, and Robust Cycle Bases." Discrete Applied Mathematics, 157(10), 2432-2438,

Knight, F.H. (1921): Risk, Uncertainty and Profit. Boston MA: Houghton Miflin and Company

Kogut, B. & Kulatilaka, N. (1994). "Operating Flexibility, Global Manufacturing and the Option Value of a Multinational Network." Management Science, 40(1), 123-139

Koopmans, T.C. (1964). "On Flexibility of Future Preferences." in M.W. Shelly and G.L. Bryan (Eds.) Human Judgment and Optimality. New York: Wiley

Koopmans, T.C. (1957): The Construction of Economic Knowledge. McGraw Hill

Kotkin, J. & Grabowicz, P. (1982): California, Inc. New York, Rawson Wade Publishers

Kotter, J. (1996): Leading Change. Cambridge, MA: Harvard University Press

Kreps, D.M. (1979). "A Representation Theorem for Preference for Flexibility." Econometrica, 47(3), 565-577

Kretchmar, L. (1989). "Auspex Serves Notice." Upside Magazine November-December: 17-18.

Krijnen, H.G. (1979). "The Flexible Firm." Long Range Planning, 12(2), 63-75

Kuhn, T.S. (1962): The Structure of Scientific Revolutions. The University of Chicago Press

Kulatilaka, N. (1986). "The Value of Flexibility." Working Paper MIT-EL 86-014WP

Kulatilaka, N. (1988). "Valuing the Flexibility of Flexible Manufacturing Systems. Working Paper MIT-EL 88-006WP

Kulatilaka, N. (1988). "Strategic Growth Options." Management Science, 44(8), 1021-1031

Kulatilaka, N. & Marks, S.G. (1980). "The Strategic Value of Flexibility: Reducing the Ability to Compromise." The American Economic Review, 78(3), 574-580

Kulatilaka, N. (1993). "The Value of Flexibility: The Case of a Dual-Fuel Industrial Steam Boiler." Financial Management, 22(3), 271-280

Lange, O., (1944): Price Flexibility and Employment. Cowles Commission for Research in Economics, Monograph #8: Principia Press

Langerhans, B.R. & DeWitt, T.J. (2002). "Plasticity constrained: overgeneralized induction cues cause maladaptive phenotypes." Evolutionary Ecology Research, 4, 857-870

Lawrence, P. & Lorsch, J.W. (1967): Organizations and their Environment: Managing Differentiation and Integration. Cambridge MA: Graduate School of Business Administration, Harvard University

Lawrence, P. & Dyer, D. (1981). "Toward a Theory of Organizational and Industrial Adaptation." Graduate School of Business Administration, Harvard University, Working Paper # HBS 80-57

Lee, G., & Xia, W. (2005). "The ability of information systems development project teams to respond to business and technology changes: a study of flexibility measures." European Journal of Information Systems, 14(1), 75-92

Lee, G, D., DeLone, W. & Espinosa, J.A. (2006). "Ambidextrous coping strategies in globally distributed software development projects." Communications of the ACM, 49(10), 35-40

Lee, H.L., Padmanabhan, V. & Whang, S. (1997). "The bullwhip effect in supply chains." Sloan Management Review, 38(3), 93-102

Lenzi, C. (2006). "Knowledge Transfer Through Job Mobility: Evidence from a survey of Italian Inventors." Università Commerciale "Luigi Bocconi", Milano, Italy, CESPRI Working Paper WP , CESPRI Working Paper #182

Lenzi, C. (2009). "Patterns and determinants of skilled workers' mobility: evidence from a survey of Italian inventors." Economics of Innovation and New Technology, 18(2), 161-179

Li, S-C., Brehmer, Y., Shing,Y.L., Werkle-Bergner, M., Lindenberger, U. (2006). "Neuromodulation of associative and organizational plasticity across the life span: Empirical evidence and neurocomputational modeling." Neuroscience and Biobehavioral Reviews, 30(6), 775–790

Liddell Hart, B.H. (1929): The Decisive Wars of History. Boston MA: Little Brown & Company

Liddell Hart, B.H. (1954): Strategy: The Indirect Approach. London: Faber and Faber

Liebskind, J.P., Oliver, A.L., Zucker, L., & Brewer, M. (1996). "Social Networks, Learning, and Flexibility: Sourcing Scientific Knowledge in New Biotechnology Firms." Organization Science, 7(4), 428-443

Lindblom, C.E. (1959). "The Science of Muddling Through." Public Administration Review, 19(2), 79-88

Lin, Z.J., Yang, H., & Demirkan, I. (2007). "The Performance Consequences of Ambidexterity in Strategic Alliance Formation: Empirical Investigation and Computational Theorizing." Management Science, 53(10), 1645-1658

Lipman-Blumen, J. & Leavitt, H.J. (1999): Hot Groups. New York: Oxford University Press

Longford, E. (1969): Wellington, the Years of the Sword. New York: Harper & Row (Wellington's original quote was published in Sir William A. Fraser, (1899): Words on Wellington: the Duke-Waterloo -the Ball. p.37 London: John C. Nimmo)

Lubatkin, M.H., Simsek, Z., Ling, Y., & Veiga, J.F. (2006). "Ambidexterity and Performance in Small-to-Medium-Sized Firms: The Pivotal Role of Top Management Team Behavioral Integration." Journal of Management, 32(5), 646-672

Luthar, S.S., Cicchetti, D. & Becker, B. (2000). "The Construct of Resilience: A Critical Evaluation and Guidelines for Future Work." Child Development, 71(3) 543-562

Lund, R. & Gjerding, A.N. (1996)."The Flexible Company: Innovation, work organization and human resource management." Danish Research Unit for Industrial Dynamics Working Paper #96-17

Lund R. (1998). "Organizational and Innovative Flexibility Mechanisms and their Impact on Organizational Effectiveness." Danish Research Unit for Industrial Dynamics Working Paper #98-23

Lutgens, F, Sturm, J., & Koleen, A. (2006). "Robust One-Period Hedging." Operations Research, 54(6), 1051-1062

MacCormack, A., Rusnak, J. & Baldwin, C.Y. (2007). "The Impact of Component Modularity on Design Evolution: Evidence from the Software Industry." Harvard Business School Working Paper Series #08-038

Maenhout, Pascal J. (2004). "Robust Portfolio Rules and Asset Pricing." Review of Financial Studies, 17(4), 951-983

Maidique, M.A. & Hayes, R.H. (1984). "The Art of High Technology Management." Sloan Management Review, (January), 17-31

Maidique, M.A. & Zirger, B.J. (1984). "A Study of Success and Failure in Product Innovation: The Case of the U.S. Electronics Industry." IEEE Transactions on Engineering Management, EM-31(4), 192-203,

Maidique, M.A. & Zirger, B.J. (1985). "The New Product Learning Cycle." Research Policy, 14(6), 299-313

Mäler, K-G. (2004). "Sustainable Development and Resilience in Ecosystems." Environmental and Resource Economics, 39(1), 1724

Mäler, K-G., Chuan-Zhong Li, & Destouni, G. (2007). "Pricing Resilience in a Dynamic Economy-Environment System: A Capital-Theoretical Approach." Beijer Institute of Ecological Economics, Discussion Paper # 208

Mäler, K-G., Aniyar, S. and Jansson, Å. (2009). "Accounting for ecosystem services as a way to understand the requirements for sustainable development." Proceedings of the National Academy of Science of the United States of America, 15(8), 9501-9506; also published in Environmental and Resource Economics, 42(1), 39–51

Malone, M.S. (2002): Betting it all. New York: Wiley

Malone, T.W. (2004). "Bringing the Market Inside." Harvard Business Review, 82(4), 106-114

Mandelbaum, M. (1978). "Flexibility in Decision Making: An Exploration and Elaboration." Unpublished Doctoral Dissertation, University of Toronto, Canada

Mandelbaum, M. & Cunningham, A.A. (1979). "The Use of Flexibility in Decision Making: Hedging Against Model Deficiencies." Paper presented at ORSA/TIMS Conference

Mandelbaum, M. & Brill, P.H. (1989). "Examples of measurement of flexibility and adaptivity in manufacturing systems." Journal of the Operational Research Society, 40(6), 603-609

Mandelbaum, M. & Buzacott, J. (1990). "Flexibility and decision making." European Journal of Operational Research, 44(11), 17-27

March, J.G. (1981). "Decisions in Organizations and Theories of Choice." in A.H. Van de Ven, & W.F. Joyce, (Eds.): Perspectives on Organization Design and Behavior. Wiley

March, J.G. & Olsen, J.P. (1976): Ambiguity and Choice in Organizations. Norway, Universitetsforlaget

Marschak, T. & Nelson, R. (1962). "Flexibility, Uncertainty and Economic Theory," Metroeconomica, 14(1, 2, & 3), 42-58

Martin, O.C. & Wagner, A. (2007). "Multifunctionality and robustness tradeoffs in model genetic circuits." Santa Fe Institute Working Paper 07-09-037

Mascarenhas, B. & Aaker, D.A. (1989). "Mobility Barriers and Strategic Groups." Strategic Management Journal, 10(5), 475-485

Mason, E.S. (1938). "Price Inflexibility." Review of Economic Studies, 20(2), 53-64

Mason, S.P. (1986). "Valuing Financial Flexibility." in B.M. Friedman, (ed.) Financing Corporate Capital Formation, University of Chicago Press

Masten, A. S. (2001). "Ordinary magic: Resilience processes in development." American Psychologist, 56(3), 227-238

Masten, A. S. (2004). "Regulatory processes, risk and resilience in adolescent development." Annals of the New York Academy of Sciences, 1021, 310-319

Masten, A. S., Burt, K., Roisman, G. I., Obradović, J., Long, J. D., & Tellegen, A. (2004). "Resources and resilience in the transition to adulthood: Continuity and change." Development and Psychopathology, 16(4), 1071-1094

Masten, A. S. (2006). "Developmental psychopathology: Pathways to the future." International Journal of Behavioral Development, 30(1), 46-53

Masten, A.S., Best, K.M., & Garmezy, N. (1990). "Resilience and development: Contributions from the study of children who overcome adversity." Development & Psychopathology, 2(4), 425-444

McKendrick, D.G., Doner, R.F. & Haggard, S. (2000): From Silcon Valley to Singapore: Location and Competitive Advantage in the Hard Disk Drive Industry. Stanford, CA: Stanford University Press

McKinsey, J. O. (1932). "Adjusting Policies to Meet Changing Conditions." American Management Association, General Management Series GM-116, July 1

Meffert, H. (1969). "Züm Problem der Betriebswirtschaftlichen Flexibilität." Zeitschrift für Betriebswirtschaftliche, 39

Meffert, H. (1985). "Größere flexibilität als Unternehmungskonzept." Schmalenbachs Zeitscrift für betriebwirtschaftlichte Forschung, 2, 121-137

Mendelson, H. & Tunca, T. (2004). "Strategic Trading, Liquidity and Information Acquisition." The Review of Financial Studies, 17(2), 295-337

Merkhofer, M.W. (1975): Flexibility and Decision Analysis. Unpublished Doctoral Dissertation, Stanford University

Merkhofer, M.W. (1977). "The Value of Information Given Decision Flexibility." Management Science, 23(7), 716-727

Merkhofer, M.W. & Saade, W.M. (1978). "Decision Flexibility in a Learning Environment." Unpublished Report, SRI International, Decision Analysis Group

Meyer, M.H. & Roberts, E.B. (1986)."New Product Strategy in Small Technology-Based Firms: A Pilot Study." Management Science, 32(7), 806-821

Miles, R.E. & C.C. Snow (1984). "Fit, Failure and the Hall of Fame." California Management Review, 27(1), 1-19

Miller, D. (1987). "The Genesis of Configuration." Academy of Management Review, 12(4): 686-701

Mintzberg, H. (1979): The Structuring of Organizations. Englewood Cliffs NJ: Prentice-Hall

Mockett, B.G. & Hulme S.R. (2008). "Metaplasticity: new insights through electrophysiological investigations." Journal of Integrative Neuroscience, 7(2), 315-336

Mom, T.J., van den Bosch, F.A.J., & Volberda, H.W. (2009). "Understanding Variation in Managers' Ambidexterity: Investigating Direct and Interaction Effects of Formal Structural and Personal Coordination Mechanisms." Organization Science, 20(4), 812-828

Montgomerie, R., Lyon, B., & Holder, K. (2001). "Dirty ptarmigan: behavioral modification of conspicuous male plumage." Behavioral Ecology, 12(4), 429-438

Moore, G.A. (1992): Crossing the Chasm. New York: Harper Business

Mulvany, R.B., Thompson, L.H., & Haughton, K.E. (1975). "Innovations in Disk File Manufacturing." In An Overview of Disk Storage Systems, Proceedings IEEE 63, 1148-1152

Nadkarni, S. & Narayanan, V.K. (2007). "Strategic schemas, strategic flexibility, and firm performance: the moderating role of industry clock-speed." Strategic Management Journal, 28(3), 243-270

Narassipuram, M.M., Regev, G., Kumar, K., & Wegman, A. (2008). "Business process flexibility through the exploration of stimuli." International Journal of Business Process Integration and Management, 3(1), 36- 2008

Nelson, K.M. & Nelson, H.J. (1997). "Technology Flexibility: Conceptualization, Validation, and Measurement," hicss, 3, 76-87, 30th Hawaii International Conference on System Sciences (HICSS) Volume 3: Information System Track- Organizational Systems and Technology

Nerur, S., Mahapatra, R., & Manglalraj, G. (2005)."Challenges of Migrating to Agile Methodologies.' Communications of the ACM, 48(5), 73-78

Nicholls, W.H. (1940). "Price Flexibility and Concentration in the Agricultural Processing Industry." Journal of Political Economy, 48(6), 883-888

Nilchiani, R., Hastings, D., & Joppin, C. (2005). "Calculations of Flexibility in Space Systems Design." Rochester NY:INCOSE 15th International Symposium

Nilchiani, R. (2005). "Measuring Space Systems Flexibility: A Comprehensive Six-element Framework." Unpublished Ph.D. Thesis, Aerospace Systems, Massachusetts Institute of Technology

Nilchiani, R. (2009). "Valuing software-based options for space systems flexibility." Acta Astronautica, 65(3-4), 429-441

Nonaka, I. & Takeuchi, H. (1995): The Knowledge-Creating Company. New York: Oxford University Press

Okhuysen, G.A. & Eisenhardt, K.M. (2002). "Integrating Knowledge in Groups: How Formal Interventions Enable Flexibility." Organization Science, 13(4), 370-386

Olsson, C.A., Bond, L., Burns, D.A. Vella-Broderick, D.A., & Sawyer, S.M. (2003). "Adolescent resilience: a concept analysis." Journal of Adolescence, 26(1), 1-11

Olsson, N.O.E. (2006). "Management of flexibility in projects." International Journal of Project Management, 24(1), 66-74

Olsson, P., Gunderson, L.H., Carpenter, S.R., Ryan, P., Lebel, L., Folke, C. & Holling, C.S. (2006). "Shooting the Rapids: Navigating Transitions to Adaptive Governance of Social-Ecological Systems." Ecology and Society, 11(1), 18-38

O'Reilly, C. A. (1989). "Corporation, Culture and Commitment: Motivation and Social Control in Organizations." California Management Review, 31(4), 9-25

O'Reilly, C. A. & Chatman, J. (1996). "Cultures as Social Control: Corporations, Cult and Commitment." In L. Cummings, and B. Staw, (Eds.) Research in Organizational Behavior, Greenwich, CT: JAI Press

O'Reilly, C. A. & Tushman, M. L. (1996). "Ambidextrous Organizations: Managing Evolutionary and Revolutionary Change." California Management Review, 38(4), 8-30

O'Reilly, C. A. & Tushman, M. L. (2004). "The ambidextrous organization." Harvard Business Review, (April) 74-83

O'Reilly, C. A. & Tushman, M. L. (2007). "Ambidexterity as a Dynamic Capability: Resolving the Innovator's Dilemma." Harvard Business School Working Paper, WP 07-088

Oosterhout, M. v., Waarts, E., & Hillegersberg, J.v. (2006). "Change factors requiring agility and implications for IT." European Journal of Information Systems, 15(2), 132-145

Oulasvirta, A. & Nyyssönen, T. (2009). "Flexible Hardware Configurations for Studying Mobile Usability." Journal of Usability Studies, 4(2), 93-105

Overby, E., Bharadwaj, A. & Sambamurthy, V. (2006). "Enterprise agility and the enabling role of information technology." European Journal of Information Systems, 15(1), 120-132

Paenke, I., Branke, J., & Jin, J. (2006). "Efficient Search for Robust Solutions by Means of Evolutionary Algorithms and Fitness Approximation." IEEE Transactions on Evolutionary Computing, 10(4), 405-420

Paenke, I., Sendhoff, B. & Kawecki, T. (2007) "Influence of Plasticity and Learning on Evolution under Directional Selection." American Naturalist, 170(2), E47-E58

Paenke, I., Sendhoff, B. & Kawecki, T, (2007). "On the Influence of Phenotype Plasticity on Genotype Diversity." IEEE Symposium on Foundations of Computational Intelligence, 33-41 2007

Paret, P. (Ed.) (1986): Makers of Modern Strategy. Princeton University Press

Paret, P. (1976): Clausewitz and the State. Princeton University Press

Patten, K. (2004). "How CIO's Balance Flexibility and Reliability in Uncertain Business Environments." International Journal of Computers, Systems and Signals, 5(1), 3-15

Patten, K., Whitworth, B., Fjermestad, J., & Mahinda, E. (2005). "Leading IT Flexibility: Anticipation, Agility and Adaptability." Proceedings of the Eleventh Americas Conference on Information Systems, Omaha, NE

Pauwels, P. & Matthyssens, P. (2004). "Strategic Flexibility in Export Expansion." International Marketing Review, 21(4-5), 496-510

Pauwels, P. & Matthyssens, P. (2005). "Strategic flexibility, rigidity and barriers to the development of absorptive capacity in business markets: themes and research perspectives." Industrial Marketing Management, 34(6), 547-554

Perrow, C. (1970): Organizational Analysis: A Sociological View. London: Tavistock

Piersma T., & Drent J., (2003) "Phenotype flexibility and the evolution of organismal design." Trends in Ecology and Evolution, 18(5), 228-233

Popper, K.R. (1972): Conjectures and Refutations: The Growth of Scientific Knowledge. London: Routledge & Kagan Paul

Porter, M.E. (1980): Competitive Strategy. New York: The Free Press

Porter, M.E. (1990): The Competitive Advantage of Nations. New York: The Free Press

Priore, M. & Sabel, C. (1984): The Second Industrial Divide. New York: Basic Books

Pye, R. (1978). "A Formal Decision Theoretic Approach to Flexibility and Robustness." Operational Research Quarterly, 29(3), 215-227

Qing, D., Dong, L., & Kouvelis, P. (2007). "On the Integration of Production and Financial Hedging Decisions in Global Markets." Operations Research, 55(3), 470-489

Quaas, M.F., Baumgärtner, S., Derissen, S. and Strunz, S. (2008). "Institutions and preferences determine resilience of ecological-economic systems." University of Lüneburg, Working Paper Series in Economics, # 109

Quinn, J.B. (1979). "Technological Innovation, Entrepreneurship, and Strategy." Sloan Management Review, (Spring): 19-30

Quinn, J.B. (1992). "Intelligent Enterprise: A Knowledge & Service-based paradigm for Industry." New York: The Free Press

Raisch, S., Birkinshaw, J., Probst, G., & Tushman, M.L. (2009). "Organizational Ambidexterity: Balancing Exploitation and Exploration for Sustained Performance." Organization Science, 20(4), 685-695

Raynor, M.E. (2001): Strategic Flexibility in the Financial Services Industry. Deloitte Research

Raynor, M.E. & Bower, J.L. (2001). "Lead From the Center: How to Manage Divisions Dynamically." Harvard Business Review 79(5), 92-100

Raynor, M.E. (2004). "Strategic Flexibility: Taking the Fork in the Road." Competitive Intelligence, 7(1), 6-13

Raynor, Michael E. and Ximena Leroux (2004). "Strategic Flexibility in the R&D Function." Research and Technology Management, 47(3), 17-23

Read, D.W. (2005). "Some Observations on Resilience and Robustness in Human Systems." Cybernetics and Systems, 36(8), 773-802

Rip, Peter (2009). Early Stage VC. Blog. Retrieved 2/25/2009 from: http://earlystagevc.typepad.com/earlystagevc/2006/09/riya.html

Roberts, E.B. (1980). "New Ventures for Corporate Growth", Harvard Business Review, July-August, 134-142

Rock, A. (1987)."Strategy versus Tactics from a Venture Capitalist." Harvard Business Review, 65, (November-December), 63-67

Rogers, E. and J. Larsen (1984): Silicon Valley Fever. New York: Basic Books

Roll, C.D. & D.M. Shibata (1991)."Resilience, robustness, and plasticity in a terrestrial slug, with particular reference to food." Journal of Canadian Zoology, 69(4), 978-987

Romanelli, E. (1987). "New Venture Strategies in the Minicomputer Industry." California Management Review, 30(1), 160-175

Rosenbloom, R.S. & Cusumano, M.A. (1987). "Technological Pioneering: The Birth of the VCR Industry." California Management Review, 29(4), 51-76

Rosenhead, J., Elton, M., & Gupta, S.K. (1972). "Robustness and Optimality as Criteria for Strategic Decisions." Operational Research Quarterly, 23(4), 413-428

Rosenhead, J. (1980). "Planning under Uncertainty: The Inflexibility of Methodologies." Journal of the Operational Research Society, 31(3), 201-209

Rosenhead, J. (1980). "Planning under Uncertainty: A Methodology for Robustness Analysis." Journal of the Operational Research Society, 31(4), 331-341

Rosenhead, J., Best, G., & Parston, G. (1986). "Robustness in Practice." Journal of the Operational Research Society, 37(5), 463-478

Rothwell, R., Freeman, C., Horsley, A., Jervis, V.P.T., Robertson, A.B., & Townsend, J. (1974). "SAPPHO Updated: Project SAPPHO." Research Policy 3(3), 258-291

Rumelt, R.P. (1995a). "Inertia and Transformation" in C.A. Montgomery, (Ed.) Resources in an Evolutionary Perspective: Towards a Synthesis of Evolutionary and Resource-based Approaches to Strategy. 101-132 Norwell MA: Kluwert Academic Publishers

Rumelt, R.P. (1995b). "Precis of Inertia and Transformation." Downloaded 12/03/2009 http://www.anderson.ucla.edu/faculty/dick.rumelt/Docs/Papers/berkeley_precis.pdf

Rutter, M. (1985) "Resilience in the face of adversity. Protective factors and resistance to psychiatric disorder." The British Journal of Psychiatry, 147(6), 598-611

Rutter, M. (1987). "Psychological Resilience and protective mechanisms." American Journal of Orthopsychiatry, 57(3), 316-331

Rutter, M. (1993). "Resilience: Some Conceptual Considerations." Journal of Adolescent Health, 14(8), 626-631

Saleh, J.H., Hastings, D.E., & Newman, D.J. (2001). "Extracting the Essence of Flexibility in Systems Design." MIT Engineering Systems Division Working Paper ESD-WP-2001-04

Saleh, J.H., Hastings, D.E., & D. Newman, D.J. (2003). "Flexibility in system design and implications for aerospace systems." Acta Astronautica, 53(12), 927-944

Saleh, J.H., Gregory, M. & Jordan, N.C. (2009). "Flexibility: a multidisciplinary literature review and a research agenda for designing flexible engineering systems." Journal of Engineering Design, 20(3), 307-323

Sanchez. R. (1995). "Strategic Flexibility in Product Competition." Strategic Management Journal, 16(9), 135-159

Sanchez, R. & Mahoney, J.T. (1997). "Modularity, flexibility, and knowledge management in product and organization design." IEEE Engineering Management Review, 25(4), 50-61

Sanchez. R. (1999). "Modular Architectures in the Marketing Process." Journal of Marketing, Fundamental Issues and Directions for Marketing, 63, 92-111

Sanchez, R. & Mahoney, J.T. (1996). "Modularity, Flexibility, and Knowledge Management in Product and Organization Design." Strategic Management Journal (Special Issue on Knowledge and the Firm), 17, 63-76

Saxenian, A. (1994): Regional Advantage: Culture and Competition in Silicon Valley and Route 128. Cambridge, MA: Harvard University Press

Schank, J., Mattock, M., Sumner, G., Greenberg, I., Rothenberg, J., & Stucker, J.P. (1991). "A Review of Strategic Mobility Models and Analysis." Rand Corporation Report R-3926-JS

Schober, F. & Gebauer, J. (2008). "How Much to Spend on Flexibility? Determining the Value of Information System Flexibility." University of North Carolina at Wilmington, Cameron School of Business Working Paper 08-015

Schroeder, D.H., Wiggins, L.L. & Wormhoudt, D.T. (1981). "Flexibility of Scale in Large Conventional Coal-Fired Power Plants." Energy Policy, 9(2), 127-135

Schoon, M. (2005). "A Short Historical Overview of the Concepts of Resilience, Vulnerability, and Adaptation." Workshop in Political Theory and Policy Analysis, Indiana University, Working Paper W05-4

Schumpeter (1934): The Theory of Economic Development. Cambridge MA: Harvard University Press

Seung-Hyun, L. & Makhija, M. (2009). "Flexibility in Internationalization: Is it Valuable during an Economic Crisis?" Strategic Management Journal, 30(5), 537-555

Shackle, G.L.S. (1938): Expectations, Investment and Income. Oxford University Press

Shackle, G.L.S. (1953). "The Logic of Surprises." Economica, 20(78), 112-117

Shank, J., Mattock, M., Sumner, G., Greenberg, I., Rothenberg, J., & Stucker, J.P. (1991). "A Review of Strategic Mobility Models and Analysis." The RAND Corporation Research Report R-3926-JS

Sherman, W.T. (1875): Memoirs of W.T. Sherman. New York: D. Appleton & Company

Shewchuk, J.P. & Moodie, C.L. (1998). "Definition and Classification of Manufacturing Flexibility Types and Measures." The International Journal of Flexible Manufacturing Systems, 10(4), 325-349

Shi, D. & Daniels R.L. (2003). "A survey of manufacturing flexibility: Implications for e-business flexibility." IBM Systems Journal, 42(3), 414-427

Shimizu, K. & Hitt, M.A. (2004). "Strategic flexibility: organizational preparedness to reverse ineffective strategic decisions." Academy of Management Executive, 18(4), 44-59

Sia, S.K., Koh, C., & Tan, C.X. (2008). "Strategic Maneuvers for Outsourcing Flexibility: An Empirical Assessment." Decision Sciences, 39(3), 407-443

Siegel, J. I., & Larson, B.Z. (2009). "Labor Market Institutions and Global Strategic Adaptation: Evidence from Lincoln Electric." Management Science, 55(9), 1527-1546

Slack, N. (1987)."The Flexibility of Manufacturing Systems." International Journal of Operations and Production Management, 7(4) 35-45

Smead, R. & Zollman, K.J.S. (2009). "The Stability of Strategic Plasticity." Carnegie Mellon University, Department of Philosophy, Technical Report # 182

Smith, A. D. & Zeithaml, C. (1996). "Garbage Cans and Advancing Hypercompetition: The Creation and Exploitation of New Capabilities and Strategic Flexibility in Two Regional Bell Operating Companies." Organizational Science, 7(4), 388-399

Sonsino, D. & Mandelbaum, M. (2001). "On Preference for Flexibility and Complexity Aversion: Experimental Evidence." Theory & Decision, 51(2), 197-216

Spur, G., Mattle, H.P., & Rittinghausen, H. (1976). "Flexible Manufacturing Cells in Multiple Station Production." Annals of the C.I.R., 329-334, 1976

Staw, B.M. (1983). "The Escalation of Commitment: A Review and Analysis." In B.M. Staw (Ed.), Psychological Foundations of Organizational Behavior, Second edition, Glenview, Illinois, Scott, Foresman and Company, 329-33

Stevens, L.D. (1981). "The Evolution of Magnetic Storage." IBM Journal of Research Development, 25(5), 663-675

Stigler, G.J. (1939). "Production and Distribution in the Short Run." Journal of Political Economy, 47(3), 305-327

Street, A., Barroso, L.A., Chabar, R., Mendes, A.T.S., & Pereira, M.V. (2008). "Pricing Flexible Natural Gas Supply Contracts under Uncertainty in Hydrothermal Markets." IEEE Transactions on Power Systems, 32(3), 1009-11017

Strotz, R. (1955). "Myopia and Inconsistency in Dynamic Utility Maximization." Review of Economic Studies, 23(3), 165-180

Suarez, F.F., Cusumano, M.A., & Fine, C.H. (1996). "An Empirical Study of Manufacturing Flexibility in Printed Circuit Board Assembly." Operations Research, 44(1), 223-240

Suchman, M. (2000). "Dealmakers and Counselors: Law firms as Intermediaries in the Development of Silicon Valley." In M. Kenney, (Ed.): Understanding Silicon Valley. Stanford University Press

Swanger, C.C. (1995). "Apple Computer: The First Ten Years." Case Study # S-BP-245, Graduate School of Business, Stanford University

Tallon, P.P. (2008). "Inside the Adaptive Enterprise: An Information Technology Capabilities Perspective on Business Process Agility." Information Technology Management, 9(1), 21–36

Tan, C and Sia, S.K. (2006). "Managing Flexibility in Outsourcing." Journal of the Association for Information Systems, 7(4), 179-206

Taylor, M.B. (1959). The Uncertain Trumpet, New York: Harper

Teece, D.J. (1987). "Profiting from Technological Innovation: Implications for Integration, Collaboration, Licensing and Public Policy." In D.J. Teece (Ed.): The Competitive Challenge: Strategies for Industrial Innovation and Renewal. Cambridge, MA. Ballinger Publishing Company

Teece, D.J., Pisano, G. & Shuen, A. (1997). "Dynamic Capabilities and Strategic Management." Strategic Management Journal, 18(7), 509-533

Teece, D.J. (2007). "Explicating dynamic capabilities: The nature and micro-foundations of (sustainable) enterprise performance." Strategic Management Journal, 28(13), 1319-1350

Teece, D.J. (2009): Dynamic capabilities and Strategic Management. Oxford University Press

Thomke, S.T. (1997). "The role of flexibility in the development of new products: An empirical study." Research Policy, 26 (1), 105-119

Thompson, J.D. (1967): Organizations in Action. New York: McGraw Hill

Tilak, A.G. (1978). "Job Shop Scheduling with Routing and Resource Flexibility." Unpublished Ph.D. Dissertation, Texas Tech University

Timoshenko,V. (1930). "The Role of Agricultural Fluctuations in the Business Cycle." Michigan Business Studies, 11(9), 1-89

Tinbergen, J. (1933). "Notions of Horizon and Expectancy in Dynamic Economics." Econometrica, 1 (3), 247-264

Tomlinson, R.C. (1976). "Operational Research, Organizational Design and Adaptivity." Omega, 4(5), 527-537

Triantis, A.J, and J.E. Hodder, J.E. (1990). "Valuing Flexibility as a Complex Option." Journal of Finance, 45(2), 549-565

Trigeorgis, L. (1996): Real Options: Managerial Flexibility and Strategy in Resource Allocation. M.I.T. Press

Trigeorgis, L. & E. Schwartz (Eds.), (2001): Real options and Investment Under Uncertainty: Classical Readings and Recent Contributions. M.I.T. Press

Trigeorgis, L. (1993). "Real Options and Interactions with Financial Flexibility." Financial Management, 22(3), 202-224

Tushman, M.L. & O'Reilly, C.A. (1992): Winning Through Innovation. Cambridge, MA: Harvard University Press

Unger, P.S., Grine, F.E., & Teaford, M.F. (2006). "Diet in Early Homo: A Review of the Evidence and a New Model of Adaptive Versatility." Annual Review of Anthropology, 35, 209-228

Utterback, J.M. (1970). "The Process of Technological Innovation Within the Firm." Academy of Management Journal, 14(1), 75-88

Vaccaro, A., Brusoni, S., & Veloso, F. (2007). "The Role of Virtual Design Tools on Knowledge Replication and Recombination: An Empirical Investigation" CESPRI Working Papers 198, CESPRI, Centre for Research on Innovation and Internationalisation, Università Commerciale "Luigi Bocconi", Milano, Italy

Vanderbilt-Adriance, E., & Shaw, D.S. (2008). "Conceptualizing and Re-Evaluating Resilience Across levels of Risk, Time and Domains of Competence." Clinical Child and Family Psychology Review, 11(1-2), 30-58

Valikangas, L. (2007). "Rigidity, Exploratory Patience, and the Ecological Resilience of Organizations." Scandinavian Journal of Management, 23(2), 206-21

Van der Vet, R.P. (1977). "Flexible Solutions to Systems of Linear Inequalities." European Journal of Operational Research, 1(4), 247-254

Van Mieghem, J.A. (1998). "Investment Strategies for Flexible Resources." Management Science, 44(8), 1071-1078

Van Mieghem, J.A. (2007). "Risk Mitigation in Newsvendor Networks: Resource Diversification, Flexibility, Sharing, and Hedging." Management Science, 53(8), 1269-1288

de Visser, J. A. G. M.; Hermisson, J., Wagner, G.P., Meyers, L.A., Bagheri-Chaichian, H., Blanchard, J.L., Chao, L. Cheverud, J.M., Elena, S. F., Fontana, W., Gibson, G., Hansen, G.F., Krakauer, D., Lewontin, R.C., Ofria, C., Rice, S.H., Von Dassow, G., Wagner, A. & Whitlock, M.C. (2003). "Evolution and Detection of Genetic Robustness." Evolution, 57(9), 1959–1972

Volberda, H.W. (1996). "Toward the Flexible Form: How to Remain Vital in Hypercompetitive Environments." Organization Science, 7(4), 359-374

Volberda, H.W. (1997). "Building Flexible Organizations for Fast-moving Markets." Long Range Planning, 30(2), 169-183

Volberda, H.W. (1998): Building the Flexible Firm: How to remain competitive. Oxford University Press

Wadhwa, S. & Rao, K.S. (2003a). "Enterprise Modeling of Supply Chains Involving Multiple Entity Flows: Role of Flexibility in Enhancing Lead Time Performance." Studies in Informatics and Control 12(1), 5-20

Wadhwa, S. & Rao, K.S., (2003b). "Flexibility and Agility for Enterprise Synchronization: Knowledge and Innovation Management Towards Flexagility." Studies in Informatics & Control, 12(2), 111-128

Walsh, J.W. (1995). "Flexibility in Consumer Purchasing for Uncertain Future Tastes." Marketing Science, 14(2), 148-165

Warren, N., Moore, K., & Cardona, P. (2002). "Modularity, Strategic Flexibility, and Firm Performance: A Study of the Home Appliance Industry." Strategic Management Journal, 23(12), 1123-1140

Watson, T. (1963): A Business and Its Beliefs. McGraw Hill

Wegener, H. (2002). "Agility in Model-Driven Software Development: Implications for Organization, Process and Architecture." OOPSLA Workshop on Generative Techniques in the Context of Model-Driven Architecture, Seattle, WA

Weick, K.E. (1982). "Management of Organizational Change among Loosely Coupled Elements." In S. Paul & Associates (eds.): New Perspectives in Theory, Research and Practice. San Francisco CA: Jossey Bass

Werner, E.E. (1986). "Resilient Offspring of Alcoholics: A Longitudinal Study from Birth to Age 18." Journal of Studies on Alcohol, 47(1), 34-40

Werner, E.E. (1993). "Risk resilience and recovery: Perspectives from the Kauai Longitudinal Study." Development Psychopathology, 5(4), 503-515

Weill, P., Subramani, M., & Broadbent, M. (2002). "IT Infrastructure for Strategic Agility." Massachusetts Institute of Technology CISR WP #329 (Published in Sloan management Review, October 15)

Wong, K.P. (2007). "Operational and Financial Hedging for Exporting Firms." International Review of Economics and Finance, 16(4), 459-470

Yao, D.D. & Buzacott, J.A. (1987). "Modeling a Class of Flexible Manufacturing Systems with Reversible Routing." Operations Research, 35(1), 87-93

Young-Ybarra, C. & Wiersema, M. (1999). "Strategic Flexibility in Information Technology Alliances: The Influence of Transaction Cost Economics and Social Exchange Theory." Organization Science, 10(4), 625-636

Zahra, Shaker, A.A., Hayton J.C., Neubaum, D.O., Dibrell, C., Craig, J. (2008). "Culture of Family Commitment and Strategic Flexibility: The Moderating Effect of Stewardship." Entrepreneurship Theory and Practice, 32(6), 1035-1054

Zhang, J. (2003): High Tech Start-Ups and Industry Dynamics in Silcion Valley. San Francisco CA: Public Policy Institute of California

Zimmerman, M.A. & Arunkumar, R. (1994). "Resiliency Research: Implications for Schools and Policy." Society for Research in Child Development, 13(4), 1-17

11 Index

Accountability.......6, 12, 123, 127, 129, 134, 136, 139, 150, 156, 157, 161
Adaptability...4, 13, 21, 22, 38, 39, 43, 56, 173
Adaptation........1, 2, 3, 4, 5, 6, 7, 9, 13, 22, 23, 30, 31, 32, 36, 40, 41, 47, 56, 57, 59, 61, 62, 71, 81, 106, 120, 150, 169, 170, 171, 172, 173, 174, 175, 176
Adaptec.....................46, 65, 72, 74
Agile Giants......................51, 75
Agility...9, 15, 18, 19, 20, 21, 23, 24, 37, 38, 39, 61, 87, 119, 120, 129, 139, 146, 173, 176
Alacritech.............................65, 74
Aligning.....11, 12, 41, 61, 95, 123, 153, 167
Ampex.....................................57
Apple Computer...6, 47, 53, 57, 59, 64, 65, 66, 68, 72, 85, 91, 103, 113, 127
Auspex 46, 59, 65, 74
Balancing........6, 9, 125, 126, 129, 131, 141, 151, 165, 171, 174
Blending..............................55, 59, 148
Boucher, Larry 2, 6, 65, 72, 74
Campus............................144, 158, 160
Centigram...........................66, 74
Clark, Jim........................29, 49, 65
Clustering Dimension.........12, 123, 129
Cohesive Dimension..........12, 129, 144
Collaboration...50, 58, 59, 60, 128, 144, 159, 162
Compensation...137, 143, 147, 148, 155
Connective Dimension...............12, 129
Conner Peripherals...........46, 64, 67, 71
Coordination.......12, 113, 124, 126, 127, 129, 130, 133, 134, 139, 145, 150, 151, 164, 166, 173
Corrective Maneuver.............91, 92, 93, 94, 95
Cross-functional Teams................2, 133
Cross-Pollinating....................11, 62, 75
Cross-Silo Forums...................134, 138
C-Suite Executives..........................139
Decision-Making 99, 127, 142, 166, 173
Deliberate Model............................100
Disk Drive Controller.............56, 59, 81
Divisional.............16, 78, 126, 130, 164
Divisional Structure....................16, 78
Donaldson Lufkin and Jenerette.........71
Downsizing..89
Elasticity.......................21, 37, 39, 173
Emergent....................52, 99, 100, 101, 103, 104, 114, 120
Emergent Model..............................101
Emotional Connectivity....125, 151, 155
Empirical Pragmatism......................171
Entrepreneurs...4, 7, 11, 13, 32, 33, 41, 43, 44, 45, 46, 48, 49, 50, 51, 54, 55, 56, 61, 63, 64, 65, 66, 68, 69, 75, 80, 82, 104, 107, 110, 118, 121, 169
Exit Strategy...........................5, 51, 55
Experimentation........10, 11, 56, 61, 75, 99, 105, 108, 109, 110, 112, 114, 115, 120, 125, 151
Exploitive Maneuver.............93, 94, 95
Failure......11, 61, 62, 68, 69, 73, 75, 80, 83, 96, 119, 120, 170
Flexibility........1, 2, 3, 4, 7, 8, 9, 10, 15, 16, 17, 18, 19, 20, 21, 22, 23, 24, 25, 26, 27, 28, 29, 30, 32, 34, 35, 36, 37, 38, 39, 40, 41, 43, 58, 59, 74, 75, 77, 78, 79, 81, 82, 84, 93, 94, 95, 96, 97, 105, 108, 110, 117, 118, 119, 120, 124, 131, 134, 142, 145, 147, 150, 165, 166, 167, 172, 174, 175
Flexible Architectures......................124
Floppy Disk Drives.................59, 71, 87
Functional Structure.........................145
GE.................................138, 147, 149
Geo-Distributed...............11, 12, 13, 15, 123, 127, 138, 141, 146, 149, 150, 151, 153, 163, 165, 175

Index

Glue..........................129, 141, 147, 148
Hard............................1, 6, 9, 11, 12,
   13, 15, 55, 69, 95, 129, 141, 154,
   156
Soft...............12, 15, 129, 141, 154, 156
Group Structure................................131
Hagstrom, Professor Stig....................67
Hambrecht & Quist.......................51, 71
Hedging...............18, 21, 25, 26, 39, 84,
   89, 173
Hennessy, John..................................49
Heterarchy...150
Hewlett Packard....7, 46, 53, 55, 57, 64,
   65, 66, 67, 80, 109, 128, 143
Houghton, Kenneth............................46
Hubs..........61, 134, 139, 140, 146, 149,
   164, 165, 174
Hybrid Structure...............................113
IBM...13, 45, 46, 49, 65, 66, 67, 71, 72,
   73, 76, 87, 88, 92, 93, 106, 107, 112
Informal Networks......................67, 167
Information Technology (IT).........6, 15,
   18, 19, 20, 23, 26, 28, 39, 49, 86, 87,
   123, 124, 130, 135, 136, 138, 140,
   147, 149, 151, 164
Innovation.......1, 8, 9, 10, 11, 12, 17, 23,
   24, 28, 29, 41, 43, 45, 46, 47, 48, 49,
   50, 58, 59, 60, 61, 62, 65, 67, 71,
   72, 77, 78, 79, 80, 82, 85, 100, 103,
   107, 125, 128, 131, 151, 161, 169,
   170
Intel.....7, 46, 47, 53, 57, 66, 67, 75, 91,
   128, 138, 143
Jobs, Steve.........................65, 85, 91, 103
Joint Venture Silicon Valley.........43, 45,
   47, 48, 50, 56
Kaleidoscopic Change............10, 17, 75,
   77, 81
Knot-holes............................16, 30, 33,
   34, 80, 82, 174,
Knowledge Generators.................44, 51
Knowledge Hatcheries.................44, 50
Knowledge Lubricants.................44, 53
Knowledge Worker......4, 6, 8, 9, 10, 11,
   12, 13, 36, 40, 41, 43, 48, 53, 61, 66,
   68, 69, 88, 96, 99, 120, 121, 124,
   125, 131, 136, 137, 141, 142, 144,
   146, 149, 150, 151, 153, 154, 155,
   156, 157, 158, 159, 160, 161, 162,
   164, 165, 167, 169, 171, 172, 176
Kuhnian Inversion................................3
Leader as a teacher..........................138
Liquidity......8, 9, 18, 19, 21, 26, 37, 39,
   51, 52, 71, 95, 120, 173
Living Dead............................7, 52, 68
Lubricants.....44, 47, 53, 54, 58, 60, 171
Malleability.........21, 27, 37, 38, 39, 173
Maneuver 10, 11, 13, 16, 18, 61, 75,
   77, 78, 79, 81, 82, 83, 84, 85, 86, 87,
   88, 89, 90, 91, 92, 93, 94, 95, 96, 97,
   171, 174
Matrix Structure 131, 139
Maxtor............................46, 74, 75, 57
Memorex 46, 67, 71, 57
Metaphor Computers..........................71
Metcalfe, Bob....................................49
Military Strategy.........15, 16, 18, 28, 77,
   78, 94
Mobility......6, 21, 28, 36, 43, 62, 66, 67,
   68, 120, 147, 159, 173
Modular Structures.....................29, 124
Mohr Davidow Ventures....................92
Moley, Richard..........................76, 109
Morphing...84
Multi-cultural....10, 11, 12, 43, 48, 125,
   137, 141, 142, 155
Multi-polar.....10, 11, 12, 127, 129, 150,
   171, 175
Napoleon 78, 83, 175
Netflix.......................106, 115, 116, 117
Netscape.......................49, 65, 80, 86, 94
Network Appliance (NetApp)......58, 74
New Ventures......50, 54, 56, 59, 61, 62,
   63, 65, 71, 75, 76, 96, 100, 146
Offshoring...43
Organic..........................30, 45, 127, 170

Organizational Challenges....... 125, 135
Organizational Design...15, 18, 29, 123, 124, 126, 129, 144, 145, 151, 152, 171, 173,
Organizational Structure....6, 22, 23, 27
Orgitechting 11, 61, 123, 174, 175
Oshman, M. Kenneth 76
PalmPilot (Palm).............. 58, 69, 70, 80, 91, 92
Palo Alto Research Center (PARC)...49, 67, 71, 80, 81
Parent-Child Leadership...12, 156, 157, 167, 172
Peer-Peer Leadership...11, 12, 153, 156, 157, 158, 159, 167, 172
Performance Management....... 143, 161
Pioneering....1, 3, 6, 11, 29, 43, 46, 49, 52, 53, 55, 66, 67, 68, 71, 73, 74, 78, 80, 90, 99, 106, 107, 110, 115, 116, 119, 126, 155
Potential Surprise 97
Pre-emptive Maneuver................ 85, 86, 87, 88, 89, 95
Protective Maneuver............... 89, 90, 95
Prototyping.......... 10, 11, 36, 61, 62, 68, 69, 94, 105, 108, 120
Quantum....................... 46, 58, 59, 69, 72, 73, 74, 75
Real-options.. 19
Recalibration..... 11, 65, 69, 96, 99, 103, 104, 105, 106, 107, 114, 115, 116, 117, 119, 120, 121, 171
Recalibration Model........................ 104
Recombinant Innovations................... 58
Re-Combining.............................. 62, 70
Recruiting......... 142, 143, 144, 148, 173
Recursive Learning...62, 68, 69, 75, 76, 108, 110
Recycling....... 10, 11, 41, 60, 61, 62, 63, 64, 66, 67, 68, 69, 71, 73, 74, 75, 76, 120, 174
Recycling Mechanisms 62, 76
   Re-combining 62, 70
Recursive learning...... 62, 68, 69, 75, 76, 108, 110
Re-financing 62, 69
Re-inventing................ 43, 62, 68, 69
Re-packaging.................... 62, 69, 70
Re-financing.............................. 62, 69
Re-inventing.................... 43, 62, 68, 69
Re-packaging........................ 62, 69, 70
Research Institutes...................... 48, 49
Resilience....... 9, 15, 18, 20, 21, 22, 23, 32, 33, 34, 35, 38, 39, 43, 119, 120, 131, 141, 155, 173, 174
Re-starts.. 65
Robust.....7, 8, 9, 13, 17, 19, 21, 22, 23, 34, 35, 37, 38, 60, 40, 123, 173, 174
Role of Headquarters........................ 146
ROLM......... 49, 51, 57, 59, 76, 80, 106, 107, 108, 109, 110, 111, 112, 113, 116, 117, 118, 119, 120, 126
SASI.. 72
Schizophrenia 13, 37
Scientific Method 105
Screening & Recruiting.................... 142
SCSI................................ 72, 74, 92, 94
Seagate............... 46, 47, 51, 57, 64, 67, 73, 74
Serial Entrepreneurs................... 56, 118
Shockley William................... 45, 46, 67
Shugart.......... 46, 64, 66, 67, 71, 72, 73, 74, 75, 80, 81, 87, 88, 102, 103
Shugart, Alan........................ 64, 71, 73
Silicon Valley.....3, 5, 6, 7, 9, 10, 11, 13, 28, 33, 34, 41, 43, 44, 45, 46, 47, 48, 50, 51, 53, 54, 55, 56, 57, 58, 59, 60, 61, 62, 63, 64, 65, 66, 67, 68, 71, 73, 74, 75, 77, 79, 80, 81, 89, 90, 96, 106, 128, 143, 144, 145, 146, 147, 153, 158, 159, 169, 171, 172
Silos......... 126, 127, 129, 133, 136, 137, 138, 139, 145, 149, 164, 173
Slack.................... 7, 8, 21, 25, 26, 95
Sollman, George.................... 66, 74, 75
Spin-offs........ 44, 46, 52, 53, 65, 66, 72,

73, 74, 75, 110
Stages of Growth...............................5, 9
Stampede Effect..................................56
Stanford.......46, 49, 50, 64, 65, 67, 102, 106, 158, 159
Stanford Research Institute..........49, 57
Stanford University.........46, 49, 67, 64, 102, 158
Stealth Start-Ups........................86, 118
Super-Flexibility....1, 2, 3, 4, 7, 8, 9, 10, 38, 40, 41, 43, 59, 75, 77, 78, 79, 81, 84, 93, 95, 96, 97, 119, 120, 150, 167, 174, 175
Supply chain agility................18, 19, 24
Sutter Hill Ventures............................54
Swarm Effect......................................56
System Industries........................72, 73
Talent Mobility...........28, 62, 66, 67, 68
Techno-Evangelists............................68
Terman, Frederick..............................46
Time Dimension..................................97
Trade-offs....12, 34, 114, 117, 118, 120, 129, 131, 149, 151
Trajectory........5, 10, 13, 15, 31, 52, 71, 77, 81, 97, 119, 124, 138
Transitioning....................................173
Triggers....3, 4, 5, 8, 11, 15, 16, 35, 39, 79, 80, 81, 82, 84, 110, 112
TVI..74
Tyabji, Hatim......................................98
Uncertainty....1, 2, 9, 17, 27, 28, 43, 80, 99, 102, 103, 109, 110, 124, 151, 165, 170
Universities.........44, 47, 48, 49, 50, 55, 59, 63, 67, 146, 159
University of California, Berkeley...49, 67
US Venture Partners...........................50
Venture Capital....43, 44, 47, 50, 51, 54, 59, 63, 65, 66, 67, 69, 70, 71, 74, 86, 92, 96, 118, 119, 146
VeriFone...133
Versatile.........7, 8, 9, 13, 22, 36, 37, 60, 95, 119, 123, 151, 166, 167
Winchester Disks...........46, 49, 59, 69, 70, 71, 72, 73, 80
Yahoo........47, 49, 57, 58, 64, 80, 82, 86

12 Biographies

Dr. Homa Bahrami is a Senior Lecturer at the Haas School of Business, University of California, Berkeley, a Faculty Director at the Haas Center for Executive Education, UC Berkeley, and on the Board of the Haas Center for Teaching Excellence. UC Berkeley. Her research, teaching and advisory work focus on organizational innovation, team effectiveness and enterprise adaptation in dynamic, knowledge-based industries. She has published widely in leading journals and is the co-author of a major textbook (with Harold Leavitt, Stanford University) "MANAGERIAL PSYCHOLOGY: MANAGING BEHAVIOR IN ORGANIZATIONS", published by the University of Chicago Press, and translated into many languages. She serves on several boards in Silicon Valley and is active in executive education, executive development, and executive coaching.

Dr. Stuart Evans is a Distinguished Service Professor at Carnegie Mellon University, Silicon Valley, where he teaches "Innovation & Entrepreneurship" and "Enterprise Innovation". He is a board member, educator and author, focusing on dynamic high tech ventures. His professional career spans research (SRI International, Stanford Graduate School of Business,), teaching (The Judge Business School, Cambridge University), consulting (Bain and Company, Menlo Park, California), investing (Sand Hill Venture Group, Menlo Park, California) and executive management (Shugart Corporation, a Xerox subsidiary, Sunnyvale, California). He has published widely on high tech venturing.

9783642431548